# ENCOURAGING VOICES

# Encouraging Voices:
## respecting the insights of young people
## who have been marginalised

**Edited by Michael Shevlin and Richard Rose**

*ndfa*

NATIONAL DISABILITY AUTHORITY
ÚDARÁS NÁISIÚNTA MÍCHUMAIS

First published in 2003
National Disability Authority
25 Clyde Road, Dublin 4
Copyright © The contributors

ISBN 1 870499 04 2


British Library Cataloguing-in-Publication Data.
A catalogue record for this book is available from the British Library.


Typeset in Ireland by Wordwell Ltd
Editor: Aideen Quigley
Book design: Nick Maxwell
Cover design: Rachel Dunne
Printed by E.G. Zure, Bilbao

# CONTENTS

## Acknowledgements

The Encouraging Voices project has been developed by Michael Shevlin (Education Department/National Institute for the Study of Learning Difficulties, Trinity College Dublin) and Richard Rose (Centre for Special Needs Education and Research, University College Northampton) in collaboration with colleagues from Ireland, the UK and Iceland. This project, to date, has involved participation in an authors' research symposium, a national conference (both hosted by the National Disability Authority) and the publication of the *Encouraging Voices* book.

We would like to acknowledge the contribution of the many people and organisations that have supported our work: The National Disability Authority has generously supported our research symposium, national conference and the publication of the *Encouraging Voices* book. We would especially like to thank the following individuals for their advice, practical help and organisational skills: Maighread Kelly, Catherine Kenny, Claire O'Connor, Donie O'Shea, Mike Timms, Christine Whyte and Marion Wilkinson.

We would also like to thank Agnes Anderson for her interview with Thomas (see Common Ground section), and Natasha Mycawka for her administrative support. We would also like to acknowledge our colleagues at the Education Department/National Institute for the Study of Learning Difficulties, Trinity College Dublin, and the Centre for Special Needs Education and Research, University College Northampton, who have listened to our ideas and contributed to our thinking.

We are delighted to recognise the contribution of the young people whose voices are recorded in this book. Their participation in the research process represents a first step towards greater societal acknowledgement of their valued place within our communities.

### Disclaimer

## FOREWORD

The National Disability Authority (NDA) dedicates itself to strive for the creation of a society in which people with disabilities have equal rights and opportunities.

Education is a particularly powerful tool in creating equality for people with disabilities in society. Early experiences of inclusion or exclusion are crucial in shaping the future participation of people with disabilities. Opportunities and barriers experienced by people with disabilities impact critically on the choices they can make in the future and the extent to which they can achieve their full potential.

Internationally there has been a concerted attempt to make education more inclusive and democratic. Legislation and research highlight the right of people with disabilities to be included in mainstream schools, but there is a distinct paucity of knowledge as to what the reality of inclusion is from the pupil's perspective.

Certain voices within our society have not always been heard. Such voices belong to those who have been most marginalised, and their voices have often been ignored, isolated and patronised as the discourse of professionals and policy makers have dominated.

This book is published by the NDA and provides a unique opportunity to explore the perspectives of young people with regard to their education, as well as crucial issues such as rights, democracy and equality in our schools.

In reality, rights and status are closely related to the ability to have one's voice recognised and heard.

*M. Claire O'Connor*
*Director*
*National Disability Authority*

# Introduction

This book represents an attempt to explore the perspectives of young people from diverse backgrounds with regard to their educational experiences. It has involved the active participation of young people from diverse backgrounds in collaboration with researchers, teachers and also adults with disabilities. Common themes were identified among the contributions, and these themes are used to highlight crucial issues for these young people. As a result, the book is divided into four sections: Voicing Concerns; Shaping Identities; Between Two Worlds; and Common Ground. However, these divisions are somewhat arbitrary, as some contributions could fit comfortably into a number of sections.

Within the Voicing Concerns section, a broad perspective is adopted to examine the views of children on critical issues such as rights and equality. Children commented on the unequal power relationships inherent in schools between children and adults, and favoured the development of a more democratic ethos and structure within schools. These perspectives form the backdrop for an analysis of the effects of exclusion on individual children who have a disability or who are subjected to bullying and harassment.

The contributions within Shaping Identities address how the identities of young people from diverse backgrounds can be influenced by their educational experiences. They report that they have to confront institutionalised stereotypes that emphasise difference as deficit. People with disabilities, for example, describe how low expectations have had a negative influence on their school careers and their subsequent life paths. However, there are also examples of good practice where pupils with severe learning difficulties are enabled to make choices and develop their own learning skills.

Between Two Worlds brings together the insights from a variety of traditionally marginalised groups. These young people have experienced mainstream education, to a greater or lesser extent, from a marginalised situation. Societal attitudes and systemic limitations have contributed to the construction of these young people as 'different' and 'less than' in the eyes of their peers. Being construed as different has damaged their sense of belonging and their ability to participate fully in the mainstream world. It may also have reinforced cultural/disability identities so that these young people only feel comfortable and accepted within their own milieu.

The Common Ground section attempts to represent a variety of perspectives, including personal reflections on education from people belonging to marginalised groups, as well as from those involved in shaping education at the levels of policy and practice. These contributions provide a reflective consideration of how a rights-based perspective can inform the educational experiences of marginalised individuals and groups. The diversity of voices produces a powerful reminder that education is a common pursuit shared by all and that continued marginalisation is invidious and unacceptable.

# List of Contributors

**Dora S. Bjarnason** is an associate professor at the Iceland University of Education, and has worked within inclusive education and disability studies for almost two decades as a researcher and a teacher trainer. Dora has written extensively in the area of inclusive education. She has worked in the US, Australia, New Zealand, Japan and Denmark as a researcher or visiting professor at various universities and research institutes. Dora is the parent of a young man with significant impairments.

**Chris Derrington** has a wide range of teaching experiences in both mainstream and special education. She has worked as a teacher of hearing impaired children, as an Inspector for Special Educational Needs, as Head Teacher of a special school and as Senior Research Officer with NFER (National Foundation for Educational Research). She is currently Senior Lecturer in Special Education in the Centre for Special Needs Education and Research, University College Northampton. A significant proportion of Chris's career has been spent on issues of multi-cultural education and as Coordinator for Traveller education.

**Dympna Devine** worked as a primary school teacher for nine years before joining the Education Department in UCD. She lectures in the areas of sociology of education and research methods and coordinates the Master of Education programme. She has completed research in the areas of school effectiveness, childhood studies (in particular children's voices on their schooling experience) and more recently ethnicity.

**Goretti Horgan** is a researcher with Save the Children Fund in Northern Ireland. She has worked as a Senior Research Officer with the National Children's Bureau, as a Research Officer in the University of Ulster at Magee and as a community development worker. She has extensive experience involving children and young people and has a particular interest in participatory research. Her publications include *Planning for children in care in Northern*

*Ireland* (1997); 'Involving children and young people in review meetings', in *Research, Policy and Planning* 3 (1998); *A sense of purpose: the views and experiences of young mothers about growing up in Northern Ireland* (2001), and, with Paula Rodgers, 'Young people's participation in a new Northern Ireland society', in *Youth and Society* 1 (2000).

**Sally Kendall** is a senior research officer at the National Foundation for Educational Research (NFER). The majority of her research activity and publication record is related to studies on pupil disaffection and adult literacy. Before joining the NFER's Northern Office in 1998, Sally worked on a number of community and adult education projects with Traveller families, and completed her Ph.D., which explored the social, cultural and spatial characteristics of Traveller lifestyles.

**Máirín Kenny,** former Principal of a primary school for Traveller children, is a research consultant. She recently collaborated in a research project on the experience of young people with disabilities in second level schools (commissioned by the South West Regional Authority). She is currently working on a research project for Pavee Point, a Traveller social policy research centre.

**Anne Lodge** is a member of the Education Department, NUI Maynooth. She previously worked as a Research Officer in the Equality Studies Centre, UCD, on the 'Equality and Social Climate of Schools' project, examining the equality climate of second level schools in Ireland with a particular focus on the perspectives and concerns of young people.

**Kathleen Lynch** is a member of the Equality Studies Centre, UCD. She directed the 'Equality and Social Climate of Schools' project. She has published widely on a range of issues relating to various equality concerns and has a particular interest in education.

**Eileen McNeela** is a primary school teacher who has lectured in Business Studies in the Institute of Technology, Blanchardstown, Dublin. In addition,

Eileen has coordinated a number of European funded projects and worked on disability-related and multi-cultural research.

**Stephen James Minton** is an educational researcher, and is currently a postgraduate student in the Department of Education, Trinity College Dublin, having previously studied at the University of Glasgow. Over recent years, he has been active in the general area of teacher education, with his primary research concerns being the prevention and countering of bullying behaviour in schools, and the enhancement of self-esteem through teaching practice.

**Kevin Myers** teaches social history and history of education at the University of Birmingham. His doctoral thesis examined the settlement and education of refugee children in Britain between 1937 and 1945 and he has published many articles in this area, including 'Policy, equality and inequality: from the past to the future' (with Ian Grosvenor), in *Schooling and Equality*, edited by Dave Hill and Mike Cole.

**Kerry Noble** is an independent consultant working on issues of disability education and rights. Her own educational experiences have been in both mainstream and special education. Since leaving university, Kerry has worked for a number of charitable organisations and has also cooperated on projects with colleagues in higher education and in local education authorities. Her previous experiences have involved working as an actress and a model.

**Margaret O'Donnell**, assistant principal teacher in a special school for students with general learning disabilities in Ireland, is at present seconded as Education Officer to the National Council for Curriculum and Assessment, where she directs the coordination of all aspects of the curriculum that relate to the provision of special education. She has taught in mainstream as well as in special schools. She has frequently lectured on issues relating to special educational provision, and she is currently engaged in developing guidelines for teachers of students with general learning disabilities at primary and post-primary levels.

**Astrid Mona O'Moore** is Head of the Education Department/Coordinator of the Anti-Bullying Centre, Trinity College Dublin. Mona has researched the experiences of young people with disabilities in school. Her current research focuses on developing anti-bullying programmes in schools and the workplace.

**Natalie Rooney** is an independent researcher with a background in psychology. She has worked on a number of research projects, including a study of the retention of students in higher education for the Counselling Service, Trinity College Dublin.

**Richard Rose** has taught in schools in several parts of England and was Head Teacher of a special school. After three years as a Local Education Authority Inspector, he joined the academic staff at University College Northampton, where he is now Head of the Centre for Special Needs Education and Research. He has co-authored a number of books in the area of curriculum for pupils with special needs and inclusion, and has published widely in journals.

**Michael Shevlin** has taught in a secondary school in Ireland and was seconded to develop curricular links between mainstream and special schools. Subsequently, he joined the Education Department of Trinity College Dublin, and for the past five years he has taught Special Education courses at undergraduate and postgraduate level. He has written about the inclusion of young people with profound and complex learning needs in link programmes and also about the school experiences of young people with disabilities.

**Donal Toolan** was born in 1966 and grew up in the west of Ireland, where he attended school between frequent periods in hospital. He briefly attended Trinity College Dublin and has worked as a broadcaster and journalist in radio and television, focusing on issues relating to disability as a rights issue. He won the award for Broadcast Journalist of the Year in 1993 for the documentary series 'In from the margins'. In 1990 he was involved in founding the Forum of People with Disabilities. He is currently an executive member of the Irish Council for Civil Liberties.

# voicing concerns

# 1

## PROVIDING OPPORTUNITIES AND LEARNING BY ENCOURAGING VOICES

### RICHARD ROSE AND MICHAEL SHEVLIN

In this introductory chapter Richard Rose and Michael Shevlin identify the context for providing opportunities for young people to play a greater role in making decisions that impact upon their lives. Taking the concerns that have been expressed by young people with regard to the plight of children who are suffering from famine, disease or oppression in many parts of the world, the authors suggest that through fuller participation in education, pupils will be better equipped to play a greater role in the increased democratisation of society.

## Why encouraging voices?

The Encouraging Voices project is founded upon a belief that all individuals, given the opportunity, can make an important contribution to our understanding of teaching and learning. The principles of developing a partnership in education, where teachers and pupils work together in mutual respect, learning from and about each other and endeavouring to overcome obstacles along the way, is an important motivating force for all the contributors to this book. During the course of the twentieth century our concept of schools, and the role they play in the education of all children, has changed. Gardner (1999) describes how, by the beginning of the twentieth century, the classroom was 'established as the locus of an effectively inescapable collective experience shaping the lives of each successive generation' (p. 125). In recent years our understanding of how children learn, our perceptions of the diverse factors — cultural, social, biological and political — that can impact upon learning, and indeed the very purpose of education itself, have been subjected to scrutiny and debate. Throughout the century philosophical concepts of childhood moved away from the perception of children as innocents to be moulded and prepared for adulthood, as espoused in earlier times by writers such as Rousseau and Froebel. Debate about the nature of childhood has followed a complex path, from a consideration of the need to exercise control and order in potentially disruptive individuals, as discussed by Durkheim (1968) and Foucault (1977), to a notion of childhood as a social construct greatly influenced by culture, social class, gender and ethnicity, as reported in the work of James and Prout (1990). At the same time, our understanding of the psychological development of children, greatly influenced by the work of figures such as Piaget, Vygotsky and Bruner, has led to a more critical analysis of the ways in which teaching may be structured in order to support the learning process.

One common feature of the expansion of the study of children, whether this has been conducted through psychological, ethnographic or sociological research models, has been a tendency to view them as interesting and challenging 'subjects'. While the intention of much of the research carried out has been honourable and has undoubtedly informed our understanding and improved our practices in child care and teaching, the focus has been on doing research *on* or *about* children rather than engaging them fully in the investigative process. The researchers who have contributed to this book are concerned to promote an approach to working with children that is based upon respect and partnership and which suggests that an important means of learning about children and childhood is by listening to and valuing their opinions. Researchers who work for the improved condition and status of children and who base their work on providing teachers and others who work with young people with the means to work more effectively, must accept that such engagement is inevitably political. The researchers who have contributed to this book have demonstrated a commitment to change, and in so doing they provide a critical commentary on current practices in the provision of education and support to individuals who have often been disadvantaged by systems that have not developed an adequate understanding of their needs. However, while much of the research conducted into education and other aspects of provision for children may be described as emancipatory, it is the commitment to involve individuals not only as the subjects of research but as partners in inquiry that has motivated the work of writers within this text.

## Pupil participation in a context of rights

In May 2002 the United Nations General Assembly in New York held a special session on children, during which delegates considered ways to improve the rights of children and young people around the world. Immediately prior to the main conference, 404 young people under the age of eighteen were invited to attend the General Assembly and to express their concerns, their hopes for the future and their desire for action to improve the lives of millions of children who are currently oppressed through war, poverty, disease or enforced child labour. The quality of their presentations and the sincerity of their expression were matched only by their concern for others who they perceived to be in greater need than themselves. Many of the young people who spoke with such eloquence about their concerns for the state of the world and the plight of their peers came from impoverished countries where the quality of life experienced by children is distressingly poor. The decision to involve young people and to listen to their opinions should be welcomed and celebrated as an indication of a commitment that was made through Article 12 of the United Nations Convention on the Rights of the Child. This article explicitly calls upon governments and all agencies who work with children and young people to take into account the views and ideas expressed by children with regard to all decisions that have a direct bearing upon their lives.

The young people who spoke in New York did so with a clear understanding of many of the issues that confront children across the world. In representing the youth of their countries they made the following statement:

> We are the world's children.
> We are the victims of exploitation and abuse.
> We are street children.
> We are the children of war.
> We are the victims and orphans of HIV/AIDS.
> We are denied good quality education and healthcare.
> We are victims of political, economic, cultural, religious and environmental discrimination.
> We are children whose voices are not being heard: it is time we are taken into account.

This statement alone may well be enough to make responsible adults take notice of the conditions that many of the world's young people are forced to endure. More impressive, however, was the clear understanding that these representatives of youth had with regard to the actions that they saw as essential if the situation was to be improved. Not least among their concerns was the need for a reform of education and, in many instances, its provision for children who are currently denied all but the most rudimentary access to formal schooling. They expressed their desire for:

> equal opportunities and access to quality education that is free and compulsory; school environments in which children feel happy about learning; education for life that goes beyond the academic and includes lessons in understanding, human rights,

peace, acceptance and active citizenship;

These young ambassadors were not only expressing their outrage at the inability of the world's adults to provide an appropriate education for so many young people, they were also able to articulate their vision of an education system that could address so many of the wrongs that they perceive. Among the many statements that they made regarding the education that they would like to see was the following cry to be heard, and for Article 12 of the United Nations Convention to be heeded.

> Through the active participation of children, we see: raised awareness and respect among people of all ages about every child's right to full and meaningful participation, in the spirit of the Convention on the Rights of the Child, children actively involved in decision-making at all levels, and in planning, implementing, monitoring and evaluating all matters affecting the rights of the child.

The 2002 meeting of the UN General Assembly was attended by many politicians and leaders from around the world who have the power and authority to make a difference in the lives of children. Their attendance and their support for children's rights may be seen as an important step towards addressing many of the injustices that affect so many children. However, an observer at this meeting might be forgiven for expressing some doubts with regard to the determination of governments at both national and local levels to take the actions that would result in the changes sought by these young people. In 1990 a World Summit for Children, led by seventy-one Heads of State, issued the Declaration on the Survival, Protection and Development of Children and a Plan of Action for implementing the Declaration in the 1990s. This document was intended to bring about radical reforms in the rights of all children. At the time, it was embraced with enthusiasm as a blueprint for development, and heralded a new era of reform. It is true to say that in many countries there has been considerable progress in addressing the rights of children and that governments who signed up to the Declaration have endeavoured to implement change in support of improvements to welfare and education. However, a report issued by UNICEF in 2002 indicates that despite outstanding examples of progress for children in the last decade, most governments have not lived up to the promises that were made. Some of the statistics provided in this report make for alarming reading:

> More than 10 million children under the age of five still die each year from preventable causes; 149 million children in developing countries still suffer from malnutrition; more than 100 million children are still not in primary school, the majority of whom are girls; millions are still caught up in child labour, trafficking, prostitution, and conflict.

Clearly there remains much to be done. It would be easy to assume that the challenges ahead are issues mainly for those countries described as 'under-developed' or 'emerging', terms that themselves give an indication of the paternalism that has characterised so many of the approaches towards supporting both individuals and groups perceived to be in need. However, this would be to deny the responsibility that all governments and all who work with children, wherever they may be, have in ensuring that the children's rights agenda is fully addressed.

Developments in the area of pupil involvement in schools in the United Kingdom, in Northern Ireland and throughout the Republic of Ireland have been considerable in recent years. A combination of legislation and policy documents has been crucial in this process. Legislation such as the Children Act (1989) and the Special Needs Code of Practice (2001) in the UK, and the Education Act (1998) in the Republic of Ireland, along with The National Children's Strategy (2000), have made important strides in enabling children to express their opinions. Such legislation has placed an onus on professionals to give greater consideration to the aspirations of individual pupils. Examples of good practice in the involvement of pupils in their own assessment and learning procedures and in decision-making processes that affect their future have been documented (Alderson and Goodey, 1998; Vlachou, 1997) and some are reported within this book. However, those who work to ensure that pupils' rights are safeguarded cannot afford to rest on their laurels.

This book attempts to draw together examples of practices that have either encouraged greater pupil participation or inhibited educational opportunities. In so doing, every effort has been made to provide examples that make use of first-hand experiences, drawing upon the authentic voice of the individual. While it is clear from each paper that efforts have been made to include young people in decision-making processes, there is also considerable evidence that there is a need to build upon existing practices in order to ensure that young people are not only 'heard', but also 'listened to'. The writers who have contributed to this book all have a commitment to working collaboratively with young people in order to ensure that a more equitable education system emerges. Some work as researchers, and have demonstrated that the research contribution to our understanding of participation can in itself be emancipatory. By researching *with* young people, rather than *on* or *about* them, they have shown how both parties can actively engage in a rewarding learning process. Other contributors have given evidence of their own experiences within the education system, and they provide important indicators of how changes in procedure or in the attitudes of individuals could have major benefits for everyone involved.

The contributors to this book come from a wide range of disciplines and backgrounds. Some write from personal experience of disability, or from experience of being a member of a minority community in an educational institution. Others report on their experience as professionals who have attempted to support groups or individuals by providing an opportunity for them to express their own views or to become more involved in their own education. A common theme that runs through all the papers is the desire to ensure that opportunities are provided for all learners, regardless of need, ability or background, to participate fully in the education process.

While making a commitment to the greater involvement of individuals in decisions concerning the management of their own learning procedures, the contributors are not suggesting that this is a straightforward process. The relationship between the teacher and the learner has always been and continues to be a complex one. Teachers need to feel confident and competent in working with pupils who may at times challenge their conventional understanding of the teaching process. In concentrating upon the often complex needs of individuals who may be described as representing minority groups, the contributors acknowledge that there are times when teachers may feel that they lack experience or understanding of the factors that affect learning and access to education encountered by some pupils. It is suggested here that the real experts in assessing needs are the pupils themselves, who have learned to live with disability, with labels associated with their culture, or with the low expectations that are often a characteristic of the approach of schools in dealing with the needs of minority groups. In suggesting that teachers and education policy makers need to give greater consideration to the ways in which they encourage greater pupil participation, the contributors recognise that this presents a major challenge and will require new ways of working in many schools. The greatest obstacle to full pupil participation continues to be attitudes that endorse traditionally low expectations of pupils from minority groups. Disability, culture and social background continue to provide excuses for failure and to produce stereotyped beliefs about what pupils can achieve. However, if negative attitudes are to be overcome, it will be necessary to ensure that professional colleagues are provided with advice and practical assistance in developing a learning environment that is supportive and beneficial for all learners. Several of the contributors have provided concrete examples of how teachers may develop approaches that ensure that all pupils play a more positive role in learning.

### What are the benefits of pupil involvement?

Teachers who have endeavoured to create systems to enable pupils to play a greater role in their own education processes have reported a number of significant benefits. Munby (1995) suggests that when pupils are closely involved in assessment procedures and planning related to their personal learning needs, they become more accurate in making judgements about their own performance and understanding. This assertion receives further support from the research conducted by Rose, Fletcher and Goodwin (1999) with pupils with severe learning difficulties. Their research further suggests that in addition to raising the pupils' self-awareness, staff gained increased understanding of pupil needs and were more focused on addressing these through their planning and through changes in pedagogical practice. Davie and Galloway (1996) suggest that when teachers are introduced to principles that appear to advocate increased pupil autonomy, they are at times sceptical and apprehensive. However, their research indicated that these teachers, once involved, could see the benefits, which in many instances have included improved behaviour and greater acceptance of responsibility. Griffiths and Davies (1995) have demonstrated that pupil involvement can begin at a very young age and that it may lead to an increasingly respectful and collaborative school culture. However, some writers (Armstrong, Galloway and Tomlinson, 1993; Gersch, 1996) have suggested that there is a need to avoid tokenistic approaches by developing systems that ensure that pupils are equipped with the skills necessary to enable them to play a genuine role in involvement (a theme returned to by Rose later in this book).

When children are not centrally involved in developing their learning skills, learning failure can result. Within an Irish context, Kenny *et al.* (2000) report that young people with disabilities are often overlooked in classroom situations, and their difficulties in learning are often attributed to their impairment. The overprotective attitude of teachers can prevent these young people from taking responsibility for their own learning and making significant progress. Yet, we have many examples where children are actively involved in constructing their own learning. Donnelly (2001) provides examples of young children engaging in higher order thinking while involved in a programme promoting philosophical reflection. Also, Day (1997) reported how children's informal talk made a positive contribution to their writing skills and enabled them to become critically aware of language processes.

## Conclusion

It is not suggested that the greater involvement of pupils will be easily achieved or that all teachers and other professional colleagues will embrace these principles easily. However, it is evident that there are many instances of good practice that have enabled teachers not only to give pupils a voice, but also to demonstrate that by doing so the standards and quality of learning can be improved. Within this book we have attempted to demonstrate a collaboration between researchers, teachers and students, giving each an opportunity to express their views or to articulate their experiences. The writers in this book are, of course, committed to this approach and convinced of its value. A number of obstacles remain in the way of making progress in this area for all pupils, particularly those who come from minorities or have disabilities. Dialogue that involves educators, policy makers and children will be a feature of good practice that can move this debate forward.

The young people who addressed the United Nations General Assembly demonstrated that they have concerns and an understanding of issues, which may well have surprised some of the adults in attendance. As responsible adults we have a responsibility to enable them to feel confident that we are addressing the agenda that they identified. The writers within this book are not suggesting that by simply encouraging voices they will bring about the changes necessary to promote a more just and equitable society. They are, however, convinced that actions at a local level can produce the kinds of positive results that may encourage others, including those in positions of power, to see the value of ensuring that children's voices are heard.

## References

Alderson, P., and Goodey, C. (1998) *Enabling education: experiences in special and ordinary schools*. London: Tufnell.

Armstrong, D., Galloway, D., and Tomlinson, S. (1993) 'Assessing special educational needs: the child's contribution'. *British Educational Research Journal* 19 (2), 121–31.

Bruner, J. (1966) *Toward a Theory of Instruction*. New York: Norton.

Davie, R., and Galloway, D. (1996) 'The voice of the child in education'. In R. Davie and D. Galloway (eds), *Listening to children in education*. London: David Fulton.

Day, T. (1997) 'The role of children's informal talk in their writing'. *Irish Educational Studies* 16, 223–34.

Donnelly, P. (2001) 'A study of higher-order thinking in the early years classroom through doing philosophy'. *Irish Educational Studies* 20, 278–95.

Durkheim, É. (1968) *Education and sociology*. Translated from the French with an Introduction by Sherwood D. Fox. New York and London: The Free Press. (Originally published in French in 1929 as *Éducation et socologie*.)

Foucault., M. (1977) *Discipline and punish*. London: Allen Lane.

Fröbel, F. (1826) *On the education of man (Die menschenerziehung)*. Keilhau/Leipzig: Wienbrach.

Gardner, P. (1999) 'Reconstructing the classroom teacher 1903–1945'. In I. Grosvenor, M. Lawn and K. Rousmaniere (eds), *Silences and images*. New York: Peter Lang.

Gersch, I. (1996) 'Listening to children in educational contexts'. In R. Davie, G. Upton and V. Varma (eds), *The voice of the child*. London: Falmer.

Government of Ireland (1998) Education Act. Dublin: Stationery Office.

Griffiths, M. and Davies, C. (1995) *In fairness to children*. London: David Fulton.

James, A., and Prout, A. (eds) (1990) *Constructing and reconstructing childhood*. Basingstoke: Falmer.

Kenny, M., McNeela, E., Shevlin, M., and Daly, T. (2000) *Hidden voices: young people with disabilities speak about their second-level schooling*. Cork: Bradshaw Books.

Munby, S. (1995) 'Assessment and pastoral care, sense, sensitivity and standards'. In R. Best, C. Lang., C. Lodge and C. Watkins (eds), *Pastoral care and personal social education*. London: Cassell.

Piaget, J. (1929) *The Child's conception of the world*. London: Routledge & Kegan Paul.

Rose, R., Fletcher, W., and Goodwin, G. (1999) 'Pupils with severe learning difficulties as personal target setters'. *British Journal of Special Education* 26 (4), 207–11.

Rousseau, J.J. (originally published 1762) *The Emile of Jean Jacques Rousseau*. New York: Teachers College Press, 1956.

UNICEF (2002) *Annual Report*. New York: UNICEF.

Vlachou, A. (1997) *Struggles for inclusive education: an ethnographic study.* Buckingham: Open University Press.

Vgotsky, L.S. (1962) *Thought and language.* Massachussets: MIT Press.

# 2

## YOUNG PEOPLE'S EQUALITY CONCERNS: THE INVISIBILITY OF DIVERSITY

### *ANNE LODGE AND KATHLEEN LYNCH*

Schools often pride themselves on being institutions that promote equal opportunities and enhance pupils' understanding of democracy. In this chapter Anne Lodge and Kathleen Lynch examine the climate of schools and give students an opportunity to describe their perceptions of the ways in which schools operate. The relationships that are established between teachers and students are of primary concern, and the authors pay particular attention to the ways in which students perceive the use of teacher power and responsibility.

## Introduction

One of the primary purposes of our study on the equality climate of schools was to investigate whether, and how, schools and those who inhabit them are implicated in the reproduction of unequal social relations. We were interested in exploring the equality agenda in schools as defined by the primary actors within educational institutions — young people, teachers and school principals (Lynch and Lodge, 2002).

Our study of educational equality climates involved twelve second level schools located across six different counties in the Republic of Ireland. Our research process involved negotiation and dialogue with participants from the outset. When we set out to study schools, we realised that no single method would enable us to understand the complex web of interactions, processes and procedures that collectively make schools. Schools are highly complex institutions (Ball, 1997); thus, the research design needed to be complex and multifaceted. We used a triangular approach and a range of research tools to explore schools and classrooms. We listened, observed and dialogued with principals, teachers and most especially students. We used different media, including informal discussion, tape recordings, essay writing, focus groups, questionnaires and observations in classrooms, playgrounds and school events, to give us an understanding of the inside life of schools.

The young people who participated in our study were keenly aware of the inequality they experienced because of their youth and lack of power vis-à-vis adults. However, they were far less aware of other equality issues, including the rights of those belonging to minority groups. There was little spontaneous awareness of the needs and rights of those whose identities rendered them socially subordinate. Furthermore, many of the attitudes expressed by the young people who participated in this study showed a marked failure to recognise and respect the cultures and perspectives of such minorities. The groups in question here include people belonging to ethnic or racial minorities, those with disabilities, those professing minority religious beliefs and those who are gay, lesbian or bisexual.

## Young people's equality concerns

The primary equality concerns expressed by the young people who took part in our study focused on the ways in which schools and teachers exercised power over them. They were particularly troubled by their lack of rights in terms of the ways in which they were controlled and punished (Lodge and Lynch, 2000). Young people were keenly aware of the fact that they had little or no consultative role or voice in school, even when it came to issues such as personal appearance which directly impacted on their daily lives. They were bothered by their lack of privacy and autonomy. Other issues of concern included their experiences of unfair punishment, particularly when they felt that they were being blamed in the wrong or labelled due to the behaviour or reputation of siblings or other relatives.

As part of our study, we asked students to write about their most pressing equality concerns and their own experiences of inequality in their school lives.[1] While almost half (48%) of all those who wrote such essays (N=1,202) expressed concern about the way in which adults exercised power and authority over them, only a tiny proportion named any minority identity as a contributory factor in their (and anyone else's) experience of inequality (see Figure 1). For example, only 0.7% of respondents named sexual orientation as a source of inequality in their experience of school.

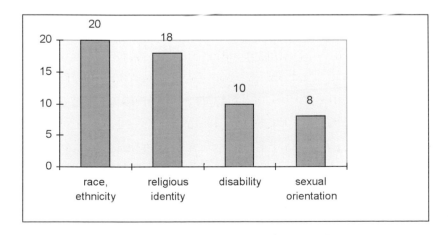

*Figure 1—Numbers of student essays in which minority identity issues arose as named equality issues in their school (Total = 1,202)*

The lack of awareness of equality and minority identities expressed by young people in schools was mirrored by a similar lack of concern expressed spontaneously by their teachers. While 12% of teachers who answered a question on important equality issues in Irish education named gender, less than 1% of these respondents named either disability, sexual orientation, religious identity, race or ethnicity as a factor contributing to educational inequality.

**Equality and the recognition of difference**

Fraser (1995) argues that there are two core models of social justice. The first of these is the distributive model, concerned with the just distribution of resources and benefits, rooted in political economy. The second is the recognition model that is concerned with respect for different identities, values and lifestyles, rooted in culture. In studies of race, ethnicity, disability, sexuality and gender, social justice is concerned not only with distributive justice, but also with issues of recognition of, and respect for, difference. Culturally marginalised groups experience inequality primarily through non-recognition, misrepresentation and lack of respect for difference.

It can be argued that all subordinate groups in society experience some forms of non-recognition, including women and working class groups. However, recognition is much more likely to be the primary source of inequality or injustice for groups that are defined by their cultural marginalisation, and who are identified as 'other' by the dominant group in society. Oppressed groups are subject to what Young (1990) describes as cultural imperialism. They are both rendered invisible (non-recognition) and simultaneously subject to negative stereotyping (mis-recognition). The *sociocultural and symbolic injustices* experienced by marginalised groups are rooted in patterns of representation, interpretation and communication. They take the form of cultural domination, symbolic misrepresentation or non-recognition, all of which lead to a lack of respect (Baker, 1987; 1998; Fraser, 1995; Young, 1990).

Negative images of oppressed groups marginalise them as deviant, ugly and threatening, thus legitimating acts of violence that can be used against them. Not only are their values, perspectives and lives rendered invisible by the life worlds of the dominant group that permeate cultural and institutional norms; this invisibility causes members of oppressed groups to view themselves through the lens of supposed 'normality'. Furthermore, they often internalise the negative stereotypes to which their group is subjected (Goffmann, 1968; Bell, 1997).

Fraser (1995) argues that for people who are gay, lesbian or bisexual, the principal cause of the injustice they experience is the failure to recognise their sexuality, the unwillingness to name it and facilitate it on equal terms with heterosexuality. Our entire culture is pervaded by a presumption of heterosexuality (Epstein and Johnson, 1994). Other groups also experience both non-recognition and mis-recognition. These include racial and ethnic minorities, people with disabilities or different abilities, and religious minorities. The level of non-recognition experienced by these different groups varies with the unique cultural and historical contexts of societies and institutions, including schools.

Inequalities of recognition are fundamentally injustices relating to identity and status. These involve institutional practices of denial, denigration and subordination (Fraser, 2000). Cultural non-recognition or misrepresentation is grounded in the practices and processes of social life, including the life of schools. Curriculum content, pedagogical approaches and organisational norms and processes can all contribute to the exclusion of students with disabilities from full participation in education, for example (Slee, 1997). Failure to consult with those students who are differently abled further compounds their non-recognition and experience of exclusion (Mason, 1990; Slee, 1998). Experiences of rejection or non-recognition of these students by their peers, including rejection or bullying, also contributes to a sense of exclusion from the life of the school.

## Acceptance and recognition of minorities by young people

The schools participating in our study were, like most Irish schools, fairly homogenous in their intake in terms of disability, race, ethnicity, and religious belief. The needs of young learners with disabilities have traditionally been met in segregated schools (Kenny *et al.*, 2000), as has been the case in Britain and elsewhere until relatively recently (French and Swain, 1997; Rieser, 2000). Traveller[2] young people have also experienced separate educational provision, the majority attending special training centres rather than second level schools (Drudy and Lynch, 1993; Kenny, 2000). The majority of Irish primary and post-primary schools[3] are denominationally controlled, a situation that is underpinned by the Irish constitution (Clarke, 1998; Glendenning, 1999). Denominational schools have the right to limit access to those of other beliefs in order to protect their own ethos.

This meant, in the first place, that there were very few young people from minority backgrounds in our study. It also meant that the students in these schools had very little experience of a diverse learning environment. Thus, they had little opportunity afforded to them in a school context to become acquainted with peers from minority backgrounds, thus enabling them to develop friendships as well as understanding and respect for difference. Instead, the attitudes expressed by many of the young people taking part in our study were negative, mocking or fearful of difference. Institutional practices in the participating schools sometimes confirmed rather than challenged the stereotypical attitudes of the young people.

## Sexual orientation — discomfort and rejection

Those who were gay, lesbian or bisexual in our study were the most likely of all minority groups to be invisible and marginalised in public discourse. The silence that surrounds sexual orientation in the education sector is reflective of a discomfort around sexual issues that has characterised Irish society over a lengthy period (Inglis, 1999). Ten of the twelve schools in our study did not deal with differences in sexual orientation in any systematic way. This was true whether schools were Roman Catholic, Protestant or multi-denominational. There was no recognised space in the education programmes of these schools where issues of sexual orientation could be discussed in a safe and inclusive way. A recent study examining the implementation of the Relationships and Sexuality programme found that no school had opted to cover the component looking at sexual orientation (O'Carroll and Szalacha, 2000).

When the subject of sexual orientation emerged, either in whole-class contexts or in focus-group discussions as part of our research, it caused a lot of discomfort and unease among both junior and senior students in general. There was similar unease among school staffs regarding sexual orientation. When we presented our attitudinal data to the staffs in all twelve participating schools indicating the high level of homophobia among students, this subject was only raised by teachers in our research discussions with them in one of the participating schools.

This institutional invisibility was reinforced by the lack of a vocabulary to name and discuss sexual differences. Students were generally not accustomed to addressing the subject of sexual orientation, so they literally did not know what to say or how to say what they did feel or know. The fact that the issue of sexual orientation was only raised spontaneously in eight of the twelve hundred essays as a cause of unequal treatment in schools is itself indicative of the silence that prevails. This is not to suggest that sexual orientation is not a sensitive or important subject in schools, but merely to point out that it was a subject on which there was great silence. The schools participating in our study were by no means unique in terms of their institutional silence and discomfort regarding sexual orientation — a recent review of Irish educational research on this topic revealed very few such studies (e.g. Glen/NEXUS, 1995; Gay HIV Strategies/Nexus, 2000).

There was very limited awareness among students about sexual differences. However, when the subject of sexual differences was named, it evoked sentiments of ignorance, fear and hostility, especially among boys:

> Set all fags on fire. (A second year student in Ballinroe [single-sex boys' school (ssb)])

> Gays should not be allowed to be educated. They have a perverted problem. (A third year student in St David's [ssb feepaying (fp)])

> Mr ... has a problem with me but maybe that's because I have a problem with him, he is GAY! He is always poking me and I think he is bent. (A third year student in Ballinroe [ssb])

Being gay was also perceived as a disorder by some:

> I think this school should be made a co-education [school] for the
> sake of the students already attending. For I'd say of the students
> that don't really mix outside they probably end up gay. (A third year
> student in St David's [ssb fp])

And teasing and bullying among boys sometimes centred on labelling their
targets as gay.

> Sometimes out in the yard, I don't like it when people call me
> names or say I'm gay. (A first year student in St Dominic's [ssb])

Students participating in the study were presented with a series of attitude
statements regarding minority groups. Through these, hostile and negative
student attitudes towards sexual orientation emerged clearly. In response to
the statement 'It is not unusual to be gay or lesbian', almost half of all students
(48%) disagreed, indicating that they considered such identities as deviant
from the dominant cultural norm. Discovering that a friend was gay or lesbian
was considered grounds for termination of friendship by a majority of
respondents. In response to the statement 'If I found out my friend was gay or
lesbian, that would end our friendship', 55% indicated agreement.

It was notable, however, that where an individual teacher or a specific
school programme had addressed the issue, as had occurred in two of the
schools, pupils in focus groups were better able to examine their own
ambiguous feelings and fears. A proactive approach by their school or teacher
was judged by them to have helped to create a space in which this aspect of
sexuality could be explored.

> [There is a need for] mass education about the normality and
> acceptability of homosexuality. There is a huge lack in sex
> education in school [on this subject}. (A sixth year male student in
> St Ita's [co-ed fp])

## Travellers and other racial minorities

Although non-recognition was most acute in relation to sexual orientation, it also pertained in relation to ethnicity (Traveller status especially), racial identity (especially colour and to a lesser extent accent), disability and religious differences. Mis-recognition in the form of deep-seated prejudice towards Travellers was encountered across most of the schools in discussions following on from essays. Students expressed fear, resentment and mockery.

In general, Travellers were regarded as 'undeserving' and unacceptable to the majority, in part because of their apparent lack of willingness to assimilate. A sixth year girl in Ollan (co-ed community college) explained during a focus group discussion that 'Travellers could fit in like anyone else; if they tried they'd fit in. They only make trouble for themselves.' Students referred to them as 'knackers' during the course of focus group discussions and in their classrooms. In some cases, mockery of a particular area or location was related to the fact that some of the people who lived there were Travellers.

For some students, deep distrust between the settled community and Travellers was an accepted part of the ethos of their locality, views held by adults and young people alike. In the course of focus group discussions, a third year boy in Ballinroe (ssb non-feepaying (nfp)) explained that 'people act on the reputation they [Travellers] have. People are used to hating them.'

A number of students believed that Travellers would not be accepted by parents or other students in their school.

> I think because this school is quite snobbish there are inequalities, which are a result of students' attitudes ... For example, although I myself wouldn't have anything against a Traveller coming to this school, I think she would get a hard time due to a large number of snobs in the school. (A sixth year student in St Cecilia's [single-sex girls' school fp])

A fifth year male student in St David's (ssb fp) explained 'my parents pay for me to have privilege and [they] wouldn't like Travellers in this school'.

The hostility and negativity expressed in comments such as those quoted above was reflected in the negative responses to attitude statements regarding Travellers and equality in the student questionnaire. In response to the statement 'Travellers would fit in well at this school', only one quarter (24%) of all respondents were in agreement. Almost all the respondents (91%) felt that 'Having Travellers in this school would make life difficult for the teachers and the pupils'. Travellers were not seen as potential friends; indeed, connection with a Traveller would result in social rejection — over half the students agreed that 'If I made friends with a Traveller, my other friends might not go around with me anymore.'

Where positive attitudes were expressed, these tended to be held by individuals who had previous or ongoing positive contact with Travellers (as neighbours or as school friends in their primary schools). Some of the students attending both urban and rural schools had been in primary classrooms with Traveller children. These students explained how they had no problems with their Traveller classmates, 'everyone got on fine'. Some of the most noticeably positive attitudes expressed by individuals were in towns or places where a proactive approach had been taken in a locality to increase understanding and acceptance between Travellers and settled people. For example, one male student in a school in one such town argued with the researcher while completing his questionnaire that a Traveller student could be offended at the content of some of the attitude statements, and that this was unfair. During the course of a focus group discussion with another class group in the same school, a male student argued 'Travellers have the right to have an education.'

The lack of any sizeable ethnic minority in most schools meant that there was no way of exploring students' responses to racial and ethnic minorities, except hypothetically. A fifth year male student in St David's (ssb fp) argued during a focus group discussion that individuals belonging to racial minorities would be tolerated, but that this would change 'if a large number of them came to the school, then people [would be] prejudiced and resentful'. Indeed, this expectation mirrored the situation in the only school where there was any evidence of a clash between different ethnic groups. This school had a sizeable minority of overseas students. As these students were a relatively homogenous group culturally, they were readily identifiable as 'different'. This is how one of the overseas students described the attitudes in the school:

> Foreigners are treated as though they are not only unintelligent, but also cheaters and wasters by the teachers ... Students treat new people who are not from Ireland like dirt and the only people who have made any efforts at nice behaviour after being here three months are the other foreign students. (A fifth year student in St Ita's [co-ed fp])

While there was some evidence of mis-recognition of individuals or groups belonging to racial minorities in schools, the attitudes expressed by students towards Travellers were noticeably more negative. Student responses to attitude statements clearly demonstrated much higher levels of negative stereotyping and rejection for Travellers than for other ethnic or racial minorities. For example, less than a quarter (23%) of respondents agreed with the statement 'In this school you would get bullied if you were black or coloured', while three quarters (76%) said that Travellers would not fit into their school.

The minority of participating students who were racially different reported an awareness of their outsider status due to experiences of being labelled as such by their peers because of differences in appearance or accent.

> I am originally English so when I arrived in this country I got some abuse because of my accent. I am also quite dark-skinned, so in this country it pertains to being a 'Nigger'. (A fifth year student in Ballinroe [ssb])

## Religious beliefs

Most Irish schools are relatively homogenous in religious terms, so it is difficult to determine whether or not students would experience religious prejudice or discrimination if they expressed a minority religious belief. The limited evidence available from the study, however, is not that encouraging.

In one west of Ireland school, with a large rural intake, junior pupils expressed worry about their ability to understand or be 'close to' a peer with a different religious affiliation. When probed, this appeared to be based on complete lack of contact with members of other religious denominations. They simply said they did not know if they could cope with difference, as they had no experience of it. A senior male student in St David's (ssb fp) expressed the view that his school's homogenous religious intake encouraged rather than challenged his own prejudices, explaining, 'I know I see Protestants, for example, as different, "not like us".' He felt that if his school had a more diverse student intake, people could become accustomed to difference.

In one school where there were identifiable religious minorities, there was a widespread belief among these minorities that the majority were not especially tolerant or respectful of their religious beliefs, particularly where those beliefs impacted on student lifestyle and ability to participate in peer culture.

> The students are very cold to you if you are smart and you don't do drugs or smoke or drink when you go out. They have problems with you if you have *any* morals or religion about your life. (A fifth year female student in St Ita's [co-ed fp])

One of our schools, with a predominantly Roman Catholic student intake, was located in a border region, and had a sizeable minority of students from a range of Protestant denominations. Students were aware of the family religious affiliation of their peers because it was a close-knit rural area. There were no prejudicial views expressed by any students during focus group discussions, nor were there any complaints regarding this issue in their essays. Senior students taking part in two different focus group discussions in this school expressed the view that the mixed religious intake in their school had a very positive effect: 'People are not bothered [about religious difference], mixing people of different religions in school helps them not to care about difference.' Friendships across religious divides were the norm in their school. They were aware of other areas nearby (closer to the border) where they believed attitudes towards religious difference were less tolerant.

In general, issues for individual students belonging to minority religious beliefs related to non-recognition rather than hostility and rejection. However, there were exceptions. One student from a minority faith in a midlands school complained:

> I am a Protestant and I am in a Catholic school. The other pupils do not understand me and give me a hard time. My last year's religion teacher nearly had a heart attack when [the teacher] discovered my religion, [the teacher] began to treat me more like I was above the class. I received a lot more attention than other class members and the class naturally assumed I was a lick. They threatened me with threats like I'll send the IRA to your gaff. Now they are only slightly better. (A third year student in a single-sex boys' school)

Individual comments made by students either during focus group discussions or recorded in more informal situations showed that, for some of them, Protestant identity was exclusively associated with Northern Ireland and unionist politics. In a single-sex girls' school, students talking informally about a teacher they liked assumed that this person was Protestant because of having a Northern Irish accent and background. In a single-sex boys' school, one focus group clearly associated all Protestants with activities and beliefs of the Orange Order, unionism and Glasgow Rangers. One of the boys in this group explained that he would not want any Protestants in his school 'because they think they're English'.

Responses to attitude statements regarding religious affiliation of peers showed a lower level of negativity and hostility than did either statements regarding Travellers or people who are gay. Nonetheless, there was some evidence of negativity, suspicion or lack of awareness regarding religious differentiation. One quarter (25%) of students agreed with the statement 'I would like my close friends to have the same religion as myself'; 14% of respondents agreed that 'Pupils of different religions should not be mixed in the same school'. Almost half (46%) of students disagreed with the statement that 'In this school it does not matter what religion any pupil has'.

The most striking aspect of any discussion regarding religious identity was its apparent lack of any relevance to the lives of young people. During the course of focus group discussions, most young people felt that religious belief was either an entirely private, individual matter, or was of no particular importance in their own lives. In some cases (and this was also evident in some essay comments), students expressed a certain tension regarding the significance afforded to religious expression or identity and the ethos and authority of their school.

> [I would like] less influence of the church on the school. The church inflicts morals and opinions which are sometimes unwanted. (A sixth year male student in Dunely [ssb nfp])

> Religion should not be [a] compulsory [subject] but there should be religion classes for those of different religions, not just Catholic. (A sixth year female student, St Cecilia's [ssg fp])

## Attitudes towards disability

The silence around the subject of disability was not underpinned by the same hostility that characterised students' attitudes towards members of the Traveller community or towards those who were gay, lesbian or bisexual. Indeed, responses to attitude statements regarding persons with disabilities were generally positive. For example, in response to the statement 'Disabled pupils are treated as well as everyone else in this school', over three-quarters (76%) of all students agreed. Rather than expressing negativity, students were more likely to pity someone with a disability.

Students who had little previous contact with disabled students defined them as deserving 'sympathy' and being 'in need of care'. In response to the statement 'Pupils who have disabilities should go to special schools', most did not accept this; however, almost one third (29%) of all respondents agreed that special schools were the more appropriate place for learners with disabilities. During a second year focus group discussion in St Dominic's (ssb nfp), students explained this in terms of the unsuitability of the environment in the school (including behaviour and attitude of students) to cater for the perceived needs and vulnerability of a person with a disability. One of the participants explained

'It's not that you wouldn't want him here — it's for his own safety.' Attitudes to disability therefore reflected assumptions about the 'dependency' of disabled people, combined with a view that having an impairment was some type of 'tragedy' deserving sympathy. The normality of impairment was not visibly part of the majority of students' awareness.

Where students had had some opportunity to mix on equal terms with disabled students in their school, there was some evidence of a 'basic rights' perspective on disability issues. Students expressed concern about the unsuitability of their school buildings (and in one case of the pushing on crowded corridors and stairs) for a person with a mobility-related impairment.

> There could be better facilities for the handicapped pupil such as a lift so he can get upstairs instead of being stuck downstairs all the time. (A fourth year student in St David's [ssb fp])

> More facilities should be provided for the disabled people and extra time between classes so they can get to class on time. (A sixth year student in St Cecilia's [ssg fp])

Where pupils had direct contact with a person with a disability in their class, or as a member of their friendship group, they did not describe that individual in terms of their 'helplessness', or with a sense of pity. Indeed, third year students participating in a focus group discussion in Our Lady's (ssg nfp) described how annoyed they felt when others (students or staff) treated their disabled classmate as different or helpless. A second year boy from St David's (ssb fp) spoke about the impact on his own attitudes of having a wheelchair user in his class:

> Before [student] came to the school if I looked at a person in a wheelchair I really didn't know a lot about them. But when [student] came I realised he's just another person.

Overall, disability was a very minor equality theme in essays, with only ten students naming it as an issue spontaneously. This does not suggest that disability-related inequalities are not important in and of themselves; rather it suggests that disability issues had not arisen for the students. The fact that there were relatively few disabled students in the schools, and only those with very visible physical impairments seemed to be identified as being disabled, resulted in little awareness of disability-related inequalities in schools.

The dominant attitudes to disabled students, both expressed in the discussions and essays, was one of ignorance combined with pity. Of those who expressed a view, most felt that disabled students would be dependent, vulnerable and requiring care. There were only a few individual students who were aware of the educational rights of disabled students, and the majority of these were either friendly with, or in class with, a disabled person.

## Conclusion

The equality focus of most of the young people in our study was primarily based on their own immediate experience and concerns. In the case of adolescents in full time education, this reflects their relative lack of power and status vis-à-vis adults in a school context. They had limited awareness of equality concerns due to a lack of recognition and respect for differences. Their attitudes towards minority groups were informed by a similar lack of respect.

Our findings indicate that the groups that experience the strongest form of mis-recognition were those who were gay or lesbian, and Travellers. The analysis of attitude statements in particular, but also essays and focus groups, indicated that those who were gay or lesbian and those who were Travellers were often regarded as unsuitable for friendship or even as school companions. Their differences were understood as inferiority, abnormality or deviancy. Comments regarding members of these groups indicated high levels of hostility, fear and rejection on the part of many students participating in the study. While disabled people, religious and racial minorities were also the subject of negative stereotyping at the time of our study[4], they did not experience the same level of hostility or disrespect as gays, lesbians and Travellers (Lynch and Lodge, 1999).

We found that male attitudes towards minority groups were more negative than were those of females. Negative views expressed by adolescent males regarding oppressed groups can be understood within a framework of masculine identity. The achievement of hegemonic masculinity involves the domination of other groups believed to be inferior. Masculinity exists within a hierarchical power relationship in which it dominates not only femininity, but also other forms of masculinity (Connell, 1995). Hegemonic masculinity exercises power over other, subordinate forms of masculinity, most notably gay males (Kaufmann, 1994).

Non-recognition and mis-recognition of minorities permeated peer culture in the schools we studied. The negative views expressed by many young people in their school environments reflect those of their immediate communities and the wider society. Schools are not insulated from cultural and social value systems. Where individual teachers attempted to address some of the more entrenched negative attitudes of their students with regard to Travellers, for example, they met with strong student resistance to engage with the material or to consider alternative views.

Young people actively reproduce hierarchical, oppressive relations in society through their own peer interactions, values, norms and culture (Corsaro, 1997; Lodge and Flynn, 2001). These attitudes and values involve the failure to recognise or respect the identities and rights of minority groups. As young people are active contributors to cultural values, norms and practices (Qvortrup, 1993), their attitudes and behaviours play a part in the ongoing oppression of these groups within society.

However, it is important to recognise that young people's cultural attitudes and values are played out within an education system which, for a long period of time, has been characterised by segregation and lack of recognition for difference and diversity in its institutional processes and structures. We found that where young people had the opportunity to study and socialise in a more diverse environment, differences (such as disability, or membership of minority ethnic groups) could cease to be seen as deviant or subordinate. Schools themselves have failed to provide an inclusive environment in which young people are afforded the opportunity to learn to respect and recognise difference.

## References

Baker, J. (1987) *Arguing for equality*. New York: Verso.

Baker, J. (1998) 'Equality'. In S. Healy and B. Reynolds (eds), *Social policy in Ireland*. Dublin: Oak Tree Press.

Ball, S.J. (1997) 'Good school/bad school: paradox and fabrication'. *British Journal of Sociology of Education* 18 (3), 317–35.

Bell, L.A. (1997) 'Theoretical foundations for social justice education'. In M. Adams, L.A. Bell and P. Griffin (eds), *Teaching for diversity and social justice: a sourcebook*. London: Routledge.

Clarke, D. (1998) 'Education, the state and sectarian schools'. In T. Murphy and P. Twomey (eds), *Ireland's evolving constitution, 1937–1997: collected essays*. Oxford: Hart Publishing.

Connell, R.W. (1995) *Masculinities*. Cambridge: Polity Press.

Corsaro, W.A. (1997) *The sociology of childhood*. London: Pine Forge Press.

Drudy, S., and Lynch, K. (1993) *Schools and society in Ireland*. Dublin: Gill and Macmillan.

Epstein, D., and Johnson, R. (1994) 'On the straight and the narrow: the heterosexual presumption, homophobias and schools'. In D. Epstein (ed.), *Challenging lesbian and gay inequalities in education*. Buckingham: Open University Press.

Fraser, N. (1995) 'From redistribution to recognition? Dilemmas of justice in a "post-socialist" age'. *New Left Review* 212, 68–93.

Fraser, N. (2000) 'Rethinking recognition'. *New Left Review* 2 (3), 107–120.

French, S., and Swain, J. (1997) 'Young disabled people'. In J. Roche and S. Tucker (eds), *Youth in society*. Buckingham: Open University Press.

Gay HIV Strategies/NEXUS (2000) *Education: lesbian and gay students*. Dublin: Author.

Glen/NEXUS (1995) *Poverty: lesbians and gay men*. Dublin: Combat Poverty Agency.

Glendenning, D. (1999) *Education and the law*. Dublin: Butterworths.

Goffmann, E. (1968) *Stigma: notes on the management of a spoiled identity*. London: Penguin.

Inglis, T. (1999) *Irish lessons in sexuality*. Dublin: UCD Press.

Kaufmann, M. (1994) 'Men, feminism and men's contradictory experiences of power'. In H. Brod and M. Kaufmann (eds), *Theorizing masculinities*. London: Sage.

Kenny, M. (2000) 'Travellers, minorities and schools'. In Sheehan, E. (ed.), *Travellers: citizens of Ireland*. Dublin: The Parish of the Travelling People.

Kenny, M., McNeela, E., Shevlin, M., and Daly, T. (2000) *Hidden voices: young people with disabilities speak about their second-level schooling*. Cork: South West Regional Health Authority.

Keogh, A. (2000) 'Talking about the Other: a view of how secondary school pupils construct opinions about refugees and asylum-seekers'. In M. McLachlan and M. O' Connell (eds.), *Cultivating pluralism*. Dublin: Oak Tree Press.

Lentin, R. (1999) *The expanding nation: towards a multi-ethnic Ireland. Proceedings of a Conference*. Vol. 1. Dublin: Department of Sociology, Trinity College Dublin.

Lodge, A., and Flynn, M. (2001) 'Gender identity in the primary school playground'. In A. Cleary, M. Nic Ghiolla Phadraig and S. Quin (eds), *Understanding children, volume 1: state, education and the economy*. Dublin: Oak Tree Press.

Lodge, A., and Lynch, K. (2000) 'Power: a central educational relationship'. *Irish Educational Studies* 19, 46–67.

Lynch, K., and Lodge, A. (1999) 'Essays on school'. In K. Lynch, *Equality in Education*. Dublin: Gill and Macmillan.

Lynch, K., and Lodge, A. (2002) *Equality and power in schools*. London: Routledge/Falmer.

McVeigh, R. (1995) *The racialization of Irishness*. Belfast: CRD.

Mason, M. (1990) 'Disability equality in the classroom: a human rights issue'. *Gender and Education* 2 (3), 363–6.

O'Carroll, I., and Szalacha, L. (2000) *A queer quandary: the challenges of including sexual difference within the relationships and sexuality education programme*. Report compiled for Lesbian Education Awareness.

Qvortrup, J. (1993) 'Nine theses about "childhood as a social phenomenon"'. In Qvortrup, J. (ed.), *Childhood as a social phenomenon: lessons from an international project. Eurosocial Report No. 47.* Vienna: European Centre for Social Welfare Policy and Research.

Rieser, R. (2000) 'Special educational needs or inclusive education: the challenge of disability discrimination in schooling'. In M. Cole (ed.), *Education, equality and human rights.* London: Routledge/Falmer.

Slee, R. (1997) 'Imported or important theory? Sociological interrogations of disablement and special education'. *British Journal of Sociology of Education* 18 (3), 407–19.

Slee, R. (1998) 'Inclusive education? This must signify 'new times' in educational research'. *British Journal of Educational Studies* 46 (4), 440–54.

Young, I.M. (1990) *Justice and the politics of difference.* Princeton University Press.

**Notes**

1  All 1,557 students in the study were invited to write a short essay on their experiences of inequality in their school, and outline their ideas as to how to make their school more equal and just; 1,202 wrote essays. The essay question was in two parts and was worded as follows:

*We would like you to write here about any time or place when you think you've been unfairly or unequally treated since you came to this school, either by other a) pupils or b) teachers.*

*To make school a fairer and more equal place, what kind of changes would you like to see in it?*

2  Travellers are Ireland's largest indigenous ethnic minority, whose economic and social structures are fundamentally based on nomadism. They have a range of social and cultural practices that make them distinctive from the settled community. They have experienced discrimination in the way that they are treated by the sedentary majority as well as by the Irish State (McVeigh, 1995).

3  Currently, 99% of all Irish primary schools are denominationally owned and

controlled. Over half (57%) of all second level schools are denominationally owned and controlled. Other institutions providing post-primary education, which are State owned, also have varying levels of denominational input, although they are officially referred to in the Department of Education and Science as 'interdenominational'.

4   Since we completed the fieldwork, there has been a very significant increase in the number of migrant workers, refugees and asylum seekers entering Ireland. Such groups are now experiencing the same type of recognition problems as the more despised indigenous groups (see Lentin, 1999). A recent study of young people's attitudes towards refugees and asylum-seekers (Keogh, 2000) reported varying levels of fear, hostility and rejection of racial difference.

# 3

## VOICING CONCERNS ABOUT CHILDREN'S RIGHTS AND STATUS IN SCHOOL

*DYMPNA DEVINE*

Dympna Devine describes a process whereby pupils from primary schools were encouraged to voice their opinions about their educational experiences. Pupil perceptions of their status within their school and their understanding of the sometimes inconsistent roles that teachers play in their lives are explored, as well as the pressures exerted through the expectations of a demanding imposed curriculum model. The school environment can be a critical influence on the ways in which students engage with the learning process. The author provides indicators of how student perceptions can provide valuable insights into the ways in which we can create democratic classrooms that are more conducive to teaching and learning.

## Introduction

While equality issues are increasingly being framed within the context of a rights discourse, the identification of children as a distinct group with minority status has only recently come to the fore. The ratification of the United Nations Convention on the Rights of the Child (1989), coupled with a growing research movement focusing on the sociological positioning of children and childhood (Corsaro, 1997; James, Jencks and Prout, 1998; Mayall 2002; Qvortrup, 1994; Wyness 2000), has drawn attention to the absence of children's voices in major policy debates both internationally and nationally, and the negative implications for their capacity to be taken seriously within society at large. Within education, children's voices have become increasingly prominent in the work of Pollard (2000; 1985), Woods (1990) and King (1989; 1978). The exclusion of children from full participation within society must be considered within the context of the dynamics of power and control that operate between adults and children within a variety of institutional contexts. This paper considers the positioning of children within one such context, that of the school, highlighting their voices on key aspects of their school experience related to what they learn, how they learn and their relationships with teachers and fellow pupils. It is argued that the nature of children's schooling experience in each of these areas shapes their sense of themselves with particular rights and status within the school. Located within the context of recent debates related to children's citizenship (Roche, 1999; Devine, 2002), this in turn, it is argued, has implications not only for their capacity as adult citizens of the future but also as engaged active citizens of the present.

## Children's rights and status in Irish education

Within the education system, debates over children's rights have been conducted primarily in terms of the right to education (Government of Ireland, 1996) rather than through any specific reference to the rights of children as a group and their experience of the system itself. Rights and status are connected with the exercise of power and the capacity to have one's voice both expressed and heard. Foucault (1979) in his analysis of the exercise of power in modern societies highlights the significance of discourse in promoting particular definitions of normality, with negative implications for the rights and status of those who are defined as 'other' or outside of the norm within the modern social sphere. Specifically he points to the range of 'disciplinary technologies' employed in modern day institutions (hospitals, prisons and schools) that divide and classify the population, defining them according to their perceived normality or 'otherness'. An evaluation of the rights and status of children within the school system can thus be made with reference to the exercise of power between adults and children, within the context of discourses that have governed adult/child relations in modern Irish society.

A socio-historical analysis of children's rights and status in Irish education reveals the changing discourse in relation to children and childhood from the turn of the century up to the present day (Devine, 1999). Prior to the 1960s it is clear that within the discourse of the period, the focus of education was upon the normalisation of children in terms of Catholic and nationalistic ideologies. Furthermore, education was seen as an act of imposition, something that teachers 'did' to children, who were perceived to be passive and in need of containment. The discourse of the period was also highly paternalistic, reflecting the view that children were ultimately the property of their parents. Issues relating to the rights and status of children did not arise — children were to be seen and not heard, with strict adherence to adult definitions of 'normal' behaviour emphasised throughout their school experience.

A change in discourse in relation to children and childhood in Irish society is evident, however, from the 1960s onward (Devine, 1999). Adult discourse of the period began to stress the innocence and vulnerability of children, with a specific focus on satisfying individual needs. Such discourse had implications for teacher/pupil relations, as well as curricular and pedagogical practices in primary schools, and was reflected in a less authoritarian approach to the teaching of children. In spite of a broader approach to the framing of children's activities, schoolwork was still carried out within a predominantly instrumental/adult-centred framework, with little impact on the subordinate status of children within the system. The focus continued to remain on the normalisation of children in terms of adult goals, although these were now expressed in terms of the fulfilment of children's needs. The discourse of the period thus failed to challenge the status differentials between adults and children in any serious way; what changed was the manner in which they were expressed.

Rights and status issues are interwoven with the capacity to have one's voice acknowledged, respected and heard. In the past ten years, significant steps have been taken to incorporate previously hidden voices into educational policy making, reflected in particular in the holding of the National Education Convention in 1994 (Coolahan, 1994). Such 'partnership in education', however, has been defined primarily in adult-centred terms, with the main users of the education system, children, excluded from the process of consultation. More recently, the revised primary curriculum (1999), devised on the basis of consultation with such partners, makes welcome reference to the need to consider children as 'active agents', yet the process of consultation leading to its formulation did not at any stage include children. Similarly, the limited rights of consultation accorded to children in the recent Education Act (1998) suggests that the definition of citizenship underlying the provision of education does not take account of children as central actors, with the right to exercise their voice at a meaningful level within the system (Devine, 2000).

This contradictory position is indicative of a particular power relationship between adults and children, governed by discourses relating to the nature of children and childhood. More recent policy, as outlined in the National Children's Strategy (2000) seeks to address such anomalies, specifying the need, as articulated in the United Nations Convention on the Rights of the Child (Article 12/13), to accord children greater rights of consultation in all matters that affect them. According children a greater voice, however, has implications for the exercise of power between adults and children. To be effective, such policy must take account, and be informed of, the dynamics of power and control currently operating between adults and children within and through the school system. Highlighting children's experience of this power relationship is important, not only in furthering our understanding of the dynamics of adult/child and teacher/pupil relations, but also in validating the perspectives and views of children themselves, and in so doing enabling them to exercise their voice in education.

## Children's perspectives on school — voicing their concerns

With this in mind, research was conducted into the views and perspectives of a sample of primary school children on their experience of school (Devine 1998). In total, three primary schools were involved, all co-educational with contrasting socio-economic intakes: 'Churchfield' was predominantly middle/upper middle class, 'Hillview' served a lower middle class population and 'Parkway' was a designated disadvantaged school. A mixed methodological approach was utilised, consisting of qualitative fieldwork over a period of one school year, continuous observations of classroom practice, open-ended questionnaires and semi-structured interviews with 133 pupils in first/second and fifth class. Questionnaires consisted of open and closed questions and covered aspects of school practice in terms of social relations, pedagogy, curriculum and evaluative systems in use in school. Teachers were not present when the questionnaires were being completed. To facilitate younger children, the questionnaires were administered in small groups; each question was read aloud, and each child was given sufficient time to complete their response. Interviews were conducted in friendship groups of three and four, and the children were free to select with whom they wished to be interviewed. This reduced the formality of the interview context and gave rise to a greater sense of ease on the part of the children in discussing issues of interest to them. The older children in the study were also asked to complete diaries, noting incidents or events that they personally viewed as being important in their school lives. Drawings of an ideal yard/classroom were also used to elicit information from the children, providing a useful context within which to identify children's sense of the use of space within the school. Semi-structured interviews with the teachers (five in total) as well as their school principals (three) were also conducted. Such interviews, beyond the scope of this chapter, focused in particular on their perceptions of children and childhood in modern Ireland, their attitudes toward education, the curriculum, pedagogy and evaluation, as well as the moral and social education of children in their care.

For the purposes of this chapter, the analysis focuses on key aspects of children's school experience, with regard to their relations with their teachers, pedagogical and evaluative practices as well as the experience of the curriculum in school. Experience in each of these domains, it is argued, contributes to children's practical consciousness (Giddens, 1991) concerning their role, rights and status within the school, in turn framing their perception of themselves as active, critical beings, with a voice to be both heard and expressed.

## Rights and status issues in children's relations with their teachers

Children form clear perceptions of their positioning within the school hierarchy in their relations with their teachers and of the resultant constraints imposed on their capacities as autonomous agents with a voice to be both heard and expressed. This is particularly evident in their definitions of a teacher: as one who is grown up, knowledgeable, bossy and free, reflecting his or her superior power, hence status, in school:

> The children have the least power 'cos they're not allowed do anythin ... say what they want ... do what they want ... the principal has the most power ... and the teachers ... they're grown-ups so they're meant to be the bosses. (5th class boy, Parkway)

From the children's perspective, the greater power of teachers is reflected not only in their greater access to facilities within the school and their apparent freedom from rules, but also in the sensitivity children feel they must display to teacher mood:

> Sometimes you can ask her a question but you never know when she is going to jump on you ... like you are just talking to her and she could jump on you and give out to you no matter what you say ... especially if she has a bad day ... she takes it out on us. (5th class girl, Hillview)

The extent of children's sensitivity to teacher power was also reflected in their constant references to the level of surveillance they experienced in school, with younger children in particular convinced of the magical powers of detection of some of their teachers:

> I think the teacher has eyes in the back of her head, 'cos when she's out of the room she knows stuff that happened and even when she's at her desk she is looking out the side of her eye to see who is even whispering. (2nd class girl, Churchfield)

The lack of reciprocity in teacher/pupil relations was also referred to by older children, indicating for them the greater power of teachers, as adults, in the school:

> In the classroom the teachers and the principal have more power 'cos we can't give out to them like they give out to us ... we can't tell them to be quiet or send them up to the office ... they are adults and they think they have more power, but kids have rights as well. (5th class boy, Hillview)

In typifying teachers in these terms, it is clear that children perceive themselves in opposite terms, as having subordinate status with the school. This is reflected not only in the fact that just 1% of children felt the school belonged to them, but also in their comments listing the most to least important people in the school:

> Mr [Principal] is the most important 'cos he runs the school, then Mr [Vice Principal], the teachers, and the children are the last ... we are important to our mams ... you don't see the children bossing others ... children don't boss adults. (5th class boy, Hillview)

> The children are the least important 'cos we are just children. (5th class girl, Hillview)

Not being taken seriously is a prime indicator of children's subordinate status, and this emerged in their accounts of not being listened to, being unfairly treated and not being given a voice in school. Their views are reflected in the following comments:

> When adults are treated unfairly they stand up and object to it ... but they don't kinda take children seriously ... they think they are just messin' or lookin' for attention. (5th class girl, Churchfield)

> Sometimes children should have a say ... if something is really hard for children and they might feel scared ... if they have a say the teacher might understand more ... but you need to know they won't say 'Oh listen to this and listen to that' ... that's what they do sometimes at staff meetings with the black book. (2nd class girl, Churchfield)

However, not all children subscribed to these views, with factors such as social class and age level mediating the level of dissatisfaction expressed. This was particularly the case in relation to children's desire to exercise a greater voice in school, with fifth class children and those of middle class origin most likely to assert their right to be respected and to voice an opinion on matters that concerned them in school. Familiar with the changing discourses governing adult/child relations in the wider sphere (typified by a breakdown in traditional authority relations between adults and children), such children question the traditional structures of domination in school, suggesting alternatives that would radically alter the nature of teacher/pupil interaction:

> I think there should be a vote over rules ... 'cos we live in a democracy ... if we could have different lunch times that would be brilliant ... we should be allowed vote about whether or not we want to go to the choir. (5th class boy, Churchfield)

> I think the children should get a say in deciding rules ... well, there are votes for Presidents or whatever, so we could put our vote in the

> box ... she'd have her rules and then we'd vote for them. (5th class
> girl, Churchfield)

While children, particularly older middle class children, were clearly
dissatisfied with aspects of their social interaction with their teachers, the study
also indicated that most children were positively disposed to the socio-
emotional climate in their classrooms. In the busy and often pressured
environment of the classroom, children in general perceived their teachers to
be kind and caring and wanted to have a positive relationship with them.
Children were particularly sensitive to teacher praise and the care and
attention received when required:

> I feel happy when I get everything right and the teacher says good
> boy. (2nd class boy, Churchfield)

> I feel good about myself in school knowing that someone cares
> enough to teach you stuff and give you a good education. (5th class
> girl, Parkway)

However, the increasing workload on older children toward the end of primary
school results in a more instrumental and disciplined approach by teachers in
working with them. This gives rise to a more qualified perspective by such
children on their relations with teachers:

> The teachers are much nicer to the younger children but as they
> get older they expect you to be more responsible ... they give us
> loads of work and expect us to do it on our own. (5th class boy,
> Hillview)

The data indicates that children are aware of and sensitive to power
differentials between themselves and the adults within the school. This in turn
has implications for their perception of their rights and status within the school,
in particular their capacity to question teacher authority and control and to

assert their voice in matters that concern them. However, it should be noted that this overarching sensitivity to teacher control does not preclude children from engaging in a range of backstage behaviours that undermine such control, while simultaneously providing some relief from the constant surveillance of adults in the classroom. Thus yard-time was replete with examples of 'forbidden' activities such as fights, 'rude' rhymes and 'bad' language, as children engaged in a world free from the glare of adult eyes:

> Sometimes there does be a big crowd and everyone gathers around and the teacher does be saying get away, get away … and the teacher is trying to find out who did it and doesn't unless someone tells … mostly children say: 'Oh I didn't see it.' (5th class boy, Hillview)

> We have lots of scraps in the yard 'cos children are calling each other names like d*** and w*** … No way would we say them in front of the teacher. (5th class boy, Churchfield)

Through child culture, children engage in a world that is free from adult control, forging friendships, forming identities and playing a host of games differentiated by gender and age. In this process of action and reaction, governed by its own series of rules and regulations (Devine, 1998), children regain some measure of autonomy, enabling them to cope with the restrictions of classroom life.

The differential status and positioning of teachers and children has implications for children's experience of all elements of school practice. In voicing their concerns about their curricular experience, for example, children spoke of their frustration regarding the absence of consultation over what and how they should learn at school. While subjects such as physical education and art proved universally popular, older children in particular recognised the importance of learning Irish, mathematics and English for future study and job opportunities. Nonetheless, dissatisfaction was expressed over the frequency of learning in the latter subjects and the time pressure to complete work that was perceived to be difficult:

> There shouldn't be so much time spent on maths ... it's always
> maths ... I know it's important but we spend about an hour and a
> half on it every day. (5th class girl, Hillview)

> Some teachers don't understand what it's like ... how hard it is ...
> like they might say, do the next six questions, and they might be the
> hardest in the book ... and twenty minutes later they say have you
> got them all done, even though they would take half an hour ... if
> they had to be children for just one day they would know it was
> hard and find out what it was like to do a question in five minutes
> ... or get extra homework. (5th class boy, Hillview)

Their views in many ways parallel those of the teachers in the study, who also complained about the heavily loaded nature of the primary curriculum. A further source of pressure related to the assignment of homework, which children viewed as an unfair intrusion into their private lives, and one over which they had little control. Indeed, for many children, homework epitomised the powerful position of the teacher, in terms of using it as a form of punishment, as well as extending control beyond the school:

> Homework is bad 'cos we work hard every day ... and then you are
> sent home to do more ... teachers give children homework to keep
> them occupied after school ... you are supposed to go home and
> relax, not do more homework ... it's like the teacher is still there
> watching you even though you are at home ... the only way you get
> out of it is if you are sick. (5th class boy, Hillview)

While many children accepted teacher authority in choosing what they should do in school (with girls and younger children most likely to accept teacher control), others questioned the exercise of power in this manner. The contrast in attitudes is reflected in their comments below:

I think the teacher should choose 'cos then there would be no arguments … some of the class like things that half the class doesn't. (5th class girl, Parkway)

Sometimes it feels like a bit like being a robot … as if the teacher is in the middle of the room with a great big remote control and you have to do everything she says or you will get into trouble. (2nd class girl, Churchfield)

The teachers don't really let you do what you want … so they don't give much power to the children … the teachers have the most power and make the children learn what they want them to learn. (5th class boy, Churchfield)

Where children were frustrated with the lack of choice or consultation afforded them, this centred primarily on the working of the timetable itself and the absence of a sufficient balance between worktime and playtime in school. Understood in the context of the exercise of power between adults and children, what children are looking for is a marrying of both the adult and child worlds, where the priorities of each group are given equal weight in the school day:

We should be allowed choose about PE or going out to the yard … we'd mix work and play more … like at the beginning of the year we could decide the timetable and have half an hour of work and an hour break. (5th class girl, Churchfield)

The fact that teachers could choose to do subjects that they liked was also a source of irritation — highlighting children's own lack of choice in such matters:

Teachers sort of choose the subjects they like … so they do that a lot … like our teacher loves Irish or when we had nuns they did a lot of religion. (5th class girl, Churchfield)

Annoyance was also expressed at the routine nature of the timetable and the fact that the hardest subjects were always chosen first:

I'd like to be able to choose more … 'cos every day we do the same thing and it gets boring … and if you want to do say history, she wants to do maths or something … she sticks to the same routine all the time. (5th class boy, Hillview)

Overall the children's comments reflect the desire to cater for child culture as well as adult expectations for learning in the organisation of the timetable, thereby balancing children's love of fun and freedom with 'real work' of Irish, English and mathematics.

While children's perception of the use of time in school highlighted issues related to their rights and status, particularly in terms of curricular choices and the organisation of the timetable, the organisation of space within the school also highlighted differences in the positioning of adults and children within the school. While most children in the study were favourably disposed to the manner in which their classroom space was organised, space as a form of symbolic power between adults and children emerged in their accounts of differences in access to resources and facilities between teachers and pupils in school. For the children, the superior status of teachers was confirmed in their access to a well-equipped staff room and furniture that was comfortable and relaxing:

I wish we had more comfortable chairs … teachers have big comfortable chairs and they have drawers in their desk … the teachers have them 'cos they are grown-ups … teachers are respected more by the principal and other teachers. (5th class boy, Churchfield)

Recreation space also differed greatly between teachers and children, with the barren appearance of the schoolyards in sharp contrast to the more comfortable space of the school staff rooms. While all children valued their yard-time, they were critical of the lack of space and facilities afforded them:

> I wouldn't call it a playground 'cos there is nothing to do except run around and we're not even allowed do that 'cos we're so squashed up. (5th class girl, Churchfield)

The control of children's time and space in school takes place within a disciplinary framework in which they are required to monitor their behaviour in line with a series of rules and regulations. Conformity to these rules is part and parcel of the process of normalisation and is tied to the exercise of power between adults and children. Interview data indicated that rules related to movement, social interaction and control of speech were foremost in children's minds, with teachers by and large making the decisions as to what the rules should be. Children's perceptions of the fairness/legitimacy of school rules drew on two contrasting discourses: one that defined children in a paternalistic light and therefore in need of containment and guidance, and another that seeks a greater voice for children in the making of rules:

> If there were no rules in school, children would be fighting all the time. (2nd class girl, Churchfield)

> It would be better to share decisions about rules with children ... at the start of the year he just comes in with a long list and says now abide by the rules ... it's like being in boarding school. (5th class boy, Parkway)

In general, girls, younger children and children from working class backgrounds ascribed to the former discourse, while boys, older children and those from middle class homes related to the latter viewpoint in their attitudes to school rules. Younger children in particular were highly ambiguous about their level of control over teachers' behaviour, suggesting a relatively unquestioning acceptance of the authority and status of adults within the school, encapsulated in the comment of one young boy that 'teachers are allowed to do everything they want'.

Older children, however, were more sensitive to the power context within pupil/teacher interactions, expressed in their desire to limit teacher control over them, as well as their resentment at the ability of teachers to circumvent school rules:

> The teachers are allowed smoke ... they're allowed walk around the classroom whenever they want ... they're allowed talk whenever they want ... they're allowed have cups of tea in the middle of school when we're not allowed even a drink of water ... they should have to follow the rules they make ... the same ones as us. (5th class girl, Parkway)

For older children the perception of double standards in teacher behaviour highlighted for them the unfairness of many rules and the uneven distribution of power between adults and children in school.

Older children's sensitivity to the power context in teacher/pupil relations was also evident in the views they expressed regarding their perceptions of teaching style and practice, with their definition of a good teacher as one who was strict and ensured adequate learning, but who exercised power in a fair manner:

> Sometimes be nice and sometimes be strict ... you can't be nice all the time 'cos children will break the rules ... a bad teacher is if they are nice all the time and don't give the children any discipline. (5th class girl, Hillview)

In contrast, younger children were more likely to focus on the interpersonal dimension of teacher/pupil interactions:

> A good teacher is someone who likes you, who cares for you and
> who minds you if you fall. (2nd class girl, Churchfield)

While the data highlighted the extent to which children's behaviour in school
is circumscribed by a range of adult-defined rules, this is not to suggest that
teacher control over children's behaviour is complete. Interview and
observational data also indicated the highly negotiated character of school
discipline. Thus teachers sought to control children by setting one subject off
another — attempting to steer the balance sought by children themselves
between worktime and playtime in school. Reduced homework or the threat of
extra homework, the promise of doing/not doing art and physical education or
watching videos, were used as a means of inducing conformity and learning
among the children.

Overall, the data highlights the centrality of pedagogical and curricular
practices to the exercise of power in schools. From the children's perspective,
to be a child in school is to have your behaviour, thoughts and gestures
controlled and defined in terms of adult norms and expectations. This is borne
out, not only by observational data detailing the content and manner of teacher
exchanges with pupils, but also by the extent of children's awareness of being
monitored and restrained in school. Children frequently spoke of their constant
surveillance by teachers, encapsulated in the comment of one child who
stated:

> I'd put the teacher's desk as far away as possible ... outside the
> classroom door ... 'cos she's watching your every move ... every
> time you even look in your bag she's watching over you ... and
> even if you want to get a head start in your homework she sees you.
> (5th class girl, Hillview).

Evaluation, both formal and informal, also formed part of the surveillance
practices used on children in school. While children generally felt that
evaluation was a necessary part of the learning process, they also viewed it in
disciplinary terms — as a means of checking who was listening and to keep

children quiet. The result of a test or the threat of a negative report had a powerful normalising effect, particularly given the public nature of much evaluation within school (Filer, 2000). A consideration of the dynamics of child culture highlights their intense scrutiny of other children, evident not only in their eagerness to find out how everyone did in a test or school report, but also in their tendency to slag and tease one another for their school performance:

> I hate when she opens up your copy and reads out the story ... say it's an Irish story and you have something wrong, like a sentence backwards ... she'd read that in front of the class and everyone would go duuuuh and you'd be sitting there embarrassed. (5th class boy, Hillview)

In terms of rights and status issues, however, it was clear that regardless of the form of evaluation used (test, report, parent/teacher meeting, public checking/reprimands), evaluation was perceived as something that was done to children or about them, and over which they had little control. Discussions over parent/teacher meetings, for example, indicated that a majority of children did not wish to be present because they feared a negative review:

> I wouldn't like to be at one 'cos if you were getting into trouble they'd both be at you ... the teacher and the parents together at the same time. (5th class boy, Churchfield)

> I do be shiverin for the meetins ... we shouldn't be there 'cos the teacher wouldn't be able to say how bad you are ... but I would like to see my ma's expression to see if she was happy or disappointed. (5th class girl, Parkway)

A minority of children, however, disliked the secrecy surrounding what was said about them and wished to be fully involved:

> I think children would like to know what the teacher said about

them … sometimes parents don't tell the truth to you … they say 'Oh the teacher said you were great or marvellous' … but the teacher might have said the opposite … I would like to know if my mum was telling the truth and I would like to tell my family 'cos it's mine … they are talking about me. (2nd class girl, Churchfield)

I would like to be there to interrupt them if they were saying something wrong. (5th class girl, Hillview)

Children's own evaluation of their school experience indicates both positive and negative views. While the importance of schooling in the promotion of future life chances is generally acknowledged, the lived experience of childhood in school is brought into question by the critical views expressed. School is a space where children are compulsorily confined and where they are subjected to a range of normalising practices, which both signify and legitimise their subordinate status relative to adults. All children, regardless of gender, age and social class, are keenly aware of this difference in status between themselves and adults in the school, although varying views were expressed on the legitimacy of such status differences, with girls and younger children in particular least likely to question the absence of children's voices in school. Their views point to the powerful impact of the hidden curriculum in the formation of social identities, with children internalising distinct messages regarding their rights and status through the curricular, pedagogical and evaluative practices employed by teachers in school.

## Conclusion

While discourse in relation to children's rights and citizenship has recently filtered into Irish governmental policy (National Children's Strategy, 2000), such discourse will only be realised in practice when the dynamics of power and control currently exercised between adults and children are brought to the fore. This paper examined children's experience in one context, that of the primary school, highlighting their views on their rights and status within the school. The strength of the analysis undertaken in this research lies in locating their views within a framework that considers the power dimension in adult/child relations, and in so doing challenges and deconstructs traditional concepts of children as immature and irresponsible. Within an adult-centred framework, the greater power that adults exercise over children is interpreted in terms of equal exchange, the benefit to teachers in terms of enabling them to carry on with the business of teaching and learning, and the benefit to children in terms of facilitating them in the promotion of their life chances. When viewed through a child's eyes, however, the paternalism inherent within such a perspective is open to question, given the sense of alienation that older children, in particular, reflected in recounting their experiences of school. This is of concern, given the enthusiasm and commitment demonstrated by younger children in the study, suggesting that as children's experience of the system grows, so too does their level of alienation and disenchantment.

To exclude children from decision-making in matters of concern to them not only undermines their experience of school as an important part of their childhood, but also detracts from developing within them the critical skills with which all citizens living in a democratic pluralistic society should be equipped (Devine, 2002; McLoughlin, 2002). For a change in children's status to take place, the structuring of adult/child relations must be informed by discourse that stresses the empowerment, inclusion and active participation of children as citizens within the school. Citizenship and the practice of democracy does not occur automatically; this can only happen through a process of training in the rudiments of argument, negotiation, planning and dealing with social realities (Fumat 1999; Holden 1999). Thus the formation of student councils, workshop education, peer support groups, circle time and cooperative learning projects, as well as children constructively evaluating their own and other's work, can all be used to create a democratic 'listening culture' within schools (Jelly *et al* 2000; Mosley 1996; Davie and Galloway, 1996). Such a culture necessitates a change in identity, however, both for adults and for children, as they negotiate new ways of 'knowing' centred on interdependence, mutual recognition and the sharing of power (Wyness, 1999; Roche, 1999). Given the socially constructed nature of personal identity (Burr, 1995), children who experience democracy in practice, in their relations with adults, will incorporate concepts of equality, difference and respect into their worldview (Bridges, 1997; Arnot, 2000). The findings of this research suggest that children may be interpreting much of their school experience in terms of subservience and conformity — concepts alien to democracy and equality. This has implications for their present lives as children, as well as their future lives as adults within society.

## References

Arnot, M. (2000) *Challenging democracy*. London: Routledge/Falmer.

Bridges, D. (1997) *Education, autonomy and democratic citizenship*. London: Routledge/Falmer.

Burr, V. (1995) *An introduction to social constructivism*. London: Routledge and Kegan Paul.

Coolahan, J. (1994) *Report of the National Education Convention*. Dublin: Government Publications.

Corsaro, W. (1997) *The sociology of childhood*. California: Pine Forge Press.

Davie, R. and Galloway, D. (1996) *Listening to children in education*, London: Fulton Publishers.

Devine, D. (2002) 'Citizenship and the structuring of adult child relations in school'. *Childhood* 9 (3), 303–21.

Devine, D. (2000) 'Constructions of childhood in school: power, policy and practice in Irish education'. *International Studies in Sociology of Education* 10 (1), 23–41.

Devine, D. (1999) 'Children: rights and status in education: a socio-historical perspective'. *Irish Educational Studies* 18, 14–29.

Devine, D. (1998) 'Structure, agency and the exercise of power in children's experience of school'. Unpublished Ph.D. Thesis. National University of Ireland, Dublin.

Filer, A. (2000) *Assessment, social practice and social product*. London: Routledge/Falmer.

Foucault, M. (1979) *Discipline and punish: the birth of the prison*. New York: Random House.

Fumat, Y. (1999) 'School and citizenship'. In A. Ross (ed.), *Young citizens in Europe*. London: CICE.

Giddens, A. (1991) *Modernity and self identity*. Cambridge: Polity Press.

Government of Ireland (2000) *Our children — their lives: the National Children's Strategy*. Dublin: Stationery Office.

Government of Ireland (1998) *Education Act*. Dublin: Government Publications.

Government of Ireland (1999) *Primary school curriculum*. Dublin: Stationery Office.

Government of Ireland (1996) *Report of the Constitution Review Group*. Dublin: Government Publications Office.

Holden, C. (1999) 'Education for citizenship: the contribution of social, moral and cultural education'. In A. Ross (ed.), *Young citizens in Europe*. London: CICE.

Jelly, M., Fuler, A. and Byers, R. (2000) *Involving pupils in practice*. Wilts: Cromwell Press

James, A., Jencks, C., and Prout, A. (1998) *Theorising childhood*. Cambridge: Polity Press.

King, R. (1989) *The best of primary education: a sociological study of junior middle schools*. London: Falmer Press.

King, R. (1978) *All things bright and beautiful? a sociological study of infants' classrooms*. New York: John Wiley and Sons.

Mayall, B. (2002) *Towards a sociology for childhood*, Buckingham: Open University Press.

McLoughlin, O. (2002) 'Citizen child: a case study of a student council in a primary school', Unpublished M.Ed thesis. Education Dept, National University of Ireland, Dublin

Mosley, J. (1996) *Quality circle time in the primary classroom*. Wisbech: Learning Development Aids.

Pollard, A., and Triggs, P. (2000) 'What pupils say: changing policy and practice in primary education'. London: Continuum.

Pollard, A. (1985) *The social world of the primary school*. Guildford: Biddles Ltd.

Qvortrup, J. (1994) *Childhood matters: social theory, practice and politics.* Aldershot: Avebury.

Roche, J. (1999) 'Children: rights, participation and citizenship'. *Childhood* 6 (4), 475–93.

Woods, P. (1990) *The happiest days? How pupils cope with school.* Bristol: Falmer Press.

Wyness, M. (2000) *Contesting childhood.* London: Falmer Press.

Wyness, M. (1999) 'Childhood, agency and education reform'. *Childhood* 6 (3), 353–68.

# 4

## PERSONAL REFLECTION ON EXPERIENCES OF SPECIAL AND MAINSTREAM EDUCATION

### *KERRY NOBLE*

Kerry Noble describes her own experiences of schooling from early years to university. Within this chapter she demonstrates how important teacher attitudes and expectations are in supporting pupils to become effective learners. Her experiences of special and mainstream schools and colleges provide an opportunity for Kerry to reflect on her life in education and also provide some important indicators of how teachers may have a more positive impact in the future.

## Introduction

My first real experience of school was when I was six years old. This was three years after my diagnosis of athetoid cerebral palsy. My parents opted for special education because they thought that the need for physical input for my cerebral palsy was essential at that point. At that time, both my parents had been serving in the army for fourteen years. After my diagnosis, the army had wanted me to attend a residential school in England, while the rest of my family were posted back to Germany. After consideration my parents decided to leave the army and remain in England to support me.

## Education

The Education Authority in which I was living at that time assessed my needs and offered a placement in a special unit for those with severe learning difficulties along with those with physical disabilities. My mother was not satisfied with the provision being offered. An alternative special school was offered, but this had a waiting list. While I was waiting for a place, I was provided with a special tutor who taught me at home alongside input from my mother. Eventually I took up a place at a centre that was referred to as a 'school' with residential provision, based in a Victorian building for pupils with all kinds of physical disabilities. I attended as a day pupil. The emphasis of the school was very much upon physical needs within a set regime. For example, set times for toileting, regular physiotherapy, speech therapy and input from a teacher of the hearing impaired (I have a slight hearing problem). So my day consisted of arriving in school, invariably late because of the school transport system, going to physiotherapy for walking and 'stretching', and toileting; and that was virtually my morning schedule. After lunch we often sat and watched television before once more boarding the transport for home. The school did not believe that I would achieve much academically, and it was left to my mother to teach me to read and write.

When I was ten, this particular 'school' closed its doors to become a home for senior citizens. I was transferred to a purpose-built special school in another part of the county. This was my first real experience of formal education. On my first day I was very apprehensive, as the other pupils seemed to be able to do so much that I couldn't do. For example, I thought that once I turned around, my right became my left and vice versa. I was really embarrassed to discover how much I didn't know. While at this school I continued a high level of physical work, but at the same time I broadened my experiences and followed a school curriculum. For the first time I experienced subjects such as mathematics, English, science and PE, the very things that my able-bodied counterparts took for granted. I learned the school regime fast. When teachers set me a piece of work I began to realise that certain teachers would praise my work regardless of the amount of effort I had made or the quality of the work produced. As a consequence of this I became lazy and did not make as much effort as I should. I suspect that if I had been able-bodied they would have had a different attitude.

Eventually a teacher from a mainstream school wanted a change of career path and decided to come to the special school. This teacher had no preconceived attitudes towards disability, having taught at all levels of mainstream schools. After a short period of teaching me and building up a rapport with me, she perceived that I had abilities that had not to that point been challenged. For the first time since I began education, and in my life in general, someone challenged me to learn. I tested this new teacher to see how far she was prepared to go in recognising and addressing my needs and potential. I submitted work that was way beneath the level of which I was capable and she rejected this work, telling me that I could do better. At this juncture I could have done one of two things: I could have curled up in a ball and cried and felt rejected, or I could accept her constructive criticisms and work harder to see what I could achieve. Fortunately, because of my stubborn nature, and with the support of my family, I chose the latter. This teacher demonstrated that she believed in me and in my potential, and for the first time someone saw me for who I was on the inside and not just my disability. I admired this teacher for her dedication and commitment and for her determination to get the best from me often, despite the adverse opinions of other teachers.

At the age of fifteen I worked towards my GCSE examinations. This was a great challenge for me as I had lost many years of structured education. At this time, to add to my challenges, it was suggested that I had many of the characteristics of dyslexia. The coursework for my examinations proved to be demanding due to my complex needs. I had to learn different strategies to overcome the many difficulties that were presented and to get my thought processes onto paper. One of the quickest and most successful ways for doing so was for my mother to support me by reading back to me the work that I had produced and to help me by correcting spellings. It always took me a long time to get work onto paper because of my physical disabilities, and the support I received from my mother was a critical factor in my success. When I sat the examinations I passed all three with good grades. This was achieved largely because of the commitment of one individual teacher. She gave up an enormous amount of time, including evenings, weekends and holidays, to support my studies. Other teachers in the school were amazed by what had been achieved, and I believe that this might have had a positive impact upon their expectations of other pupils.

## Moving on

On leaving school, my options for continuing education were to attend a local mainstream further education college that offered a vocational course alongside students with a range of physical and learning disabilities; this would involve attending just one afternoon per week and doing what I regarded as a range of rather tedious and meaningless activities. An alternative was to attend a local residential special college to concentrate upon life skills. I chose neither of these, preferring to do my own research into the range of provisions available elsewhere in the country. I gave particular attention to two colleges in Gloucestershire and Coventry. One of these was again concentrating on life skills training, so I opted for the other more 'academic' institution. This college required formal qualifications for entry. Another reason for choosing this establishment was that it was adjacent to a mainstream college with which it had an association. I believe very strongly that if you have a disability you must make the first effort to participate alongside able-bodied peers. This was influential in my choice of college placement. I took more GCSEs — two based at the special college and one in the mainstream college. I gained a high grade in the subject taken in the mainstream college, and I believe that this was due to working alongside my able-bodied peers and being the only disabled person on the course.

Having gained my extra GCSEs, I investigated a social care course as, at this point, I wanted to work in a caring profession. I was presented with rather negative responses when I applied for my chosen course. The tutor who interviewed me was somewhat reluctant to offer me a place. She identified many obstacles that she said would prevent me from successfully completing the course. For example, having discovered my dyslexia, she insisted that I should dictate an essay to her to prove that I could manage the written aspects of the course. This was not a requirement for any able-bodied student with dyslexia. I was then faced with the challenge of her perception that I would not be able to undertake work experience because of my disability. I convinced her that I had done several placements before, which had involved caring for people. Obviously the placement I would take up would have to be a suitable one, but it was not impossible. She then mentioned that I would have to complete a first aid course, which would prove too problematic. However, I informed her that I had been the only disabled member of the local Red Cross first aid team for several years. At this point she realised that the more obstacles she presented, the more determined I was to show what I could do.

Having won a major battle to enter this two-year course, I enrolled but was faced with a number of hostile reactions from my fellow students. I tried my utmost to become part of the group and to contribute fully to the life of the course. I felt that there was considerable pressure on me to make my involvement in this course a success. For the duration of my time at this college I was faced with constant hostile attitudes towards my disability, coupled with numerous occasions when students deliberately pushed chairs and tables into the back of my wheelchair. Despite such reactions I was determined to complete the course in order to show both the individual teacher and the institution that a disabled person with my level of disability could achieve in the same way as others. For most of the time I coped alone, with some additional support from the lecturer, who provided copies of her notes. On one occasion I was presented with a practical exercise where I needed additional support. I therefore arranged for an amanuensis (scribe) to be present during this time. This was the first input during structured learning time that I had from the residential college I was attending. The support worker was amazed at the hostile reaction of the other students and the tutors. Oblivious to my own ideas, she reported the bullying that I was experiencing. As a consequence of this reaction, the head of the Faculty of Social Sciences arranged to come to address the group. I was at the group session that she attended and felt embarrassed, isolated and confused. Obviously the students knew that the incidents referred to involved me. During the meeting the eye contact from several of the students was so intense that I felt sick. As a result of this meeting the bullying increased dramatically.

Fortunately at this time I was provided with an opportunity to have some time away from the college. This came about as a result of my auditioning and gaining a role in a television production called *Skallagrigg* alongside actors Bernard Hill and Billie Whitelaw. The tutor was reluctant to let me go because at first she didn't believe that the opportunity to be in this programme was real. When she understood that this was a genuine proposal, she required me to complete my coursework two months before the deadline set for other students. I achieved this before leaving to join the film crew. I did obtain one promise prior to leaving, that she would not let the other students know what I was doing. I thought that if they did know my reasons, there was a danger that the bullying would increase on my return. After returning to the college I gained top grades in all my subjects and felt vindicated for everything I had done.

After this I decided to take a year out from my studies. This gave me time to evaluate my experiences of college. During this time I gained a number of other experiences, including learning to drive in an adapted car. It was at this point that I decided to further my studies and investigate the possibility of university. I applied to five universities, as is usual within the UK system, and was fortunate to be accepted by four. I identified universities that claimed to have good access and a clear policy on disability. However, on visiting the sites where I had been offered placements I found that the reality was quite different. Having experienced so much bullying in the past, and having also been the first disabled person on a course, I was rather apprehensive about having further bad experiences. From special education to university was a huge leap and I didn't want to set myself up to fail. As a result I chose a university that had already accepted other students with my level of disability. I felt that this was essential to my success both academically and socially. The chosen university arranged all my support requirements and access needs.

Upon arrival they grouped all the new disabled students and support workers together, expecting us to gel together as a minority group. However, I had different ideas. This was my first opportunity for full-time 'integration' and I wanted to make the most of my time and be a 'real student'. I was fortunate to have a support worker who lived near the university and therefore during her time off she was happy to spend time with her own friends instead of mixing with other support workers. This left me free to enjoy all aspects of student life to the full.

At university I followed a combined degree course, majoring in sociology and women's studies. I found the course to be very demanding and particularly so because of my complex needs. I found that I had to produce my work way before other students, as I was reliant upon an amanuensis. This was quite a difficult process to which I had to adapt as my able-bodied peers were going out and leaving their coursework while they had a good time. I found myself trying to adapt to a student lifestyle that involved a lot of socialising while trying to study. This led to dramatic problems with my cerebral palsy, resulting in extreme bouts of spasm, which required the attentions of the local hospital. As a result of this episode I was forced to take two months away from my studies. Everyone at the university and at home was surprised but supportive in enabling me eventually to return to the course. Some had assumed that I would give up, but I wasn't going to be defeated, and consequently I took my first year examinations late but I passed. I adjusted my lifestyle during my second and third year, having learned a hard lesson in the first.

I experienced several problems with my support arrangements, and therefore in the third year I arranged my own provision. This proved to be more successful. I required limited personal assistance as I had a car, and my fellow students were willing to exchange the provision of limited help for the occasional lift to the shops or elsewhere!

At the end of my course I graduated with a 2.1 honours degree in sociology and women's studies. I received a special mention in the Vice Chancellor's address, coupled with a standing ovation when I received my degree. After leaving university I went through a low patch because I couldn't get a job as a result of my care needs. I was advised to seek counselling help. After a long period of time I discovered that I hadn't been able to accept my disability as being part of me. This was mainly due to not having dealt with or talked about the bullying that I had experienced at college. However, such an experience has certainly made me a stronger person, as I am now used to people's reactions.

## Conclusion

Reflecting on my experiences of education, I believe I have succeeded because I received tremendous support and encouragement from parents and friends. I am stubborn, determined and outgoing, some might even say bloody-minded, and this has certainly contributed to the approach I have to my disability. I am not really interested in politics, and perhaps this has been helpful in enabling other people to approach me and my disability. I'm Kerry and what you see is what you get! If I was starting out again, what would I want to be different? A good disabled role model would certainly help, which is why I now spend so much time in schools working with children, both physically disabled and able-bodied. Higher expectations from teachers is an essential element in any child's success. I certainly needed access to physiotherapy and speech therapy, and this should be a normal part of education that is accessible in all kinds of schools. For me, inclusion means social acceptance as opposed to academic success. If I had been educated in a local school I would certainly have more friends than I do now, though I am not sure that such schools could have addressed all of my learning needs.

The downside of special education for me was that I didn't have the opportunity to mix with my able-bodied peers and therefore failed to realise the negative reactions that form a part of everyday life.

I personally feel that as more babies with complex needs are surviving to school age as a result of medical advances, there will continue to be a need for special schools. There is a need to review how we establish better links between such schools and the mainstream. This may involve pupils moving both ways between schools. Attitudes toward disability would improve if children were allowed to gain direct experience of each other from an early age.

My life now is very busy. I divide my time between work in mainstream and special schools. I teach able-bodied children about disability, in particular cerebral palsy, in a variety of practical ways. I also act as a positive role model for other children who have special educational needs. I'm vice chair of the governing body of a special school and often work in collaboration with colleagues at a local university. This involves giving input on courses for teachers and learning support assistants who work in a wide range of schools. From a beginning in education where the expectations of what I could achieve were very limited, I feel that I have now progressed to a position where I can influence others to have much higher expectations of all children.

# 5

## THE HIDDEN VOICE OF BULLYING

### ASTRID MONA O'MOORE AND STEPHEN JAMES MINTON

In this chapter the authors examine the destructive effects of persistent bullying. Children offer insights into the causes of bullying behaviour and suggest remedies within a school context. In the past, children who have been bullied have been marginalised and silenced. Here the authors offer constructive ways of tackling bullying behaviour and ensuring that the voice of these children is heard and recognised.

It's grand at home and on the bus to and from school. I really enjoy it, but school is like a paradise of loneliness and fear. (A first year, 2nd level pupil)

## Background

Since its inception in January 1996, the Anti-Bullying Centre at Trinity College Dublin has listened to many heartfelt accounts of victimisation. The ugliness of human nature is given expression by either the victims themselves or those who care about them.

Norway, Sweden and Finland were among the first countries to draw attention to the destructive effects of bullying on school children (O'Moore, 1988). For example, three bullying-related suicides in Norway prompted the implementation of a national campaign to prevent and counter peer abuse (Roland and Munthe, 1989).

Following the first European Seminar on School Bullying, which was held in Stavanger, Norway, in 1997, a wealth of statistics have emerged from within Europe illustrating the extent of bullying worldwide (Smith *et al.*, 1993). Ireland is no exception to this trend.

In a nationwide study (O'Moore, Kirkham and Smith, 1997) that was carried out during 1993/94, 31.3% of primary school children between the approximate ages of eight and twelve reported that they had been bullied in school. Of those, 4% were bullied once a week or more often. In our post-primary schools, 15.6% of pupils (aged approximately twelve to eighteen) reported that they were bullied. Approximately 2% were bullied once a week or more frequently. In relation to bullying others, 26.5% of primary school children reported that they had bullied others; 1.4% reported that they bullied others once a week or more often. In post-primary schools, 14.9% of pupils stated that they had taken part in bullying others in school; 1% reported that they had bullied others once a week or more frequently.

Based on these figures, it was possible to estimate that one in twenty school children at primary level and one in fifty at post-primary level were subjected to frequent (serious) peer bullying. Thus there are, out of a possible 870,000 school-going children, 20,000 primary and 7,400 post-primary school children whose education may be undermined or diluted in quality. Also they may be suffering from a real sense of despair, hurt, fear, social isolation and hopelessness.

It should be noted that these figures exclude children who were bullied going to and from school, and those who were bullied by any other person other than their peers, for example teachers, family and neighbours.

What was particularly disturbing about the results of the Irish nationwide study was the high proportion of pupils who felt unable to tell their teachers or anyone at home that they were victimised. For example, of the 3,089 pupils who were victimised in primary schools, 65% reported that they had not told their teachers. The reluctance to tell was even greater among post-primary pupils: out of the 1,660 post-primary victims, 84% stated that they had not told their teachers of their victimisation. While more children reported that they had told someone at home that they were bullied at school, as many as 46% of primary school pupils and 66% of post-primary pupils did not tell anyone at home.

| Primary | No. of Victims | Have not told teachers | No. of Victims | Have not told anyone at home |
|---|---|---|---|---|
| 3 | 303 | 53.8 | 320 | 33.7 |
| 4 | 1075 | 62.0 | 1091 | 41.2 |
| 5 | 975 | 65.8 | 996 | 49.7 |
| 6 | 726 | 74.0 | 730 | 53.7 |
| **Post-Primary** | **No. of Victims** | **Have not told teachers** | **No. of Victims** | **Have not told anyone at home** |
| 1 | 714 | 82.2 | 714 | 60.9 |
| 2 | 550 | 83.3 | 550 | 69.3 |
| 3 | 185 | 82.7 | 714 | 63.5 |
| 4 | 73 | 87.7 | 550 | 68.1 |
| 5 | 89 | 92.2 | 189 | 78.9 |
| 6 | 46 | 84.8 | 72 | 79.9 |

*Table 1—Percentage of 'victims' in primary and post-primary schools who report not having told their teacher or anyone at home about being bullied.*

Table 1 shows the increasing reluctance of pupils as they advance through primary and post-primary schools to tell either teachers or anyone at home of their victimisation. However, in sixth year, the final year of senior school, there appears to be an easing among pupils in relation to telling their teacher.

To encourage children to tell of their own or their peers' victimisation is possibly the single greatest challenge for professionals who wish to develop or conduct anti-bullying programmes. Much bullying goes undetected; thus, a resolution is only made possible if the identity of the perpetrator is made known.

The following fictional account of bullying entitled 'Peer Pressure', written by a third year post-primary pupil, was forwarded to the Anti-bullying Centre in Trinity College by his teacher, and illustrates most realistically the tragic consequences that victimisation can have when the voice of the victim and of bystanders remain silent.

## Peer pressure

*(Essay by Barry Fleming, 3rd Year, Coolmine Community School)*

I just couldn't understand it. What thrill were we getting out of this by bullying him? Ya see, last month, half way through the year, this new boy called Sean came into our class from Cork. At first everybody liked him and in the canteen at break we would gather around him to talk. Then, when Joseph, the 'messer of the class', as one of our teachers called him, came back from suspension, it all changed.

Joseph was the dude of the class and everybody liked him and agreed with him. Even if Joseph said snow was hot, we would agree with him. Sadly Sean got on the wrong side of him. That was a regrettable mistake.

'*Ya little Cork bogger!*' Joseph whispered to Sean, hitting him as they walked into our Irish class. We walked in and waited for Miss to call the role. As she started, Joseph stabbed Sean with a compass from behind.

'*Sean O'Shea,*' Miss called out.

'*…is a Cork bogger,*' Joseph muttered under his breath, but it was loud enough for the whole class to hear, and they did. Sean went bright red but he faked laughter as if he were taking it as joke.

During the class Sean would continuously be stabbed by Joseph, but even this was never as bad as what would happen in the next class, religion. Since we only had RE once a week the teacher would put us in alphabetical order in an attempt to associate names with faces. To most of us it was a doss, but to Sean it was a nightmare because, once again, he had to sit beside Joseph. Sean would purposely come to class late and try to get out of it as soon as it started. All this just to avoid sitting beside Joseph. However, there was really nothing that he could do to stop the torture dished out by Joseph. Ya know, really clever things like writing on Sean's face and punching him in the arms. Sean, again, would try to laugh along with Joseph who, with his stupidity, was triggering off great laughter from all around.

The next day Sean and Joseph got into a slagging match and Sean said some really bad things to Joseph, who replied to him in a threatening voice that he was dead. Sure enough, that day after school, as we gathered outside like swallows on electrical wires waiting to make the annual migration home, Joseph kept his word. When we walked into the woods two of the boys held Sean's hands behind his back and Joseph started hitting him. Then they switched.

*'Fintan come over here and join the laugh.'* Joseph started over to me. He must have noticed me standing back watching him beat up Sean. They eventually let go of Sean and he fell to the ground as if he were a puppet with his strings cut.

*'Well, what are ya waitin' for? Hit him.'* Joseph insisted with me, with a sick sour smile on his face. I looked down at the blood-covered ground in the woods where Sean was holding his stomach and coughing. I paused. I didn't know what to do. The silence was terrible. Then in panic, I broke it by kicking him in the stomach. After all, what could I do? If I had let down my friends imagine the slagging I'd get. We walked away, and it started to rain.

The next day while walking home with Sean, neither of us

referred to what had occurred in the woods, but I listened to Sean as he told me how much he hated Joseph and how he hated the way he made fun of him in front of the whole class. For the first time he told me about Cork and how much he missed it. As I walked up the front path to my house, Sean called out to me over the wall separating our two gardens.

*'Fintan, call in for me tomorrow will ya, when we're going to school?'*

'Yeah, sure.' I was a bit surprised that he asked me that, because in fact, I usually did call into him on my way to school in the mornings. The next morning, however, I understood only too well why he asked me to call.

I hopped over the wall into Sean's garden. It was overcast. As I was about to ring the doorbell I noticed that, curiously, the door was slightly opened. I'll never forget it. As I touched the door to open it wider, a big bright bolt of lightning broke through the dark clouds overhead followed by a spine-chilling rumble of thunder that echoed across the cloud-covered sky. With hesitation, I walked into the house calling Sean's name. Then as I made my way into the kitchen I went down on my knees. There, suspended from the ceiling with a noose around his neck, was Sean's badly bruised, blue and purple body. His corpse spun around slowly like a wheel on its axis. His tongue was hanging out of his mouth and his neck stretched beyond repair.

In the climate of growing awareness and concern about peer abuse, the teacher, struck by 'a starkness so realistic', could not help wondering whether the author of the essay might himself be a victim of bullying or an eyewitness to a bullying incident.

Wisely, the teacher had the essay read and discussed by the boy's parents, their school counsellor and some others in the area of counselling, as well as by the executive members of the Parents' Association.

Fortunately they found no grounds for concern. However, the essay illustrates the depth of understanding among school-goers of the nature of bullying and the potential consequences of peer abuse. Above all, it underpins the difficulty that children have in resisting joining in with bullying and the extraordinary reluctance on the part of victims and their peers to report behaviour that they clearly know is so hurtful and damaging.

Anti-bullying initiatives so far reflect little or no increase in the number of victims who tell either a teacher or a parent about being bullied. Eslea and Smith (1998) argue that the insignificant post-intervention changes in the number of victims who report being bullied may reflect that staff members are more vigilant and the children more assertive.

While there may be some truth to this viewpoint, it is more probable that our understanding of the causes and the remedies is as yet incomplete, and the will is not there to eradicate it. Hopefully the situation has improved somewhat, but in 1995 it was found that teachers did not regard bullying as a serious problem (O'Moore, 2000a; 2000b).

Most of our knowledge of bully/victim problems has predominantly been derived from quantitative empirical studies. The aim of this paper is to report on qualitative data that was gathered as part of an intervention study to counteract bullying in national schools in Donegal.

To hear the children's own view, for example, as to what they consider bullying to be, how it arises and how it can be stopped, should help to provide a greater understanding as to how it can be better prevented and countered.

There were 822 pupils in 35 national schools in Donegal who took part in the post-intervention study in summer 2000. As well as completing the modified Olweus Bully/Victim Questionnaire (Olweus, 1989; Whitney and Smith, 1993), they also completed a qualitative questionnaire, concerning their own understanding of and feelings about bullying. This questionnaire was specially designed by one of the authors of this chapter (O'Moore). It consisted of five open-ended questions, from fictional scenarios upon which they were asked to comment, and a 'yes/no' item.

A content analysis of the results obtained from this questionnaire was then undertaken, and the results of this are presented below. The percentages refer to the percentage of response types obtained from the entire sample, rather than the pupils themselves — practically, this means that the pupils often indicated more than one category type in their response to a question.

## What do children think is the worst sort of bullying?

School bullying takes many forms. The main forms, as listed in the National Guidelines on Countering Bullying Behaviour in Primary and Post-Primary Schools (Department of Education and Science, 1993), are:

- Physical aggression
- Damage to property
- Intimidation
- Name-calling
- Bullying of school personnel
- Isolation
- Extortion
- Abusive telephone calls
- Slagging

A more recent and popular form of bullying that can intimidate without anyone else knowing is that of e-bullying (Houde, 2002).

The children in the Donegal study thought that physical bullying was the worst form of bullying, followed by verbal bullying (see Table 2).

| Response Type | Percentage |
|---|---|
| Physical bullying — hitting, kicking, etc. | 41.7 |
| Verbal bullying — name calling, etc | 30.5 |
| Threatening people | 7.5 |
| Excluding people | 5.2 |
| Emotional bullying | 3.2 |
| Stealing from people | 2.4 |
| Spreading rumours | 2.3 |
| Racism | 2.1 |
| Blackmailing people | 1.1 |

*Table 2—'What do you think is the worst sort of bullying?' Percentages of pupils' response types.*

Response types that each accounted for less than 1% of the total were 'sending to Coventry'; 'all types of bullying'; 'ganging up on people'; 'locking someone in a room'; 'picking on younger people'; 'spitting'; 'abusing'; 'putting someone's head down the toilet'. Additionally, three children said they did not know and seven others made no response at all.

### How do children feel when they are bullied?

When the pupils were then asked how they thought children feel when they are bullied, the pupils reported a range of negative emotions, chiefly sadness, hurt, anger and loneliness (see Table 3).

| Response Types | Percentage |
|---|---|
| Sad, unhappy, upset, etc. | 32.6 |
| Left out, alone, lonely, etc. | 16.4 |
| Hurt | 15.4 |
| Scared, afraid, frightened, etc. | 15.2 |
| Worthless, useless, not good enough, etc. | 7.7 |
| Angry, annoyed, etc. | 5.9 |
| Stupid | 2.1 |

*Table 3—'How do you think children feel when they are bullied?' Percentages of pupils' response types.*

Response types that each accounted for less than 1% of the total were: 'ashamed'; 'embarrassed'; 'guilty'; 'sick'; 'not nice'; 'hope it would end'; 'wish I was at home with my mother'; to 'want to cry'; 'stupid'; 'confused'; 'disgusting'; 'disappointed'; 'threatened'; and 'suicidal'. Five children said that victims of bullying probably feel as though 'something is wrong with them'; six stated that they did not know. Only four made no response at all.

### Actions children would take if bullied

In terms of what the pupils said they would do if they were bullied, a large proportion said that they would report it to teachers and parents (see Table 4).

| Response Types | Percentage |
|---|---|
| Tell the teachers and my parents | 29.5 |
| Tell someone (unspecified) | 24.0 |
| Tell the teacher only | 17.1 |
| Stand up for myself/fight back | 10.7 |
| Get away from the bullies | 5.9 |
| Tell my parents only | 5.0 |
| Tell my friends | 1.7 |
| Tell the bullies to stop | 1.2 |
| I don't know | 1.2 |
| No response | 1.0 |

*Table 4—'What would you do if you were being bullied?' Percentages of pupils' response types.*

Response types that accounted for less than 1% of the total were 'to pretend it had no effect on me'; 'I'd want to tell, but I'd be too scared'; 'tell the Gardai'; 'tell the principal'; 'ignore it'; 'feel terrible'; and 'to want to cry'. Seven children said that they did not know and six others made no response at all.

However, in practice, as was evidenced in the nationwide study (O'Moore *et al.*, 1997) and again in the Donegal intervention study (O'Moore and Minton, forthcoming), bullying is reported less frequently than these figures would indicate. The Donegal intervention study found that even after the introduction of the anti-bullying programme, there were a high proportion of victims, 50.5%, who had not told their teachers, and 35.6% who had not told their parents.

It would seem as though there is a reason, or a set of reasons, as to why this should be the case. Besag (1989) provides a comprehensive list of reasons as to why victims do not tell that they are being bullying.

## Why children do not tell

In the Donegal study, reasons for not telling were probed by a question in which (responding to a fictional scenario) pupils were asked to respond as to why two fictional characters should not report the bullying that they were suffering (see Tables 5 and 6).

| Response Types | Percentage |
|---|---|
| No response | 87.0 |
| The bullying would get worse | 5.7 |
| One would be beaten up | 2.5 |
| One would be called a 'tell-tale' | 2.1 |

*Table 5—'If you think it is not a good idea for Tony and Ann to tell their teacher, please write down the reasons you think they should not tell.' Percentages of pupils' response types.*

| Response Types | Percentage |
|---|---|
| No response | 93.4 |
| The bullying would get even worse | 1.7 |
| There would be trouble if one's parents came into the school | 1.3 |

*Table 6—'If you think Tony and Ann should not tell their parents, why not?' Percentages of pupils' response types.*

From Tables 5 and 6, it can be seen that most pupils did not, in fact, respond with reasons as to why the characters should not tell someone that they were being bullied (non-response was 87.0% for 'Why should they not tell the teacher?' and 93.7% for 'Why should they not tell their parents?'). This was largely because most thought that they should tell (88.2% for 'They should tell the teacher' and 91.6% for 'They should tell their parents').This left only a minority of pupils who provided reasons as to why they should not report being bullied.

Chief among these was the expression of the fear that the bullying would get worse if they told anyone. This could, it was reported, end up in being beaten up, being called a 'tell-tale', losing friends and, as one pupil pointed out, 'the bullies could deny it'. Other reasons given for not telling the teacher were: 'the teacher might not believe it', 'be made fun of if your parents came in' and 'when I told the teachers I was being bullied, they did not believe me'.

Further insights for not telling parents can be gained from the responses that accounted for less than 1% of the total. These were: 'it is better to tell teachers if the bullying is in school'; 'parents might get worried'; 'could be in trouble with parents for not telling before'; 'parents may not believe it'; 'they are hurt and sad'; 'don't want other people to get into trouble'; 'parents would make a big fuss'; 'I'd be too embarrassed to tell'; and 'they might think that you're stupid'.

From most of the reasons given by the pupils, it seems that they are only too keenly aware of possible repercussions of seeking support to put an end to bullying. Thus, in the current climate, the price is yet too high for telling; reprisals and the stigma associated with telling carry greater certainty than a cessation of the bullying. From listening to the pupils, it is clear that they know that they should report bullying, but they do not believe that it will be safe for them to do so. This, undoubtedly, also contributes to the considerable unwillingness of the peer group to intervene or report bullying that they are witness to.

**What children do when they see someone else being bullied**

In the Donegal study, when pupils were asked, prior to the intervention programme, what they usually did themselves when they saw another pupil of their own age being bullied, 15.9% stated: 'Nothing, it's none of my business.' Another 22.2% reported that they also 'Did nothing, but they felt they ought to help.' Results from the nationwide study in Ireland showed that the unwillingness of pupils to help their bullied peers increases with age (O'Moore, 2002).

Readiness to help dropped by 21% from third class in primary school to fifth year in post-primary school. The boys were less willing than the girls in each class or year group to help a fellow pupil who was being bullied.

If schools have clear anti-bullying policies, with provisions made for detecting, reporting and dealing with bullying on which all staff are agreed and act, then the pupils can feel confident in reporting bullying behaviour that they witness and experience. For as long as this remains a grey area, reporting may always seem to carry a risk.

**How can children be encouraged to seek help?**

To reinforce pupils to report incidents of bullying, it is critical that adults learn to respond sensitively and seriously to all allegations of bullying that come to their attention. Messages received from children through the nationwide study and the Donegal study indicate that both teachers and parents are guilty of not only trivialising but ignoring complaints of bullying.

For example, one sixth class primary school pupil had this to say: 'A boy from fourth class jeers me and if I hit him he gets an older person after me. I told the Principal on yard duty but he said, "Go away, he wouldn't do anything like that."' Another pupil had this to say: 'It feels as if they [the teachers] don't care.' Yet another pupil, eleven years of age, undermined by her parents, reported that, 'My brother picks on me and calls me names. Sometimes he hits me. My parents say it's only because we're brother and sister but it's not, he's eighteen.'

Prior to the intervention study in Donegal, only a little over half of the pupils (52.6%) felt that their teachers tried to stop the bullying. Of these, 17.2% reported that teachers did so 'sometimes' and 35.4% 'almost always'. While the pupils reported an improvement after the programme in the frequency with which teachers intervened, there was a considerable discrepancy between their reports and those of their teachers. The children reported that 45.6% of their teachers stopped the bullying 'almost always', whereas 97.6% of the 83 teachers who participated in the study reported that they 'always tried' to stop bullying 'when they saw it happening'. The remainder (2.4%) stated that they 'usually try to stop bullying'. The reason for the discrepancy is not clear, but a contributory factor may well be the differences found between the adult and the child's view of bullying (O'Moore, 2002b).

The definition of bullying usually sets out certain basic criteria. These are that bullying includes verbal, psychological and physical aggression, that the behaviour is repeated over time, that there is an imbalance of power between victim and bully, and that the behaviour is intentional. However, there is evidence that children do not place the same emphasis on the imbalance of power, or on the repeated or intentional nature of bullying. Rather, the younger the children are in age, the more they focus on the effect on the victim and the victim's interpretation of the incident. Thus, by relying on the more traditional, contrived or adult definition of bullying, it is to be predicted that teachers will overlook or even reject many aggressive acts that children would interpret as bullying. There is also the problem that children may refrain from bringing bullying incidents to the attention of the teacher for fear of them not being judged as bullying. As one twelve-year-old boy stated in the nationwide study,

'I don't know whether you would say that they are bullying me, but what they are doing is really hurting me.'

Sports can also cause great distress to pupils who are targeted, as it can so readily legitimise bullying, allowing aggressive acts unrelated to the sport to go undetected and or uncorrected. A second year post-primary pupil in the nationwide study illustrated this when he stated, 'I was pushed to the ground at all games of football and have been kicked and my hair pulled.'

Thus, to overcome the unsatisfactory level of detection and consequent apprehension of bullying, it would be advisable if all future policies on countering bullying in schools redefine bullying in such a way as not to restrict opportunities to correct aggression that is inappropriate and hurtful to the victim. No amount of encouraging victims and passive spectators of bullying to report acts of aggression is going to help to eradicate bullying unless there are effective programmes of prevention and correction of aggressive behaviour.

## What else could the school do to counter bullying? Pupils' suggestions

It is a salutary lesson that even in the Donegal project, nearly two-thirds (63.7%) of the children believed that their school could do more to stop bullying. When the children were asked for their views on how to stop bullying, the suggestions largely focused around punishing those caught bullying — detentions, suspensions, expulsions, removing privileges and the like (see Table 7).

| Response Types | Percentage |
|---|---|
| No response | 55.0 |
| I don't know / I have no ideas | 10.0 |
| Punish bullies more severely | 5.7 |
| Keep bullies inside at break and lunchtime | 5.7 |
| Tell the bully's parents | 3.7 |
| Suspend/expel bullies | 3.3 |
| Encourage pupils to report bullying | 3.0 |
| Put more teachers on yard duty | 2.6 |
| Teachers should talk to their classes about bullying | 2.2 |
| Put up security cameras in the school | 1.3 |

*Table 7—'If you have any ideas to help stop bullying please write them down.'*
*Percentages of pupils' response types*

Response types that each accounted for less than 1% of the total were: 'tell the Gardai'; 'make a leaflet'; 'show a video'; 'put it on The News'; 'make anti-bullying posters and signs, and put them up in school'. Some pupils suggested that the matter should be discussed 'at staff meetings' and 'at PTA meetings'. Others suggested that the staff could 'talk to bullies' in order to 'find out why they do it' and 'to explain to them what could happen in bullying'. Still others suggested that the school could employ an anti-bullying expert, or that staff should 'look for the warning signs', or that 'there should be two teachers in every class so there's no trouble if one has to go out for something'. One child cautioned that 'sometimes it's better not to interfere', and another stated that 'there are no bullies in my school'; three suggested that older pupils should look after or look out for younger children in the school; two children suggested that the school could put a 'bullying box' in place — where children could write down confidentially and anonymously their concerns about bullying so that these could be addressed.

It is clear from the children's responses that punishment is seen as a means to decrease the frequency of a behaviour. While undoubtedly widely used in schools, the difficulty is finding punishments that are appropriate and effective. Punishments all too often teach children that conflicts are managed through aggression and coercion. It would be preferable to teach them ways of dealing with bullying that do not rely on force but rather on empathic response.

The 'No Blame Approach' (Maines and Robinson, 1992) and the 'Common Concern Method' (Pikas, 1989) have yielded successful results for their positive and rehabilitative approach to dealing with bullying incidents. In their programmes of correction, the empathic response in the perpetrators of bullying is encouraged and the pupils learn to take responsibility for their negative behaviours. Also by apprehending the antagonists but not applying punishment in the strict sense of the word, the victims and the peer group see that the risk of reprisals diminish. As a result, children who are victimised or their witnesses are more inclined to seek help.

However, lessons from two decades of research into bullying in schools have demonstrated that all intervention strategies so far have met with limited success, and on some occasions with failure (Smith and Brain, 2000).

Nonetheless, research has found that those schools that do the most achieve the most (Smith and Sharp, 1994; Roland and Munthe, 1997).

## Why do children bully?

A contributing factor in the limited success, and in some cases failure, of intervention strategies, may be the tendency to overlook the causes of bullying. Intervention strategies tend to take a blanket approach in dealing with the problem of bullying. But, as with good medical practice, it is not enough simply to deal with the symptoms of the presenting complaint, but rather to arrive at the underlying root cause of the complaint. Only when the cause is known can the appropriate treatment be found and tried. In some instances, multiple treatments are necessary.

Lowenstein (2000) has examined the causes of bullying and holds the view that 'progress in the measurement of bullying as a group process and the success of intervention strategies may depend on finding clearer distinctions between the ringleader, the bullied and the children who help them reinforce the behaviour'.

In the Donegal study, the pupils were asked why, in their opinion, do pupils bully others. The percentage of pupils' response types can be seen in Table 8.

| Response Types | Percentage |
|---|---|
| To show off / to look cool | 15.0 |
| I don't know | 12.2 |
| Don't like the people they bully | 10.9 |
| The bullies are jealous of the people they bully | 10.8 |
| The bullies have been bullied themselves | 9.8 |
| To feel big / powerful / better about themselves | 6.3 |
| The bullies have problems at home | 6.0 |
| They think that bullying is fun / enjoy it | 5.9 |
| Bullies think that they are great / the best / more important | 4.6 |
| To get attention | 3.2 |
| Bullies are bad / selfish / angry / cold-hearted, etc. | 3.2 |
| The victims have done something to the bullies in the past | 2.6 |

*Table 8—'Why do children bully other children?' Percentages of pupils' response types*

Response types that each accounted for less than 1% of the total were 'bullies are angry at the people they bully'; 'copying older pupils'; 'to hurt people'; 'to start a fight'; 'bullies have nothing else to do'; 'to get money'; 'bullies are sad and unhappy people'; 'to make people sad'; 'to have bigger friends'; and 'because they want to'. One child informed us that bullying is 'good fun'. Six children made no response at all.

From Table 8 it can be seen that the most frequent responses were 'to show off' or 'to look cool' or 'because they don't like the people they bully'. Sadly, both of these responses could, in certain cases, legitimise bullying behaviours — if one 'shows off' or 'looks cool', then bullying must, among certain sections of the pupil population, be a desirable or status conferring act.

In the case of 'not liking' someone, it seems that reaction against someone one does not like is also fairly common. For example, in the fictional scenarios, although almost all pupils said they would 'tell a teacher', 'tell the person to stop', or 'tell someone' (unspecified), there were 10.9% who said that they would make up and use a hurtful nickname for someone who had used a hurtful nickname against them. It seems that once struck against, retribution is cast as an option — and bullying is seen by some pupils as a legitimate manifestation of such an option.

Other pupils see the reason for bullying as a problem that the bully has, such as jealousy, or the fact that they have been bullied themselves, or that they have problems at home. Still others looked at what the bully hopes to achieve by her or his behaviour. To 'show off', 'to get attention', 'to feel big', 'to feel powerful', and 'to feel better about themselves' were all mentioned. This seems to evidence the need for an esteem gain, which might have been expected in the light of the findings of O'Moore *et al*.'s nationwide study (O'Moore and Kirkham, 2001; O'Moore, Kirkham and Smith, 1997).

Essentially those who bully have low self-esteem and their bullying behaviour may be a misguided esteem-enhancing activity. Also, it would appear that pupils have the knowledge that the bully is not necessarily the oafish bully lacking in social skills but rather, as Sutton *et al*. (1999) have shown, a cold, selfish, manipulative expert, thus able to easily organise gangs and use subtle, indirect methods. It is with such children that the traditional reprimand or single method is inadequate. This was understood by one second year post-primary pupil who, in the nationwide study, conveyed that 'if the teacher talks to a bully, the bullying doesn't stop, it just happens more discreetly'.

Research has found that a proportion of children who bully have been found to have conduct disorders (O'Moore, 1995; Salmon *et al.*, 2000). While conduct disorders occur frequently in childhood, most are transient in nature. However, Luk (2001) reports that in 5% to 10% of children, the problems persist for more than six months and do not resolve spontaneously. He points out that persistent conduct disorders are serious mental health problems that require comprehensive assessment and multiple treatments. Such findings need, therefore, to be factored in to prevention and intervention programmes to address bullying behaviour if there is to be a significant reduction in bullying behaviour.

## Conclusion

In order to overcome the strong hidden voice of bullying, it is clear from listening to the children that greater efforts will be needed by teachers, schools as a whole, parents, professionals and policy makers to strengthen their resolve to prevent, reduce and counter bullying in school communities.

There is little doubt that whole school approaches to countering bullying help to reduce the level of bullying, as shown in the Donegal anti-bullying project (O'Moore and Minton, forthcoming). However, if we really try to address what the children are telling us in the Irish nationwide and Donegal studies, then greater attention needs to be given to providing children with cast iron reassurance that telling is safe.

It is clear from their responses that too many children stay silent for lack of a sympathetic ear and action that puts a stop to bullying. Maybe schools themselves also contribute to the silence. As one child put it, 'We are never told who we can turn to if we are being bullied. It might help if we were.'

Also children need to see teachers consistently respecting the needs and feelings of others. No child should be given cause to feel, as one child did, that 'my teacher isn't very nice — sarcastic and just horrible — putting you down'. Such behaviour makes a mockery of any anti-bullying message.

Greater attention also needs to be given to finding ways to encourage the peer group to take a more active role in stopping bullying that they witness or are encouraged to take part in. The Donegal study, for example, showed that there was a sizeable proportion of pupils (19.2%) who do not help, but who would like to help a child that they see of their own age being bullied. Might one reason be that they are, as was remarked by one child, 'Not sure how to help'?

The fact that there was a significant proportion of pupils (9.2%) in the Donegal study who, post-intervention, proposed that they would do nothing to help a fellow pupil whom they saw being bullied and furthermore that there were 12.8% of pupils who would be willing to join in bullying a pupil whom they did not like, suggests that more multiple prevention and treatment strategies may be necessary to curb the persistent bullying that is still so widespread in our schools.

The challenge is to find measures that can target the different root causes of bullying. Thus whole school based intervention methods will need to be supplemented when necessary with child-focused treatment, family-focused treatment and community-based interventions.

Attention must be directed at those children who are at risk of bullying others. They need to be carefully monitored as they progress through school. If problems persist, comprehensive assessment and treatment programmes should be carried out. For too long there has been a tacit acceptance that the victim owns the problem. The sensitivity and ability to restrain oneself from aggressive counter-attacks is all too often seen as a weakness.

It is this perception that undoubtedly contributes to the high reluctance of victims to tell of their victimisation. Yet there is no shortage of evidence, anecdotal or scientific, that indicates that victimisation can result from being in the wrong place at the wrong time. Indeed, the atrocities of 11 September 2001 in New York illustrated on a worldwide scale the defencelessness of the individual in the face of ruthless strategies.

To be true to our children's voices, as heard nationwide and in particular in Donegal, and to provide children with an education in an environment where they feel safe and spared the oppression and humiliation of bullying, there will need to be a significant improvement in the level of commitment from the Government Department of Education and Science to support initiatives, both practitioner and research based, that endeavour to make a difference.

It would be enormously beneficial if the Department of Education and Science were to draw the parties together who have developed an expertise in the area of prevention and intervention of bullying, in order that they may develop and implement plans for a safer and more fulfilling school environment than has been possible heretofore.

## Acknowledgements

We wish to thank the Calouste Gulbenkian Foundation, the Department of Education and Science, the North Western Health Board, and the Arts and Social Sciences Benefaction Fund of Trinity College Dublin for the financial support and encouragement that they gave to the Donegal Anti-Bullying Project.

We would also like to thank Sally Bonnar of the Donegal Teacher Centre and Ann McAteer of the North Western Health Board for their help in coordinating the project. Finally we wish to especially thank the principals, teachers and children of the schools involved in the project for their cooperation and enthusiasm.

## References

Besag, V. (1989). *Bullies and victims in schools*. Milton Keynes: Open University Press.

Eslea, M., and Smith, P.K. (1998) 'The long-term effectiveness of anti-bullying work in primary schools'. *Educational Research* 40 (2), 203–18.

Houde, C. (2002). 'How e-bullying can intimidate without anyone else knowing'. *The Irish Times*, 30 October.

Lowenstein, L.F. (2002). 'Bullying: recent research into the causes, diagnosis and treatment'. In M. Elliot (ed.), *Bullying: a practical guide to coping for schools* (3rd ed.). London: Pearson Education, Kidscope.

Luk, S. (2001) 'Persistent conduct problems in childhood'. *International Journal of Clinical Medicine, Modern Medicine of Ireland* 31(12), 17–24.

Maines, B., and Robinson, G. (1992) *Michael's story: the 'no-blame approach'*. Lame Duck Publishing, 10 South Terrace, Redlands, Bristol B566TG.

Olweus, D. (1989) *Bully/victim questionnaire for students*. Department of Psychology, University of Bergen, Norway.

O'Moore, A.M., and Minton, S.J. (forthcoming) 'Ireland: The Donegal Primary Schools Anti-Bullying Project'. In P.K. Smith, D. Pepler and K. Rigby (eds), *Bullying in schools, global perspectives and interventions*. Cambridge University Press.

O'Moore, A.M. (2002) 'Teachers hold the key to change'. In M. Elliot (ed.), *Bullying: a practical guide to coping for schools* (3rd ed.). London: Pearson Education, Kidscope.

O'Moore, A.M., and Kirkham, C. (2001) 'Self-esteem and its relationship to bullying behaviour'. *Aggressive Behaviour* 27, 269–83.

O'Moore, A.M. (2000a) 'Critical issues for teacher training to counter bullying and victimisation in Ireland'. *Aggressive Behaviour* 26, 99–111.

O'Moore, A.M. (2000b) *Defining violence: towards a pupil-based definition*. Novas Res, Italy, 1999–1577001–INO Project. www.commune.torino.it/novasres

O'Moore, A.M. (1988) *Bullying in schools*. Council of Europe Report, DECS-EGT (88) S-E, Strasbourg: Council for Cultural Cooperation.

O'Moore, A.M., Kirkham, C., and Smith, M. (1997) 'Bullying behaviour in Irish schools: a nationwide study'. *Irish Journal of Psychology* 18 (2), 141–69.

O'Moore, A.M. (1995) 'Bullying behaviour in children and adolescents'. *Children and Society* 92, 54–72.

Pikas, A. (1989) 'The common concern method for the treatment of mobbing'. In E. Roland and E. Munthe (eds), *Bullying: an international perspective*. London: Fulton.

Roland, E., and Munthe, E. (eds) (1989), *Bullying: an international perspective*. London: David Fulton Publishers.

Roland, E., and Munthe, E. (1997) 'The 1996 Norwegian programme for preventing and managing bullying in schools'. *Irish Journal of Psychology* 18 (2), 233–47.

Salmon, G., James, A., Cassidy, E., and Javaloyes, M. (2000) 'Bullying' — a review: presentations to an adolescent psychiatric service and within a school for emotionally and behaviourally disturbed children'. *Clinical Child Psychology and Psychiatry* 5 (4), 563–79.

Smith, P.K., and Brain, P. (2000) 'Bullying in schools: lessons from two decades of research'. *Aggressive Behaviour* 26, 1–9.

Smith, P.K., and Sharp, S. (eds) (1994) *School bullying: insights and perspectives.* London: Routledge.

Smith, P.K, Morita, Y., Junger-Tas, J., Olweus, D., Catalano, R., and Slee, P. (1993) (eds), *The nature of school bullying: a cross-national perspective.* London: Routledge.

Sutton, J., Smith, P.K., and Swettenbaum, J. (1999) 'Social cognition and bullying: Social inadequacy or skilled manipulation?' *British Journal of Developmental Psychology* 17 (3), 435–50.

Whitney, I., and Smith, P.K. (1993) 'A survey of the nature and extent of bullying in junior/middle and secondary schools'. *Educational Research* 35, 3–25.

# shaping identities

# 6

## SHAPED IDENTITIES

### DONAL TOOLAN

Donal Toolan's account of a series of life experiences is interwoven with reflections on how his experiences of education and life after school as an individual with a disability may be seen as typical of those in similar situations. The attitudes and ideas expressed by individuals in positions of power, whether these are teachers or members of the medical profession, can have a lasting impact upon individuals who may need to exhibit considerable determination in order to overcome prejudice and ignorance. Donal Toolan suggests that a lack of focus on the construction of the collective experience of people who have been discriminated against, marginalised or ignored as a result of their disability has inevitably resulted in a persistent negation of human rights.

## Introduction

Early experiences can act to shape futures. I spent the first four years of my life in hospital and other quasi-medical environments, and I can see some of the traces of that experience in the life I presently live. My response to such early circumstances is in many respects concerned with challenging the necessity and the outcomes of such an experience and the subsequent path it presented me with. I currently work as a coordinator of a rights-based organisation of disabled people, which seeks to promote a rights perspective of our identity and in effect challenge the medical model within which society has traditionally sought to locate our lives.

## Feeling different

If one were to look at my early formal education, through report cards and so on, it would probably be seen as no different to that of my siblings or indeed any of the children in the rural community of east Mayo in which I grew up. Why should it? Perhaps it should not, but having a physical impairment in a culture that is (at a minimum) passively uncomfortable with perceived difference, I have grown up constantly seeing my experiences as *having been* different or *going to be* different. Despite what a paper check of my early formal education might suggest, my actual experiences *were different*. Different not just because they felt different, but because the more significant influences in shaping my sense of self, and thus my capacity to learn, were shaped outside the formal educational experience of my able-bodied peers. Because of my experience of disability and how society engaged with that experience, I occupied at least two distinct worlds from birth up until my teenage years.

At birth I was seen to have a physical impairment that necessitated my spending practically the first four years of my life in hospital. This period, which is seen to be significant in emotional development, is something of a blur to me. I have the physical scars of surgery on my legs and I remember being somewhat confused about ideas of home, family and so on. From there up until I was fifteen or sixteen I spent a number of weeks, sometimes months, out of each year in rehabilitative or hospital environments.

The very fact that I was spending a portion of my life on the other side of the country, in a Dublin hospital, is in itself enough to engender a sense of difference. Spending time in a clinical, institutional space away from family and community was difficult, as was the rehabilitative process I was going through and what it was telling me about myself and my identity. I was spending time in these environments not only engaging in tests to determine why my muscles did not allow me to walk, but also painfully learning to walk at other people's bidding. I was (as the name of the hospital I attended suggested) being *rehabilitated*. No, I had not committed a crime nor was I a child drunk; but my body was perceived to have something wrong with it, so I was being *rehabilitated* so that I could fit into society. Which on the face of it retrospectively still seems like a lousy deal. Because society creates certain physical and psychological requirements for participation, I must be physically and psychologically oriented to fit into that society.

Aside from the huge ethical, social and moral questions as to the changing of children into something they are not, without informed consent, this process is most damaging because of how we were made to feel about ourselves. As a child in these environments, the first question I was asked and learned to ask other children was 'What's wrong with you?' This was usually satisfied by throwing out cerebral palsy or spina bifida polio and so on. Since my medical gurus had not cooked up a title for me until I was nearly twelve, I proved even more of an enigma to my disabled peers. Not having a label could be as exotic as it was excluding. I was clearly just trying to be different.

When I finally did get a medical diagnosis, the result of a basic muscle biopsy, it was patently clear to my medical mentors that no amount of standing in sandboxes wearing braces was going to enable me to walk without support. I recall at this time a young medical intern informing me solemnly, 'Of course you realise you were not ever going to walk.' I felt almost obliged to break down and feign absolute distress, pleading 'Why, oh why?' Actually I was thinking 'Did I ever want to walk? Did anyone actually ask me in the first twelve years of my life if I wanted to spend time away from home and school in an environment where I learned to recognise myself as someone who had something wrong with them?' A place where, on arriving as a child, I had to give up my own clothes 'for safe keeping' until the time came for me to go home again. I hated the clothes thing, not because mine were particularly trendy or glamorous, but because they were my clothes, and linked me to my mother, who had bought them, and my family, whom I missed. It was almost as if by wearing these hospital clothes we were being robbed of a last piece of connection to the outside world of our families, communities and schools.

After a few weeks, I would leave the hospital in south County Dublin, where authoritative, articulate professionals clipped along polished corridors trading over who had jurisdiction over our physical or mental parts, and return to the other world I inhabited, where I attended a two-roomed, turf-heated school in east Mayo with my brothers and sisters.

## Education

In this world I learned to speak Irish badly, to trust in God's will, and that we as a people had been oppressed by the British for some eight hundred years and in 1916, through the brave heroes pictured above the proclamation at the back of the classroom, we had won our freedom. The brave heroes had all been executed, which added to the anger we felt towards the Brits and indeed fuelled the pride we felt at having a Republic won out of a noble bloody war like the French or American Revolution.

I, like many of such an impressionable age, somehow believed this piece of paper, which talked of cherishing all the children of the nation equally. In this world I learned many other myths and legends, though I never made it at GAA. The two worlds I occupied had little in common, except me. Both worlds were as decidedly uncomfortable with me as I was with them. What was common to both of these worlds was their inability to confront the reality of who I was and what I might need. The two-room national school put in a ramp on the insistence of a social worker from a disability organisation, who, as I recall, was equally horrified by the outside toilets that we were using at the time.

The ramp had not been overlooked by the school out of any malicious intent, it just had not been considered. My family did not know they could consider such things and so, without a process in place on the part of the state's education system, it fell to a voluntary body to provide the flash cards. I was lucky in contemporary terms to have attended such a small school, whose student population as a whole was around fifty students. That meant an average of eight children in each class. Each family supplied turf for the school fire and in many ways there was a simple, familiar rhythm to school life within a community where people generally were supportive and helpful. In this world I was not hugely conscious of my difference, and children and community accepted without question my being a part of that space. Nonetheless, I grew to expect from an early age that people would stare at me and talk about me as if I was not there. This could be hurtful and isolating, particularly without a process to address such feelings.

## Identity

From an early age I found myself having to come to terms with my identity alone. I was the second youngest of seven children from a low income farming background. Money was hard to come by and my parents did not have the capacity to devote more of their energies to what was going on with me. In some ways this was difficult, as it heightened the sense of isolation, loneliness and confusion I felt. In the rehabilitative and educational worlds, and indeed in the world of my family, there was no language available to talk about any of this. So it was presumed I was content to spend twelve years learning to walk. It was also presumed that I was comfortable living in these diverse and confusing worlds. For example, in the quasi-medical rehabilitative world of hospital, I was, along with the other children around me, confronting mortality in a very real way. Not just in seeing young friends die, but also in asking each other, 'What's wrong with you?' We were also feeding our obvious insecurities as to whether we were going to die because of these medical labels. What was our future? This and a thousand other repetitive, insignificant but deeply pattern-shaping details come with living in institutional environments where people eat, sleep, go to physiotherapy, go to occupational therapy and see psychologists at the direction of those who are perceived to be more articulate and powerful than themselves.

Another aspect of the rehabilitative world was the power of the hospital in our lives. A bit like a government department, there was a sense that what they said must be important. Another aspect of this environment was that personal privacy was not seen as a priority. So the personal hygiene and care of children and even adults became everyone's concern and at times their public obsession. While the majority of the individuals with whom I came in contact were conscientious, humane people, the system and its rehabilitative/medical focus created a culture that did not recognise the individual's right of privacy and personal integrity. The fact that it was a Dublin hospital gave it a weighted authority in our disaffected peripheral lives.

The ways I negotiated these worlds varied from taking charge to manipulation and whatever else came to hand. The advantage in having to take charge of such issues at an early age was that when I was twelve or thirteen, before starting secondary school, I decided that I was not going to walk anymore. I told my parents that 'the doctors said it was not necessary'. I didn't have the same impediments as others whose parents are more hung up on their children walking. While I did not fully appreciate the psychological import of what I was doing, I was aware that this was important — I was letting go of this side of me even if I had never really wished to walk anyway. My motivation was merely to find the fastest and most efficient way of getting from A to B. Dragging myself around on crutches, wearing heavy callipers that enabled some semblance of walking, did not to this thirteen-year-old suggest either fast or efficient.

Using a wheelchair was not the source of stigma for me that it was for others. That was a whole other psychological ballgame, which again significantly impacted on my sense of self. I was for the first time buying into my being a Disabled Person. Although it was some time before I found the language to engage more fully with the identity of what being disabled meant, I was shifting the focus from what was apparently wrong with me to the reality of how I was. That this decision coincided with the beginning of my secondary education in a school of six hundred students meant I had little time to objectively consider this transition. In contrast to many of the children I met in hospitals who were attending special schools, or living permanently in school hospitals, in the 1970s and 1980s I would be considered some sort of success, as a disabled student who had an 'integrated education'. However, to suggest my experience worked might be stretching the truth somewhat.

## Integration in schools

What does this concept of integration mean anyway, when used by those involved in education? During my years in school, education was designed to equip people with a rounded education so as to enable them to access further education or employment based on their intellectual and physical capabilities. The focus was not on what was going in the individual's physical or emotional life, but rather on their capacity to perform within clearly structured margins. The experience of disability was hugely stigmatising for families not assisted in educational terms by the dominant church's role in the management of education, whose perceptions and teachings have done much to reinforce stigmas.

I am not suggesting that in the educational or rehabilitate environments I was in, I did not experience great humanity, resourcefulness and even flexibility on the part of different committed professionals. There was much of what was beneficial in intellectual and inspirational terms, and I was supported by many dedicated people. My comments relate to the design of the system. I was lucky to have encountered some excellent teachers, but the system increasingly discourages such individual supportive approaches, as our consumer-driven economy impacts upon every aspect of our lives. I can honestly and objectively say that most of what I have learned that is of use to my professional and personal life did not take place within formal education. I would also add that much of what impeded my capacity to learn in different environments, as it impedes many of the people I have facilitated in learning environments, was the inability of the formal education system to regard the individual holistically.

Why does the education system still not take into account the physical, social and emotional well-being of students as part of any appraisal of their intellectual or physical abilities? Some arguments put forward by professionals include that they are not trained or equipped to address such issues or needs. Or that such issues and needs are best addressed, if addressed at all, in a specialist environment. These arguments have seen many of the disabled people from my childhood dumped from the special schools and hospitals into the special training centres and living in so-called 'homes', where getting up in the morning, going to the toilet, eating and drinking are likely to be determined more by the availability of staff than by any individual need. These arguments see the Jamie Sinotts of the world and their families forced into courts in order to demand even basic educational rights. What has always struck me as flawed about these arguments, both in my own educational experience and as a journalist and advocate, is that changing the dominant system of education, with some limited integrated opportunities available, might make it less relevant or accessible to others. If a teacher had to spend more time with a disabled student, it might disadvantage other students. Engaging with the emotional well-being of the student may also be seen as inappropriate or requiring additional training, and this is not what teachers are trained for.

While this may ensure that all is well within the dominant education system, how many others does it fail when an education system is increasingly focused on people's capacity to produce and consume? A system designed with scant regard to our human make-up. Look at figures in Ireland for addiction, suicide, teenage pregnancies, early school leaving in disadvantaged areas and basic literacy levels. These figures are high by international standards. Is it not strikingly obvious that a greater emphasis on developing the emotional well-being of students is as relevant as directing people on how to access cyberspace? The reasons why disabled people are not accessing meaningful education, as demonstrated by an estimated 80% unemployment rate and high rates of segregated or excluded living opportunities, are endless.

## Conclusion

The real reason disabled people are not accessing meaningful education is because of the lack of legislative and other institutional support for such provision. This is not a priority because disabled people are not perceived as being equally productive and therefore not an asset within a 'consume and produce' society. As a society, we determine our values increasingly in material terms. Also, as a society, we are uncomfortable with difference. We are unclear how we feel about disabled people, because for a variety of reasons, including a difficulty to process constructively or talk about our experiences, we are collectively unclear about how we feel about ourselves — what constitutes person, identity or self.

If our sense of our identity is to be seen purely in economic terms, or in terms of a narrow definition of what is the norm, then those we perceive as different will be perceived as a threat to that notion of identity. The Traveller, the refugee, those whose skin colour is different, gays and lesbians, those with different religious beliefs, and disabled people, all represent a threat to this narrow notion of success that is promoted by an influential elite. In recent years I have spent time in New York, a place where everyone is an outsider. So while I may still expect in such a place to be stared at or seen as an oddity, I make up the majority who are comfortably staring back. Such a multi-cultural space exists from the very experience of lots of difference, but also from the system actively working to protect the rights of the 'other'.

# 7

## EDUCABLE: DISABLED YOUNG PEOPLE IN NORTHERN IRELAND CHALLENGE THE EDUCATION SYSTEM

### *GORETTI HORGAN*

The notion of participatory research is one that is only just beginning to gain momentum in terms of the involvement of young people with special educational needs. In this paper, Goretti Horgan demonstrates that through a commitment to involving young people in a major research project, both experienced researchers and research users can gain new insights into students' school experiences. The young people involved in this research reveal a series of critical issues that need to be addressed if a more equitable education system, which meets the needs of all students, is to be achieved. The low expectations that result from current practices and an inability to translate good intentions into policy and practice are seen as obstacles to the development of a more inclusive education environment. The voices of young people emerge strongly from Goretti Horgan's paper and provide a reinforcement of the view that they have opinions that can inform and improve our current educational approaches.

## Introduction

Although the United Kingdom government ratified the UN Convention on the Rights of the Child in 1989, there is little evidence of Article 12 of the Convention being taken seriously. In this regard, Northern Ireland is no different to the rest of the UK. Article 12 commits us to 'assure to the child who is capable of forming his or her own views the right to express those views freely in all matters affecting the child, the views of the child being given due weight in accordance with the age and maturity of the child'. This paper reports on a research study initiated by Save the Children (Northern Ireland) as part of its commitment to promoting the rights of children and young people, in this case disabled young people, under Article 12, to participate in debates about policy and practice issues that affect them.

In Northern Ireland, the right of children to have their views ascertained and taken into account is legally recognised in only a handful of situations. The Children (NI) Order of 1996 requires that statutory agencies and the courts take account of children's views when making decisions about them. However, this applies only to issues such as the child's choice of residence in custody cases or where the child is in public care. The Code of Practice for Producing Statements of Special Education Need, appended to the Education Order of 1996, similarly requires the child's views to be taken into account, again in a very limited circumstance.

In addition to these rights enshrined in legislation, two legal rulings in the British courts have been adjudged as extending to Northern Ireland, and these provide children and young people with significant rights to have their views considered. The Gillick Judgement of 1986 concerned the right of children under the age of sixteen to seek information about contraception without their parents' consent. The House of Lords ruled that parental rights to make choices for children diminish as the child grows in maturity and reaches sufficient understanding to be capable of making an informed decision for themselves. A subsequent ruling in 1992 found that the child's right to make decisions in relation to medical treatment extended only to the right to give consent to, but not to refuse, treatment. Thus, until the age of eighteen, parents retain the right to give consent for treatment on behalf of the child, even where the child has refused treatment (Lansdown, 1995). However, the right of children and young people to participate in the institutions and decision-making that affects them is rarely vindicated in Northern Ireland (Horgan and Rodgers, 2000). The majority of schools (77%) do not have a student representative body in the form of a student council/student union (NI Youth Forum, 1999). Inevitably, then, there has been little work done to involve children and young people with a disability in shaping the decisions and institutions that affect them.

## Involving young people with disabilities in research

Experience in consulting and involving children and young people in research is still relatively new, and the involvement of children and young people with disabilities in research projects is rare (West, 1995; Save the Children (NI), 1996; Kirby, 1999; SCF (UK), 2000). There has been relatively little research that seeks the views of disabled young people, and still less that involves them in the research process itself (Ward, 1997). As Beresford (1997) points out, disabled children are 'doubly disadvantaged' when it comes to being involved in research because:

> Methodological and ethical arguments, together with a simple failure to accept the value of the child's viewpoint, have precluded children in general from being accepted as bona fide participants in research. Having an impairment, or illness, marginalises some children even further.

Over the last twenty years, as the disability rights movement has developed, so too has the debate about the extent to which research is a social process. There is a strong argument that researchers can and must make the research process more democratic. They can strive to redress the balance of power between groups who are 'being researched' (who are usually among the more disadvantaged in society) and those who are 'doing the research' (who are usually relatively advantaged). Disability rights activists have insisted that disability research must be more 'emancipatory' and seek to empower people with disabilities in the process (Oliver, 1992).

The research reported here was entirely controlled by disabled young people. It is, as far as we know, the only research project carried out in these islands that involved young people with disabilities in every aspect of the research: planning, developing the methodology, carrying out the fieldwork, analysing the data and writing the report. There were clear advantages to this way of working. Certainly, the young people in the special schools who took part in group discussions and those in day centres who were interviewed said they appreciated the fact that the researchers themselves were disabled and so they were more relaxed because of this. The young researchers picked up cues that the professional researcher (who accompanied them on all school visits) did not (or perhaps could not). For example, one student who uses a wheelchair mentioned that she went regularly to a particular cinema. One of the young researchers immediately asked her how difficult that was since the cinema has steps outside. When they visited a school for young people with severe learning disabilities, the young researcher who shared that label acted as a 'translator' for the other young people.

> Young researcher: 'Did you have a choice about the school you
>   went to?'
> No reply.
> Young researcher: 'Did anyone talk to you about what school you
>   would go to?'
> Young researcher labelled as SLD: 'Did your Mam and Dad tell you
>   you're going to this school or did they ask you if you wanted to?'
> Student: 'Mammy told me'.

There were, of course, also disadvantages to having the research carried out by young people, but these were certainly outweighed by the advantages in terms of the quality of the qualitative data gathered by the young researchers.

**Educable and discrimination against disabled young people**
Educable was a group of nine young people with various disabilities who came together in 1998, with the support of Save the Children and the Youth Project of

Disability Action, to do some research. After a lot of discussion, the group decided to call itself 'Educable' because they felt:

> It sums up the message we hope to get across. The word means 'able to be educated'. We believe that all young people, however severe their disability, are able to be educated. It is just a matter of working out the best way for that individual.

Educable consisted of (in alphabetical order): Orlaith Cassidy, Anita Gracey, Zelda Holland, Katrina Ives, Martin McCafferty, Margaret McMahon, Caroline Millar, Chris Mussen and Michael Smith. Each of the young people has a significant disability. All had attended special school, except Anita, whose disability did not really start to affect her until her late teens. Honorary, non-disabled members of the group were the two Disability Action youth workers, Alison Davidson and Marian McKinney, and the author, Save the Children's researcher, Goretti Horgan.

Before settling on educational choices as the topic to research, the young people had long, interesting and often very lively debates about the issues that affect their lives. Several were about the language used about disability — the nasty and patronising as well as the over the top politically correct. Many of the discussions were about the segregation of young people with disabilities — in education, in social life, in relationships.

When the group started to organise some social events, the (non-disabled) professional researcher and the two youth workers were shocked to discover the level of casual, often indirect discrimination against young people with disabilities. It was almost impossible for us to have a night out together as a group. Most pubs, clubs, restaurants or theatres can accommodate one or two people using wheelchairs. But a group that includes five or six people using wheelchairs and two or three others with mobility difficulties found few venues open to them.

In a discussion about sex education at school, the one group member who had attended a mainstream school said they had been shown videos of very difficult births in order to scare girls off having sex and getting pregnant. Those who had attended special schools were amazed at this. In special schools, they said, teachers 'would have been too frightened to talk too much about sex or relationships'. One of the young women in the group had strong views on this issue. She said it was typical of the way special schools treated students that it simply would not occur to them that a girl with a disability might get pregnant before leaving school.

> They couldn't let you do that [talk about having sex] because the cotton wool would be broken. The cotton wool that they wrap you up in the day you start. Then by the time you leave, the cotton wool has pretty much smothered you.

Another area of discrimination relates to the extra costs of having a disability, especially one that affects mobility. Getting taxis everywhere costs a lot and if someone uses an electric wheelchair and needs transport with a hydraulic lift, then it is both expensive and scarce. We found that taxis that advertise as 'wheelchair friendly' charge people who use wheelchairs more than they do other passengers. This is technically illegal, but the young people felt there was little they could do about it as they depended on the taxis for any kind of a social life. The young people were adamant that 'the more disabilities you have, the more expensive it is for you to have a life'.

Educable was clear that 'as a group we have one thing in common and that is a determination to live our lives in the fullest and most independent way possible'. They felt that their ability to do this was undermined by the fact that they were 'let down by the education system' and not stretched to their full potential. So, the young researchers agreed with official government policy that disabled children should, as far as possible, be educated in mainstream schools. However, most of the group felt that mainstream education had not been an option open to them and that they had had little choice either of schools to attend or of subjects studied. Some felt very strongly that having to go to a special school was the start of the segregation they have faced ever since and that the lack of choice in schools and subjects had limited the options available to them now that they had left school. They felt the schools they had attended had very low expectations of them. Those low expectations were exposed, they felt, by their involvement in the research project. That involvement showed that:

> We are able to think things through and do work usually done by university graduates. Yet, of those of us who attended a special school, no one left school with more than three GCSEs at Grade C or above. That is why we decided to research the choices available in education for young people with disabilities. (Joint statement by Educable members)

## Methodology and fieldwork

At first, all the young people saw research as being about getting as many people as possible to fill out questionnaires. After discussion and training, they decided to use a qualitative method of collecting the information and opted for discussion groups. It was hoped that young people who were shy would open up more if they were in a group with their friends. At first, the young researchers wanted to visit every special school, further education college and day centre in Northern Ireland, but because of time constraints and the difficulties of travel and access to schools they decided to visit four special schools in the greater Belfast area. Three of these schools were for children and young people with a physical or sensory disability, the fourth for those with a learning disability. Two of the schools have boarding departments that accommodate children from across Northern Ireland. They also visited a day centre to talk to young people under the age of twenty-five about their schooldays and spoke to Disability Action's Young Women's group. Altogether, the young researchers spoke to over fifty young people ranging in age from fifteen to nineteen, all of whom had a significant disability.

The initial response from some of the school principals was poor, due they said to the many requests schools receive from researchers. The fact that these researchers were a group of young people with disabilities seems to have helped gain access to the students. Once they agreed to participate, the schools were extremely helpful. Each school was sent a leaflet for students and their parents introducing the group and the research. The principal then arranged a suitable time and provided a room for the discussions.

Before the fieldwork started, a lot of time was spent on group work skills and practising how to conduct a discussion and preparing the questions to ask the students. It took several weeks of hard work for the group to put together five sets of questions for each focus group to discuss. These covered why the pupils were at that particular school and what they liked and disliked about special school; choices of subject at their school; what the young people thought of the attitudes of teachers, parents, friends and relatives towards them; if they thought school was preparing them for life; what they wanted to do when they left school; and what they liked to do in their free time.

The long preparation paid off and the students in most of the groups to which the young researchers spoke were happy to talk openly about their lives. The students were asked if they minded the discussion being taped to ensure their words could be quoted accurately in the research report. These tapes were then transcribed, ready for coding and analysis using the NUD*IST qualitative data analysis package. The use of NUD*IST allowed the young researchers to be involved in the analysis of the transcripts in a meaningful way. They developed the coding framework as a group, and coded most of each of the transcripts themselves, leaving the professional researcher with the essentially technical job of inputting the codes and getting back what the young people said about each of the areas in which the Educable group were interested.

Writing up the report was also a group effort. The NUD*IST findings were fed back to the group and their discussions about the findings were recorded. The young researchers could not agree with some of what the young people still at school said. They argued from their own experience that those still at school could not know how hard it can be 'out in the big bad world'. They knew they had to report the research findings accurately but wanted still to take account of their own views and experiences. After some consultation with a range of professional researchers, the Educable group decided to include their own voices in the research report, to give the study the benefit of their own hindsight. (Quotes from members of the Educable group are attributed to them. All other quotes are from disabled young people who were part of a discussion group or an individual interview.) In particular, the young researchers spent several sessions looking for solutions to the issues raised by the students in the discussion groups and by young people who had recently left school. This process provided a range of recommendations from the group, which they hoped would contribute to improving the education of young people with disabilities. All of this was taped and then written up in the research report, which, again after much discussion, they decided to title *No choice: no chance*, to reflect their own views of the special education system.

## No choice and low expectations

The students seemed to have had very little choice about which school they would attend. Many of them, well over half, had been at the same school since they were two or three years old. Other students had managed in mainstream education in their primary school years and only started in special school when it came to secondary school. Others had started in mainstream but began to struggle when they were seven or eight years old, in about Primary 4 class. Lack of physical access and appropriate aids and equipment were the main reasons for their move to a special school. The experience of the young people in the school groups mirrored that of the young researchers. The majority of the Educable group went to special school because their local schools lacked access and, for some, vital physiotherapy, speech therapy and occupational therapy services.

> I know physically I wouldn't be as independent or able now if I hadn't gone to [School A]. There I got the amount of physio that I needed. (Educable member)

Even when the young people were able to cope with the work at a mainstream school, the way the other children treated them was sometimes a problem. This ranged from leaving them out of games to very nasty bullying. Again, the experiences of the school students were very much like those of the young researchers. Bullying of children with a disability seems to be widespread in mainstream schools.

> At my last school, I was left out of a lot of the activities because my friends that were all able-bodied they would go off and do their thing and leave me out and they just wouldn't really bother. I was just put to one side and that was just it for the rest of the group in the playground and stuff.

> When I was in the mainstream I got bullied and I kept it inside myself and I went and told the headmaster I was getting bullied … He did nothing about it at all. Brushed it under the carpet, like nothing was happening … I looked for a new school in the meantime and then one day I got kicked down the stairs, two flights of stairs because I was different. (Educable member)

A few young people got the chance to change schools if they wished, but decided not to, mainly because they thought they would not be able to cope with the workload in a mainstream school.

> I've been at this school since I was two years old. At one point, they did ask me would I like to go to a mainstream school, maybe at the age of fifteen or sixteen, but I decided not to. I knew the workload would be too much for me to cope with. There's enough for me to cope with in this school.

It is noteworthy that none of the young people to whom the young researchers spoke complained about the pressure of schoolwork. Some, especially in School C, talked about homework taking up a lot of their time outside of school hours. But none of the young people complained about the pressure of schoolwork in the way able-bodied fifteen to eighteen-year-olds often do. When asked about the amount of homework they had, they were generally happy with it. Some wanted to drop subjects in order to concentrate on the ones they were taking in examinations, but were discouraged from doing so. Yet dropping some subjects is relatively common in mainstream schools if a young person is unlikely to get a lot of GCSEs. This emphasis on covering a wide range of subjects, rather than concentrating on a few in order to gain qualifications, is the exact opposite of what happens in mainstream schools and is part of the pattern of low expectations from teachers.

> I: What sort of languages are you doing?
> R: Well, last time we done German and last year we did French.
> I: Do you do a different language every year?
> R: Yeah, we're trying to.

The young researchers identified with what the students said about the workload and had contradictory perceptions on the question. They agreed that there was little or no pressure put on them by teachers in special schools to work as hard as, say, their able-bodied siblings were expected to study. Yet some of them had spent hours doing relatively small amounts of homework that took an inordinate amount of their time because they did not have the computers and other aids, or personal support, needed to assist their study.

> Without a computer at home, it took me so long to do even a little bit of homework. It could take me an hour to write two sentences that I could type in five minutes. I was waiting for a laptop computer for home, but by the time I got it, I had left school. (Educable member)

In all the schools, the students said there were few choices, but they were very understanding about why a small school cannot provide a range of choices. However, in some schools, they said it was teachers, not students, who made most of the decisions about subject choices.

> I would have liked to have done geography but I couldn't because I done history … You can have a choice between history and geography but the teachers decided that we would do history.

> For the course I want to do at university, I would need more

specialised science subjects, but the school only does general science … I know I'm the only one in the school who wants to specialise in science and they can't put on a class just for me. But I wish there was a way around it.

It is clear from the research that science is done in special schools only as a very general subject. Even the brightest young scientist has no chance of doing subjects like chemistry or physics for GCSE or A level. From their own experience, the Educable group could see that the schools are afraid a student will get hurt during experiments and, with some disabilities, students might need extra help. In discussing the problems faced by the special schools, they summed them up as:

> The schools are small and resources are limited. Some of the teachers aren't very enthusiastic. Someone with a disability might need extra help, say, to do a science experiment and the school maybe doesn't have the money for that extra help. Plus, the length of the day in a special school is about two hours shorter than your average secondary or grammar school and all these things together could limit choices. (Educable member)

But for the Educable group, who had already left school and were struggling to be independent and get a job, the lack of subject choice at special school had become emblematic of the difficulties they faced in breaking into the labour market.

> My sister is at grammar school now and I can see the choice she gets and I realise what a bad deal I got. We're forced to go on to further education really because the education we got at school wouldn't get us a job. (Educable member)

Worse than the lack of subject choice, however, are the low expectations that the Educable research revealed teachers have of children and young people with disabilities. Some teachers don't expect disabled students to do well in examinations and this can become a self-fulfilling prophecy. Students are allowed to enter for only a limited number of subjects in GCSE examinations, and no special school in Northern Ireland prepares students for A levels. Some of the Educable group were very angry at the way certain teachers just assume a disability means that students are not able for particular subjects and for exams. They felt that, instead, teachers should try to find a way around the difficulties caused by disability. Since computers 'can do almost anything these days', they argued it should be possible to overcome most of the obstacles that are in the way of young people with physical and sensory disabilities.

> I find it very patronising to be told 'you shouldn't do that because it's not for you and wouldn't suit you'. And 'we're really thinking about you, you know'. And actually it's not us that has to change. It's the environment that has to change; it's the exam system that has to change; it's the schools and the teachers that will have to re-organise themselves to allow young people with disabilities get a decent education. (Educable member)

> It's not that I couldn't do them [exams], they just never gave me a chance to do them and I had seen other people doing exams and I thought, why can't I do them? Every time I asked them, it was like 'because' all the time. When I went to Pathfinders [support scheme in FE Colleges for disabled students], I put the emphasis on them that I want to do an exam in whatever and they said 'no problem, go for it', and I left there with GCSEs. (Educable member)

Many of the students complained about not being allowed to do various examinations. For those who attended mainstream primary schools, being excluded from the Eleven Plus exam was the first experience of this:

> I never done my Eleven Plus when I was in P7 because they said I couldn't because of the prep and all that.

The students spoken to in the course of the research were mainly very happy in their schools and said they preferred special school to mainstream. The younger ones especially loved the small, family-like feeling in most of the special schools, while the small class sizes mean pupils are able to get a lot of help with their work. Most of the students were hostile to the idea of integrating with a mainstream school.

> I:     What would be bad about going to a non-disabled school?
> R:     They're too big, the steps and they laugh at you [School B].
> I:     Would you like the school to be integrated more?
> R1:    It is, there's Catholics and Protestants both here.
> I:     With mainstream, I mean.
> *All eight young people say no, bar one, a young man who has been disabled for just two years.*
> I:     Why not?
> R1:1   Because I love it the way it is.
> R2:1   The classes would be all bigger.
> R3:11  I think it would go back to just being like an ordinary mainstream school ...
> R2:1   1where we'd be insulted and ...
> R3:1   bullied.
> R4:1   If a lot of people, able-bodied children, joined the school, they would just take over, we would be left to the side.
> R5:1   It's sort of as well, small numbers of pupils means you can build up a relationship with the teachers, which you couldn't do in mainstream school because you don't get that much time, you know. It's really great because I mean you can go and talk to the teachers and they're really understanding and you know you wouldn't get that in a mainstream school, they wouldn't even know you [School C].

**Young people's participation in decision-making in special schools**

The young people whose voices are heard in the Educable report are clear that they are undervalued by the present education system and are not involved in shaping their own learning experiences, despite being the clear experts about their own abilities, likes, dislikes, strengths, weaknesses, aspirations and ambitions. Yet there is a strong body of evidence that suggests that when children are encouraged to participate in their own learning 'by expressing needs, by negotiating and setting objectives and by reviewing their own progress, they are likely to be better motivated, place more value on their successes and have a more certain knowledge of their own strong and weak points' (Wade and Moore, 1993). In fact, a working group looking at the teaching of English in England and Wales concluded:

> Self-assessment by pupils, even at the primary stage, has a part to play by encouraging a clear understanding of what is expected of them, motivation to reach it, a sense of pride in achievements and a realistic appraisal of strengths and weaknesses that need to be tackled. (Department of Education and Science and Welsh Office, 1988)

Making children and young people partners in the education process is important also in overcoming the problem of low expectations highlighted in the Educable research report. Research shows that the young people were absolutely right to see teachers' expectations of them as a key concern. There is much evidence, dating back to the 1960s, of the effect of teachers' attitudes and expectations on pupils' achievements in lessons. Hargreaves (1967) demonstrated the effect of streaming on expectations of how pupils would perform. The work of Rosenthal and Jacobson (1968) suggests that pupils' achievements actually *match* the expectations of their teachers. More in-depth research by Rutter and others (1979) shows what any young person could tell us: that teachers' expectations affect pupils' attitudes and behaviour as well as their academic performance in class.

There are several ways of raising teachers' expectations of their pupils, including several recommended by the young people in Educable. Given the extent to which we are only now learning about the effects of some disabilities on learning, it is understandable how even the best of teachers can come to have low expectations of their disabled pupils. While the literacy difficulties faced by many of the Educable group are not due to a learning disability, rather a physical one, it is possible to see how their difficulties in acquiring such skills would affect teachers' expectations. Yet a fourteen-year-old boy who entered Cambridge University last year had far worse literacy difficulties than anyone in the Educable group and had to be provided with a scribe to take examinations. All the Educable young people agreed that with that level of assistance they could have done much better in examinations. This illustrates the effect of expectations on the success of a young person's education: the Cambridge entrant has a hidden disability (dyslexia) and is labelled 'extremely gifted'. As a result of this label, huge resources were made available to him to allow him to access university at an early age. The Educable young people, on the other hand, have very visible disabilities, all of which make accessing education difficult for them. So, their literacy problems are seen as insurmountable, their educational potential limited and few resources are offered them. Involving the individuals themselves in planning their education can help overcome this obstacle to the education of disabled children and young people. Teachers may be surprised by the level of self-awareness many disabled young people demonstrate, and by how realistic yet high their expectations of themselves are when explored. Thus, involving them can raise the expectations of both teacher and pupil and bring about a marked improvement in achievement.

It may be more difficult to involve some young people in planning their education. The Educable group found that young people with learning difficulties seemed quite unused to being asked their opinions and so at first found it difficult to contribute to the research. However, those who had been involved in Disability Action's Youth Project, and so were more used to being listened to and having their views valued, were able to make a valuable contribution to the research. This has clear implications for the education of young people with learning difficulties at school and in day centres: the more they are consulted, the more they open up and contribute.

None of the schools visited had a school council or other forum where the students could be involved in decision-making about broader school policies and problems. Some of the schools have consulted students about particular issues, for example, discipline and bullying policies. However, students in two of the schools complained about the policy on uniforms and the fact that their views are not listened to except 'when it suits them' (the teachers/principal). In one of the schools, the students spent most of the discussion complaining about the attitudes of teachers, and in particular the principal, towards them, which they felt demonstrated a total lack of respect. It is worth noting that these young people were all seventeen years of age or older. Under law and in most schools, they have a right to have a say in the decisions that affect their lives. As is clear from the discussion quoted below, the young people very much want a voice in their schools. All the respondents quoted below are young men, apart from YP2 (YP=young person), who is a young woman.

YP4: The management in this school have their own ideas — like we have to wear uniforms but not all the time [laughs, because all are wearing football shirts] … How come she [Principal] is always able to give us big lectures like every Friday morning in Assembly but we can't put our point of view across?

YP7: There's no respect. She just lectures us like children.

YP2: Lecture, lecture, lecture, lecture, lecture.

YP3: There used to be a regular meeting between teachers and student representatives and, okay, maybe it was mostly about silly things but she just done away with it.

YP4: And she done away with …

YP3: We used to have student representatives but she did away with them. She decided that we couldn't elect the Head Boy.

YP2: And no Head Girl.

YP3: That's right.

YP5: Another boy is Deputy Head, there's no Head Girl.

YP2: There should be something like a council.

The lack of respect from teachers and the school principal reported by some young people should not be tolerated in the twenty-first century. On the other hand, the pride that some young people showed in their schools, and their enthusiasm, ought to be harnessed in the interests of both school and pupils. There is now considerable evidence that involving students in decision-making in schools, through a forum like a school council, elected by the pupils and with real powers over some areas of school life, would help on both counts (Sutton, 1999; Alderson, 2000). The school councils would challenge the disrespect shown to some young people and build the confidence and self-esteem of all (Davies, 1999).

**Conclusion**
The Educable research demonstrated that young people with disabilities in Northern Ireland are 'being failed by the education system whether we attend mainstream or special schools'. Although the young researchers in the Educable group are completely opposed to segregated schools for disabled children, the young people they spoke to liked the small classes in special schools and appreciated the easy availability of aids and equipment to help them learn. They also recognised that special schools provide physiotherapists, occupational therapists and speech therapists, which are difficult to access in the community. The small size of special schools, which is helpful when a pupil is younger, means that subject choice is limited, and that in turn limits career choices. The question of low expectations is probably the most serious challenge to be faced, however. As the Educable young people say in the conclusion to their report:

> No one expects us to do well in exams and go on to have a career or even a decent job. Changing this means challenging a mindset that sees the disability, not the person, and that fails to recognise that while it might take a young person with a disability longer to achieve their goals, we can still do it ... As a group of young people with disabilities, Educable has shown that we can do quite a lot. We have done something few non-disabled young people have: we've

decided to do some research, planned it, learned how to do it, then did it and analysed the results. We think we came up with a lot of good recommendations …[and] that our ideas would make school life better for all young people, not just those with a disability.

Not only are the young people being failed in relation to formal education preparing them for examinations, they are also being prevented from practising their skills as young citizens through participation in decision-making in their schools. Today, when fewer than one in four post-primary schools in Northern Ireland has a forum such as a school council through which students can have even a minimal say in the running of the school, the idea of a school council in a special school may seem a radical proposal. Yet, over seventy-five years ago, Marxist educationalists and psychologists in revolutionary Russia developed an education system where pupil self-government was the aim of the committees of pupils, parents, teachers and ancillary staff that ran the schools. This included schools set up to educate disabled children, many of whom, for example deaf/blind children, had traditionally been seen as ineducable. Taking into account the arcane nature of the language, this description of life in a school for the profoundly deaf proves that not only are children and young people with significant disabilities able to be educated, they are able to run the schools themselves!

The chief principle on which our schools are based is that education is considered part of social life; school is an organisation where children participate in the life which surrounds them. The bringing up and education of children must proceed within society, through society and for society … The world's first experiment in self-governing among deaf and dumb children has been made in our schools. The children organise their own life; they have their own school governing body, with sanitary, cultural and other committees and all these interests go to make up their whole life. As a result, social habits, conscious instincts, initiative, organising abilities, collective responsibility are developing and strengthening through this system. (Vygotsky, 1925)

## References

Alderson, P. (2000) 'Education and civil rights: students' views about their rights in schools'. *Childright* 163 (Jan/Feb), 6–8.

Beresford, B. (1997) *Personal accounts: involving disabled children in research.* London: HMSO.

Davies, L. (1999) *School councils and pupil exclusions.* London: School Councils UK.

Department of Education and Science and Welsh Office (1988) *English for ages 5–11.* London: HMSO.

Hargreaves, D.H. (1967) *Social relations in a secondary school.* London: Routledge & Kegan Paul.

Horgan, G., and Rodgers, P. (2000) 'Young people's participation in the new Northern Ireland society'. *Youth and Society* 32 (1), 107–37.

Kirby. P. (1999) *Involving young researchers: how to enable young people to design and conduct research.* York: JRF.

Lansdown, G. (1995) 'Children's rights to participation: a critique.' In C. Cloke and M. Davies (eds), *Participation and empowerment in child protection.* Chichester: Wiley.

Northern Ireland Youth Forum (1999) *Students' councils and career education in schools and colleges.* Belfast.

Oliver, M. (1992) 'Changing the social relations of research production?' *Disability, Handicap and Society* 7 (2), 101–115.

Rosenthal, R., and Jacobson, L. (1968) *Pygmalion in the classroom.* New York London: Holt, Rinehart and Winston.

Rutter, M., Maughan, B., Mortimore, P., Ouston, J., and Smith, A. (1979) *Fifteen thousand hours: secondary schools and their effects on children.* London: Open Books.

Save the Children and Joseph Rowntree Foundation (2000) *Young people as researchers: a learning resource pack.* London: SCF (Save the Children).

Save the Children (NI) (1996) *Out of our mouths not out of our heads: a report on drugs and drug use in West Belfast, compiled by and for young people.* Belfast: SCF (Save the Children).

Sutton, F. (1999) *The school council: a children's guide.* Birmingham: SCF (Save the Children).

Vygotsky, L. (1925) 'Principles of social education for deaf and dumb children in Russia'. In R. van der Veer and J. Valsiner (1994) *The Vygotsky reader.* Oxford; Cambridge, Mass.: Blackwell.

Wade, B., and Moore, M. (1993) *Experiencing special education: what young people with special educational needs can tell us.* Milton Keynes: Open University Press.

Ward, L. (1997) *Seen and heard: involving disabled children and young people in research and development projects.* London: Joseph Rowntree Foundation.

West, A. (1995) *You're on your own: young people's research on leaving care.* London: SCF (Save the Children).

# 8

## ENCOURAGING PUPILS WITH LEARNING DIFFICULTIES TO UNDERSTAND AND EXPRESS THEIR OWN LEARNING NEEDS

### *RICHARD ROSE*

In this chapter Richard Rose explores how pupils described as having severe learning difficulties have been enabled to play a role in their own assessment and learning procedures. He suggests that teachers have a responsibility to examine the skills and understanding that pupils need in order to become more independent in recognising their own learning needs, and that a commitment to support pupils in acquiring these skills should become a critical part of the teacher's role.

## Introduction

Teachers who work with pupils described as having severe learning difficulties have for many years been striving to find innovative approaches that might assist these pupils in becoming more effective learners. Many of the interventions that they have put into place have been focused on teaching approaches that are in some way compensatory or that attempt to analyse the challenges to learning presented by perceived pupil deficits (Farrell, 1997). In recent years more teachers have come to realise that the potential of pupils with severe learning difficulties may in the past have been underestimated and in some instances inhibited by limited approaches to teaching (Downing and Demchack, 1996). It is generally accepted that pupils who can gain an understanding of their own learning strengths and needs are more likely to be able to build upon these and address their shortcomings. It is further suggested that teachers should strive to enable pupils to become more self-reflective and should support them in taking greater responsibility for their own learning.

This paper is written on the premise that all pupils, including those who are often perceived to face the greatest challenges in learning, can benefit from being more directly involved in decisions about their own needs and targets. It describes a small-scale research project that focused upon the involvement of pupils with severe learning difficulties in assessment, planning and learning procedures in order to give them an opportunity to take responsibility for aspects of their own learning.

## Motivation for the research

Examination of the role of pupils in the teaching and learning process may be inspired by a wide range of motivations. Similarly, the timing of any such research may be an important factor in determining the level of impact that any findings and conclusions reached may have upon policy or classroom practice. The motivations of the researcher and his colleagues for the work discussed within this paper can be seen to have been influenced by a variety of factors. Some of these may be described as circumstantial and related to national educational policy, such as the Code of Practice on the Identification and Assessment of Special Educational Needs (Department for Education,

1994, subsequently revised in 2001), which is discussed below. Other sources of motivation may have their origins in a philosophical belief about pupils' rights, based on many years' experience of working in schools. However, for research to have validity and to be of value to policy makers or classroom practitioners, it is necessary to provide a foundation on which theories and ideas may be tested and challenged and to collect data that may enable a clearer picture to be developed and disseminated. While many of the teachers who were involved in the research described here were committed to pupil involvement and believed that this had a positive impact upon learning attitudes and achievement, the evidence for such assertions were largely based on anecdotal evidence. The enthusiasm of these teachers and their determination to pursue opportunities for pupil involvement can certainly be seen as a starting point for the research and a critical motivating factor for the researchers. There are, however, important considerations to be made in respect of any research that begins from such a motivation. The need for objectivity can be more difficult to maintain when undertaking research in such an environment and demands approaches that are rigorous and researchers who are prepared to be subjected to critical scrutiny.

Within the UK education system, decisions about the structure of education and the legislative processes required to ensure that good standards and quality are maintained in schools are, quite rightly, a major concern of central government. Successive legislation throughout the twentieth century aimed to ensure that all children received their entitlement and rights to an education that would equip them for post-school life. As the demands of society have changed, new policies and structures have been developed that have aimed to assist schools in preparing pupils for life in, for example, an increasingly technological working environment or employment in a post-industrial age. Educational change inevitably promotes political debate (Kogan, 1978), and certainly discussions regarding issues such as curriculum content, statutory assessment and the composition of schools and classroom groupings have proved contentious in recent years. The introduction of a National Curriculum within the UK has been seen by many teachers (Hill, 2001) as providing an imposed content that, in its avowed intention of providing all pupils with a broad, balanced and relevant curriculum, has not necessarily succeeded in meeting the needs of the less able or more vulnerable members of the school population. Similarly, a structure of increased national testing has been seen as providing an obstacle to the inclusion of pupils with special educational needs, at the very time when government intentions to increase opportunities for pupils to be educated in mainstream schools has been asserted (Booth, Ainscow and Dyson, 1997; 1998; Rose and Howley, 2001).

While the limitations of many of the curriculum structures that have been put in place are apparent, it is important to recognise that the nature of pupil involvement is an issue that has not been ignored by policy makers. From its very inception the National Curriculum identified consultation and discussion with pupils as being an essential element of good practice in curriculum delivery (National Curriculum Council, 1990; 1992). In particular, elements of pupil self-assessment were encouraged and it was suggested that all pupils could play a part in self-evaluation. This encouragement of pupil involvement was in keeping with the spirit of the United Nations Convention on the Rights of the Child (1989), Article 12, which states that

> Parties shall assure to the child who is capable of forming his or her own views the right to express those views freely in all matters affecting the child, the views of the child being given due weight in accordance with the age and maturity of the child.

With regard to the rights of pupils with special educational needs, one might question the phrasing of this particular article. For example, who determines the capability of the child or, for that matter, their levels of maturity? It might be suggested that assertions regarding capability and maturity have been critical elements of the repression of pupils with special educational needs for many years. At one level such a statement could be seen to encourage paternalism and to provide an excuse for excluding pupils from their right to involvement. However, the positive intentions of this article have been reinforced through legislation and in particular the 1994 Code of Practice on the Identification and Assessment of Special Educational Needs. This important document aimed to ensure that all pupils with special educational needs were subjected to informed and accurate assessments and the production of a structured programme of intervention to meet their needs. Paragraph 2:37 of this document states:

> Schools should consider how they:
> — Involve pupils in decision-making processes.
> — Determine the pupil's level of participation taking into account approaches to assessment and intervention which are suitable for his or her age, ability and past experiences.
> — Record pupils' views in identifying their difficulties, setting goals, agreeing a development strategy, monitoring and reviewing progress.
> — Involve pupils in implementing individual education plans.

In the revised Code of Practice (2001) these principles have been further endorsed, with a whole chapter devoted to pupil participation (chapter 3).

While the principles of pupil involvement have been clearly asserted, the practice may well be falling some way short of the intent. A survey conducted by the author and colleagues two years after the introduction of the original Code indicated that while some schools had made considerable progress in considering how pupil involvement might be achieved, many had failed to begin to address the issue (Rose, McNamara and O'Neil, 1996). Undoubtedly since this time there has been an expansion of work in this area, with writers such as Lawson (1992) providing excellent examples of how pupils may be involved in record-keeping procedures, and also with the burgeoning of accreditation systems such as ASDAN that demand that greater attention is given to pupil participation.

It is not suggested that seeking to involve pupils in their own learning procedures will be easily achieved. Indeed, many genuine obstacles to greater pupil participation do exist. Lewis (2001) has emphasised the need to move beyond a simplistic acceptance of the right of the pupil to be heard, to a greater analysis of the complexities of elicitation and interpretation. It is true to say that many pupils are eager to please and may indeed be suggestible. Caution is needed when attempting to involve pupils in the expression of their opinions and ideas, and even greater care must be taken with regard to the ways in which these are interpreted. This paper describes the processes adopted by a single school to encourage greater pupil participation, but with a recognition that our understanding of this approach remains at an early stage of development.

The legislative framework and developments in this field have led to a climate that is conducive to enquiry related to pupil involvement. This, coupled with the undoubted increase of activity by teachers attempting to address greater pupil involvement, suggests that opportunities for research into the efficacy of the approaches being used to support this involvement are likely to present themselves. This was certainly the case with respect to the work described in this paper, which was conducted in collaboration with teachers who were not only concerned to meet the requirements established in the Code of Practice, but also had a firm commitment to pupil rights and to finding the means to support pupils in overcoming obstacles to expressing their own opinions and asserting their needs.

**The research questions**

The research was conducted in an all age day special school that provides education to pupils described as having severe learning difficulties. This school was self-selecting for the research, having approached the researcher with a request that he should examine the approaches that were being taken to involve pupils in setting their own learning targets. A visit to the school revealed that teachers working in the senior department of the school, with pupils aged between fourteen and nineteen years, demonstrated a considerable commitment to pupil involvement. Pupils were engaged in a weekly assessment of their own performance, discussing their work and identifying their own successes and difficulties. On the basis of these weekly meetings they were setting further targets to be addressed and producing record sheets on which to record their progress. The work seen was certainly impressive and indicative not only of the commitment to the process shown by staff, but also of the enthusiasm of the pupils involved in the work. Staff spoke with confidence about the increased independence that they had seen in pupils since formalising the procedures for involving them in assessment and target setting. In particular they commented on the ability of pupils to remain more focused on their individual learning needs, the pride that pupils exhibited on attaining their targets and the purposeful manner in which pupils went about working towards their agreed objectives. These assertions certainly concurred with those of other writers in this area (Griffiths and Davies, 1995; Munby, 1995; Bennathan, 1996) who suggest that pupil involvement may lead to improved behaviour, greater accuracy in work and increased levels of independence. However, time spent in the school was useful not only for the opportunity to see some interesting practice, but also in raising a number of critical questions which formed the basis of the research.

The first of these questions was: 'Why had specific pupils been selected to be involved in target setting?' The process was being undertaken with students in the senior department of the school but not with younger pupils. Teachers in the school expressed the view that in the senior department pupils were being carefully prepared for post-school life, where they would need to take more responsibility for their own actions and to demonstrate a higher level of independence. This view meant that a greater emphasis was given to pupil involvement, as it was seen as providing them with the skills needed as part of the preparation for school leaving. However, this decision appeared to have been made simply in terms of the chronological age of the pupils and their movement into the senior department of the school, and did not relate in any way to maturity. The range of pupil needs within the school is considerable and this means that pupils who enter the senior department have a diverse range of needs and abilities and vary considerably in terms of their maturity. When questioned, teachers within the school admitted that on entry to the senior department some pupils were more 'ready' for involvement in self-assessment and target setting than others and that some presented a significant challenge to the system that had been put into place. Article 12 of the United Nations Convention appeared to have some significance in terms of the school's approach. Pupils were certainly being identified who were deemed as not yet 'capable' or 'sufficiently mature' to engage with the target setting process.

The notion of 'readiness' is an important one because, while it did not detract from the determination of the school to involve its pupils, it did provide the basis of some detailed discussion, which led to the second critical question to be researched: 'What are the skills which pupils need to acquire if they are to become effectively involved in their own learning and assessment procedures?' Observation of the target setting sessions had shown that some pupils were more proficient and more comfortable with identifying their own needs, setting targets and assessing their progress than others. Teachers were very conscious of some of the challenges of working with pupils who were often eager to please and could therefore be suggestible. This required that teachers were careful about the language they used in order not to lead pupils into making decisions.

As the school was fully committed to pupil involvement, they were keen to establish an approach that would prepare pupils fully for the process of target setting and decision-making by developing the necessary skills from an early age. This provided the third research question: 'How could teaching throughout the school be organised to take full account of the skills which pupils would need to acquire in order to become more independent learners?'

## The research approach

The research conducted was managed within an action research model that aimed to address the research questions raised above, while providing the school with a model for further development of pupil involvement procedures. As an early stage of the research an analysis was made of the field notes gathered during observations of target setting sessions to ascertain successful practice and also to identify the obstacles that teachers and pupils had to overcome. Particular consideration was given to identifying which pupils were selected for participation in the target setting process, the means and effectiveness of communication between teachers and target setting pupils, and the role that each played during the sessions. At the same time, a scrutiny of target setting documentation examined the records of progress made by pupils and the nature of the targets set, and sought evidence of the specific skills demonstrated by the pupils involved.

This initial stage of the research was followed by the development of an assessment procedure. This was used to ask specific questions about pupil skills and understanding, and was designed to enable teachers to have a clear understanding of pupil needs and abilities and to plan for developing and strengthening the potential of pupils to play a full role within the target setting process. This procedure was trialled, modified and re-trialled over the course of a school year until it became a useful working document that could be consistently used within school.

## What did the research reveal?

Observation of pupils in target setting sessions revealed that those who were successful in playing a full role in the process had developed specific identifiable skills. While the positive attitudes of staff and their commitment to pupil involvement was critical, it became clear that those pupils who were most successful in playing a full role had identified a group of skills that enabled them to be both confident and competent. These could be placed within three distinct categories, which the researchers described as (a) *negotiation, (b) self-knowledge — recognition of potential,* and *(c) prediction skills — concept of time.* Each of these categories was interdependent and where pupils exhibited difficulties in any one of them, they were less able to fully engage in determining their own learning needs.

After a period of observation it was possible to list specific skills under the three headings and to develop an assessment checklist that enabled teachers to identify priority areas for teaching that would support pupils in becoming more effective participants in assessment and learning procedures. It quickly became apparent that in some instances limited teaching approaches had resulted in pupils becoming dependent upon teachers and other adults to advocate on their behalf and had limited their own competence in respect of critical functions. The specific skills identified as critical for the development of greater autonomy in assessment and learning under the three headings identified above were as follows:

*Negotiation*

Can state an opinion with confidence.

Can disagree with confidence.

Takes part in a two-way conversation.

Can say 'Yes' and 'No' in response to requests.

Seeks clarification and help when unable to understand.

Expresses personal feelings and needs.

Maintains and develops a topic of conversation effectively and appropriately.

Stands up for self – can represent own views and feelings in an assertive and non-aggressive way.

Makes suggestions and gives opinions in the correct context.

Has well-developed skills of refusal that are used effectively and appropriately.

Achieves a good balance between listening and responding.

Is able to initiate conversations successfully.

Adapts behaviour and language to the context and listener.

*Self-knowledge — recognition of potential*

Recognises/identifies personal achievements.

Knows when something has been achieved.

Identifies personal strengths and weaknesses.

Identifies likes and dislikes.

Identifies possible future leaving (post-school) needs.

Recognition of having had an effect upon decisions.

Identifies something which cannot be achieved.

Recognises something which cannot be done yet, but which can be achieved with time.

Identifies possible learning strategies, including the need for support.

Recognises something which the target setter could not do, but can do now.

Acknowledges and identifies difficulties or non-achievement experienced.

Understands concepts of hard, easy and manageable.

*Prediction skills — concept of time*

Understands the concept of time in relation to the target set.

Understands differences in time scales — day/week/term, etc.

Identifies/recognises/states the benefits of achieving a target.

Having identified these key skills, it was possible to assess pupils to define where their current strengths lay and to identify areas that required further attention. In this way it was possible to build a profile for individual pupils and for teachers to support pupils in the development of those skills that were perceived as insufficiently developed to enable full pupil participation. Having completed assessments, teachers felt more focused upon the needs of pupils and expressed themselves to be more aware of their own teaching styles. Teachers became conscious of the need to provide opportunities to address the listed skills for individual pupils, and were also more thoughtful about their general approaches to ensure that pupil participation was encouraged.

Further observation of teachers working in class showed that they were very aware of the needs of individual pupils and were taking account of these in their teaching. For example, teachers were observed to be encouraging pupils to express their opinions about activities and lessons, to comment upon their own performance and to discuss how they might build on lesson content in later sessions.

## Discussion

The development of the assessment instrument was certainly helpful in enabling teachers to support pupils in becoming more involved in self-assessment and planning. More importantly, it led to a discussion and debate about more fundamental issues such as when the process of pupil involvement should begin and what form it might take in the earlier years of schooling. A commitment to pupil involvement, which had been strong within the senior department of the school, came to be seen as a process that must be built upon early procedures to ensure that pupils entered this department more ready to function as effective decision-makers. Because of this, the assessment procedure was adopted right through the school, and teachers became more aware of the ways in which they could begin to encourage pupils to become more autonomous learners and to play a greater part in their own assessment and planning.

Revisiting the original research questions at the end of the project enabled a number of important observations to be made.

*'Why had specific pupils been selected to be involved in target setting?'*
The notions of capability and maturity are important in our understanding of why certain pupils were selected. Bearing in mind that all of the pupils involved in this research were described as having severe learning difficulties, it might be anticipated that expectations in terms of both capability and maturity might be lower than would be the case with a 'more able' population. This is not to be critical of teachers in the school, who had shown considerable commitment to pupil involvement and had a determination to make all pupils as independent as learners as they could be. In terms of capability, the work revealed that simply making a judgement because a pupil has a label of learning difficulty is not acceptable. In order to become autonomous learners and decision makers, all pupils need to learn specific skills as identified in the assessment procedure developed as part of the project. However, it may be the case that for some pupils, including those who participated in this study, there is a greater need for teachers to be aware of the underlying skills required and to make a more conscious effort to incorporate opportunities for addressing them within their day to day teaching. At a most fundamental level, this includes the provision of opportunities for pupils to make simple choices, possibly regarding materials to be used in lesson, and for teachers to seek the opinions of pupils with regard to their likes and dislikes and how they perceive their own performance in class.

Many pupils described as having severe learning difficulties are not perceived by adults as having the ability to make decisions. The commonly held belief that such pupils remain immature even in their later years of schooling can be seen as an obstacle to the development of greater independence. Certainly many pupils with learning difficulties take longer to acquire the fundamental skills necessary for full participation. However, a starting point must come from higher teacher expectations related to pupil achievement and the creation of a teaching environment which, rather than reinforcing dependency, creates greater demands upon pupils to take some responsibility for their own learning. For reasons that are wholly understandable, many adults have created an artificially protective environment for pupils who have severe learning difficulties. While for many this approach, based upon benevolence and concern, needs to be continued, it needs to be tempered by a more detailed examination of the relationship between actions that are dependency creating and the provision of opportunities to promote greater autonomy. This will only be achieved through the establishment of a partnership between teachers, parents or carers and the pupils themselves, which focuses upon the preparation of a plan of action that ensures that the necessary skills for greater independence are addressed from an early age and planned throughout the school. An important indicator of maturity is the ability of the individual to take some responsibility for their own actions and to make decisions. This is a process that must start early for all pupils, including those with severe learning difficulties.

*'What are the skills which pupils need to acquire if they are to become effectively involved in their own learning and assessment procedures?'*
The observations conducted as part of the research had identified specific skills needed by all pupils if they are to become more autonomous learners. However, acquisition of these skills alone would not prove sufficient in developing high levels of independence. Clearly pupils need opportunities to generalise their abilities beyond the classroom. Pupil involvement in decision-making that takes place only within the school context is unlikely to lead to greater independence. Partnership between home and school will be essential to ensure that the skills and understanding required are taken forward into all aspects of a pupil's life. For some parents, whose primary function may be perceived as one of nurturing and care, it may be difficult for them to see how the encouragement of high levels of pupil involvement may be a priority, particularly in the earlier years of schooling. Discussion regarding the nature of independence and the preparation of pupils for the wider world must involve all interested parties from the earliest stages of education.

The skills that were identified by researchers and endorsed by teachers working on this project are undoubtedly important. However, there remains a need to continually re-examine these skills, to further our understanding of how they may be taught and to identify the type of classroom environment and teaching approaches that promote their development. It is clear that a starting point for any school must be the belief that pupils can achieve, and a commitment to effect the changes in teaching practices that may enable pupils to become more effective independent decision-makers.

*'How could teaching throughout the school be organised to take full account of the skills which pupils would need to acquire in order to become more independent learners?*

A first principle adopted by the school at the heart of this research has been to start early. False beliefs that pupils can begin to play a greater part in their own assessment and learning procedures when they enter the senior department of the school have been disproved. Maturity is to some extent defined by the opportunities to develop skills of independence, and this must begin as early in the education process as possible. Certainly, as pupils move higher in the school, they need to be encouraged to take on ever-increasing responsibility for their own actions and learning. However, from the earliest stages of schooling, teachers need to have an awareness of the skills that pupils will need to acquire in order to become independent learners. They will further need to make decisions about how they can organise their classrooms and adopt principles that encourage the acquisition of these skills.

One of the key skills that teachers themselves must learn is that of listening effectively to the young people with whom they work. Pugh and Rouse Selleck (1996) suggest that this is not so easily achieved as might have been assumed. They have identified both skills and attitudes that need to be adopted in order to create a school climate that encourages pupils to express themselves and to understand their own learning. Key among the challenges that they perceive is that of extending children's thinking, developing what they describe as 'conversational reciprocal exchanges', in which pupils are encouraged to communicate their thoughts, ideas and opinions. For many pupils with severe learning difficulties, such a challenge will inevitably take a considerable time, but this is no reason for not trying and may indeed be all the more reason to begin the process early.

## What do the pupils themselves believe?

Fletcher (2001) has continued to work within the school in encouraging greater pupil involvement. As part of his and the whole school's commitment to developing more independent pupils who, on leaving school, are prepared, have a clearer understanding of their own strengths and weaknesses and can identify their own needs, he has been careful to record the reactions of pupils to the systems put in place. He has many examples of the ways in which pupils perceive both their own needs and their views of involvement in self-assessment and planning. For example, one pupil expresses not only his understanding of what he is trying to learn, but also an appreciation of how the acquisition of a specific skill might have advantages:

> I'm working on telling the time to ten past the hour. I chose it with a bit of help. When I leave school, I want to be able to tell the time properly. Some bloke might ask me the time — it would be nice to tell him.

Another pupil recognises that he is on route towards greater independence, but that he still has some way to go:

> We look through our folders, choose what we've found difficult and then think it over with a member of staff. A lot of people need a lot of help, I need a bit too.

Yet another is able to see how the process of pupil involvement will be of benefit in the post-school years:

> It's important so when you leave school you know what you want to do and what you don't.

These pupils, all of whom are described as having severe learning difficulties, have demonstrated that they can learn to play a full part in assessment and learning. The full benefits for them and for their teachers and families are yet to be fully understood. What is clear is that to deny any pupil the opportunity to acquire the skills and understanding necessary to play a full part in making decisions that affect their lives is unacceptable, and to use labels such as 'learning difficulty' as an excuse for not trying to support such processes can no longer be tolerated.

## References

Bennathan, M. (1996) 'Listening to children in schools: an empirical study'. In R. Davie and D. Galloway (eds), *Listening to children in education*. London: David Fulton.

Booth, T., Ainscow, M., and Dyson, A. (1997) 'Understanding inclusion and exclusion in the English competitive education system'. *International Journal of Inclusive Education* 1 (4), 337–55.

Booth, T., Ainscow, M., and Dyson, A. (1998) 'England: inclusion and exclusion in a competitive system'. In T. Booth and M. Ainscow (eds), *From them to us*. London: Routledge.

Department for Education (1994) *Code of practice on the identification and assessment of special educational needs*. London: DfE.

Department for Education and Skills (2001) *Special educational needs code of practice*. London: DfES.

Downing, J.E., and Demchack, M. (1996) 'Determining individual abilities and how best to support students'. In J.E. Downing, *Including pupils with severe and multiple disabilities in typical classrooms*. Baltimore: Paul H. Brookes.

Farrell, P. (1997) *Teaching pupils with learning difficulties*. London: Cassell.

Fletcher, W. (2001) 'Enabling students with severe learning difficulties to become effective target setters'. In R. Rose and I. Grosvenor (eds), *Doing research in special education*. London: David Fulton.

Griffiths, M., and Davies, C. (1995) *In fairness to children*. London: David Fulton.

Hill, D. (2001) 'The national curriculum, the hidden curriculum and equality'. In D. Hill and M. Coles (eds), *Schooling and equality: fact, concept and policy*.

London: Kogan Page.

Kogan, M. (1978) *The politics of educational change.* Glasgow: Fontana.

Lawson, H. (1992) *Practical record keeping for special schools.* London: David Fulton.

Lewis, A. (2001) 'Reflections on interviewing children and young people as a method of inquiry in exploring their perspectives on integration/inclusion'. *Journal of Research in Special Educational Needs* 1 (3).

Munby, S. (1995) 'Assessment and pastoral care: sense, sensibility and standards'. In R. Best, C. Lang, C. Lodge and C. Watkins (eds), *Pastoral care and personal social education.* London: Cassell.

National Curriculum Council (1990) *Curriculum guidance 3: the whole curriculum.* London: NCC.

National Curriculum Council (1992) *Curriculum guidance 9: the national curriculum and pupils with severe learning difficulties.* London: NCC.

Pugh, G., and Rouse Selleck, D. (1996) 'Listening to and communicating with young children'. In R. Davie, G. Upton and V. Varma (eds), *The voice of the child.* London: Falmer.

Rose, R., McNamara, S., and O'Neil, J. (1996) 'Promoting the greater involvement of pupils with special needs in the management of their own assessment and learning processes'. *British Journal of Special Education* 23 (4), 166–171.

Rose, R. and Howley, M. (2001) 'Entitlement or denial: the curriculum and its influences upon curriculum processes'. In T. O'Brien (ed.), *Enabling inclusion: blue skies … dark clouds.* London: The Stationery Office.

# 9

## LIVING AND LEARNING: THE SCHOOL EXPERIENCE OF SOME YOUNG PEOPLE WITH DISABILITIES

*MÁIRÍN KENNY, EILEEN MCNEELA AND MICHAEL SHEVLIN*

In this paper it becomes evident that many students have a clear view of what they expect from their schools. This paper provides an opportunity for pupils with disabilities to express their own views with regard to their expectations. It is clear that many have formed impressions of their local or designated schools well before they are offered a placement. A strong theme that emerges from the research described in this paper relates to the desire of pupils to be accepted as part of a local education community. The students who contributed to this research accept that at times they will need assistance over and above that expected by their peers. Of particular interest is the way in which they are able to articulate the type of support they require and how this may best be provided.

## Introduction

It has generally been assumed that young people with physical or sensory disabilities have benefited significantly from the movement to integrate young people with disabilities into mainstream schools. According to the OECD (1994), this type of integration has been 'a goal of education for many countries and is a significant trend in almost all OECD countries' (p. 3). The integration rationale has developed on the basis of well-constructed legal, educational and psychological arguments. Stukat (1993) asserts that enabling these young people to participate fully in education constitutes a moral choice for society. While it has been acknowledged that integration is a complex process, there has been little recognition of the difficulties encountered by young people with physical/sensory disabilities in gaining full access to participation in all aspects of school life (Kenny *et al.*, 2000; O'Keefe, 1997). Rather uncritically, it was believed that placement within mainstream schools would ensure that these young people were fully included in school life. This expectation failed to take account of a complex set of intersecting factors that shape provision for these young people. These factors include: the lack of an infrastructure to support integration initiatives (Colgan, 1998), the failure to equip schools and teachers with adequate resources and training, and the lack of awareness of the impact of societal attitudes on school experiences for these young people.

Despite increased government attention to special educational needs issues, as documented in a series of reports (Department of Education, 1993; 1995; National Council for Curriculum and Assessment, 1999), measures implemented by the government have tended to undermine the thrust towards integration. For example, the 1998 Education Act along with the Employment Equality Act (1998) and the Equal Status Act (2000) adopt a definition of disability based on the seriously flawed functional deficiencies model. This effectively ignored the strong recommendations made in the Department of Equality and Law Reform Report (Commission on the Status of People with Disabilities (CSPD) 1996) that the social model of disability should be used in framing and developing educational policy and practice. It can be strongly argued also that government commitment to integration must be seriously questioned in the context of the failure to guarantee access to education for those young people with the severest disabilities (Booth and Ainscow, 1998), and of the need for parents to fight for these rights through the law courts. In addition, Lynch (1995) reported that teachers felt unprepared to teach students with disabilities in mainstream schools. Also, little account was taken of existing research that suggests that an individual and tragic view of disability has tended to dominate 'both social interactions and social policies' (Oliver, 1990). Societal attitudes towards people with disabilities have been characterised by ambiguity and a degree of goodwill. As Lewis (1995) reported, mainstream students, not unexpectedly, tend to share the ambiguity of their elders in relation to their disabled counterparts. These misconceptions can cause difficulties in social interactions between young people with disabilities and their peers.

Irish research on the experiences of young people with physical/sensory disabilities within mainstream schools is extremely scant. O'Keefe (1997) and Kitchin and Mulcahy (1999) concur that young people with disabilities are often isolated and dispersed throughout mainstream schools without adequate supports or even an understanding of their individual needs. As a result of these disturbing findings, the exploratory study on which this paper is based was devised to examine in more detail the complex realities of mainstream schooling for young people with physical/sensory disabilities.

**Overview of findings, and paper focus**
Participants in this survey discussed issues relating to all the key aspects of their school experience — choosing their school, following the various courses, relationships with teachers, socialising with their peers in and out of school, sitting examinations, and facing their post-school future. A strong theme linking all facets of their school experience was the social dimension: every decision about school, every academic struggle, and of course every interpersonal interaction with education deliverers and peers, was achieved in the social domain. In all their talk, participants presented their school experience as a search for normality, for normal life as members of their teenage peer group. This was chronically blocked or skewed by inadequate provision for them as people with disabilities. The topic of this paper is this social achievement, and the focus is on data relating to the participants' everyday experience of school

as it impacted on their peer relations.

Section 1 of this paper is an overview of the research procedures used in the 'Hidden Voices' project. Section 2 is an analysis of selected data on life in school, and Section 3 addresses participants' experience after and out of school. The paper closes with a general commentary.

## Survey procedures

The 'Hidden Voices' project was designed as a small-scale exploratory qualitative research survey. The key objective was 'to register the experience of young people with disabilities in second level schools; so that it shapes developments in system policy and practice' (Kenny *et al.*, 2000). Particular attention was devoted to adopting research procedures that respected and validated the experiences of young people with disabilities (Atkinson and Williams, 1990; Beresford, 1997).

The survey was conducted by means of semi-structured audio-taped group interviews with young disabled people. Potential participants were contacted via involved agencies, and sixteen young people agreed to participate. They were interviewed in three groups. Given the focus of this chapter, some detail on the research process is appropriate, both to show how the findings were gathered, and because it helps to reveal the participants' wider social context. Besides, the interview process itself was a social experience for all concerned and, as will be seen, its phased structure yielded interesting insights.

## Group composition

Statistical information on people with physical and sensory disabilities in Ireland is not available (Department of Equality and Law Reform, 1996), but the population is known to be small, scattered, and diverse in relation to criteria such as range of disabilities, socio-economic status, ethnic status, family factors, gender and urban/rural locational continuum. Therefore the concept of a 'representative' sample was considered to be problematic. For this reason, and given the scale of the project, the researchers opted for cluster sampling. Invitations to participate were issued via agencies involved with young disabled people.

A few points relating to the participants warrant consideration. All participants in this project were either already in or intended to enter third level or further education. Female participants outnumbered males by two to one — the reverse of the gender balance in the general population of people with disabilities. This may have been circumstantial, given the small scale of the survey. There were five rural and eleven urban participants. Participants' disabilities included significant and minor physical disabilities, sensory disabilities and specific learning difficulties. In this paper, contributions from participants with dyslexia are included for two reasons: participants' social experiences had strong common themes across the board, and many had more than one disability or had both a disability and a learning difficulty.

**Interview procedure**

In order to maximise participants' involvement in the research, the interview process was conducted in two phases. The first phase sessions were designed to gather participants' initial accounts of their experience; the second phase sessions gave them an opportunity to reflect on their accounts and to critique the researchers' interim analysis of them. For the first phase interviews, the researchers devised a topic checklist to ensure that issues identified in current literature would get aired at some stage in the group discussion; other issues were added in the course of the interview discussions. From initial analysis of transcripts of these discussions, an interim statement of findings and a modified checklist were drawn up, and these formed the framework for the second phase interviews.

Interviews were taped, and tape transcripts were analysed using discourse analytic methods (Potter and Wetherell, 1989; van Dijk, 1998). Potter and Wetherell note that the essential criteria for discourse analysis procedures can be observed, whatever the level of detail. Discourse analysis focuses on:

> what is actually said or written, not some general idea that seems to be intended ...Analysis is made up of two closely related phases. First the search for pattern in the data ... Second, concern with function and consequence ...[and] forming hypotheses about these. (Potter and Wetherell, 1989, p. 168)

Close textual readings of data yielded the findings presented here; review of the full data body in the light of these findings indicates that more detailed analysis would probably not generate further insights.

Official texts (Department of Education and Science documents on provision for students with disabilities) were examined in the light of participants' accounts, and the role of system context in shaping their experience was identified.

This study validates the argument for consulting students regarding their own education (Lewis and Lindsay, 2000). More importantly, the issue of returning findings to research participants is of ethical significance. An interview experience, and processing it, is part of the life of the participant and can have diverse knock-on effects. Each interview provided participants with a context wherein they could reflect on their experience, place it in a wider context, and develop their thinking about issues that affected them. The two-phase structure offered participants a chance to push their thinking further. They valued their role as research partners, and wanted to know if the report would promote effective inclusion policy and practice in the school system. That in turn highlights the ethical imperative of disseminating research findings, and promoting change in policy and provision to reflect these findings.

**Data presentation**

Where quotations are presented in sequence without intervening commentary, it should be assumed that each paragraph comes from a different speaker and a separate location in the discussion. Where a paragraph series is a string of conversational interactions, it is stated in the commentary, and speaker-labels S1, S2, etc., are used.

Key elements of participants' experience, particularly with regard to their school experience, were shared by all, whatever their disability/difficulty, gender, or location. When a participant is speaking about how her/his experience is specifically related to one of these factors, this is named in the commentary, but otherwise quotations will not be 'tagged' with disability, gender or locational labels, in order to respect and highlight the commonality of experiences.

**Curriculum access: a social and personal experience**

In the following review of elements from participants' discussions of their experience in second level schools, it will be clear that accessing the curriculum is at once a social and an academic achievement, that students' social lives intersect with, shape and are shaped by, 'school work'.

Students with disabilities are entitled to a normal school career — to real opportunities for full access to the curriculum, and full involvement in the social life of the school. A fundamental prerequisite for such access is the achievement of being present and engaged where the curriculum is being delivered and wider activities are being pursued. This physical presence and engagement prerequisite has a number of levels, the most obvious of which are: choosing a school; accessing classrooms; using equipment; using transport. This sounds too obvious to need stating, but the experience of participants in this study revealed that the need to be present and engaged is far from fully appreciated in the delivery of school services.

## School entry

For participants, social considerations were foremost in the first and most basic step involved in accessing any curriculum: choosing a second-level school to attend. The following speaker considered enrolling in a 'designated' school (a mainstream school resourced to support students with disabilities):

> I had one look at that [designated school] and I said no, that's not the school for me — I don't know, I didn't like the look of it. I had two cousins [and] all my friends going to my local school so basically I'd know everyone going there. It was only across the road from the primary school. No one was going [to the designated school], it would be like making new friends all over again. That's why I said no.

He named two grounds for opting for what might be termed 'complete normality': he disliked the distinctive 'look' of the designated school, and he far more lengthily depicted flow of his peers to the local school. As the next speaker said about her mainstream school:

> It was different, you know it was nice like, it was nice being with the
> normal crowd. Like to see what everybody else was doing.

Not all participants shunned support issues in their choice of school. The next
speaker needed support to access the curriculum, and she valued it:

> I thought it was a good school, it catered for disabled people and it
> had two resource teachers and if you needed help with any subject
> they'd give you special tuition on a one to one basis.

But in some schools, dominant perceptions of disability could intervene to
inhibit the struggle to maintain a discourse of normality:

> I was going to go to the carry-on from primary [second level
> school], but the headmistress wouldn't allow me to do home
> economics because I might spill something on someone, or
> biology because it was on the top floor. So I instantly removed
> myself from that school and went to another that would allow me
> to do the subjects I wanted.

This participant's ambitions collided with perceptions of her in the 'carry-on'
school, where she found herself categorised entirely in terms of her disability.
No one else mentioned point-of-entry barriers of this type, but as will be seen,
many encountered them within the school.

It should be noted that school choice issues are engaged with during a
transition between levels of formal education provision. So they can usually be
kept private to the young person making the transition and to her/his guardians
and chosen confidants. In this study, the transition in question is from primary
to second-level, but the same considerations pertained to experiences of
transition to third level, both for these participants and for participants in
another research project among third level students with disabilities,

undertaken by the researchers for AHEAD (Kenny *et al.*, 2001).

## Getting around

However, once a participant was enrolled in a school, he or she encountered levels two and three of fundamental access to the curriculum. Level two is the achievement of getting into the classrooms or other physical spaces where the curriculum is delivered. Virtually all the participants with physical disabilities encountered difficulties accessing at least some teaching spaces: as one said, if classmates didn't carry him up to second-floor subject classrooms, he 'just didn't go to that class'. As his comment shows, social considerations were now embedded in peer relations, the struggle was engaged with under the gaze of classmates:

> The first year or so took me a while to settle in — there was one other person I think with a disability in the school so it was kind of difficult just to basically get around. And asking for help — I found that difficult, I didn't like asking the same person all the time and you know it was difficult finding somebody different every day or you know some people would make a fuss over me and other people wouldn't think. It was a mixture of reactions.

In the absence of physical facilities to enable her to move independently around the school, this participant's disability became an omnipresent identity marker, skewing her social interactions. She cringes at the memory of its 'difficult ... difficult ... difficult' impact on her peer relations. The next speaker's comments show just how much some people with disabilities must bring their personal needs into the public domain:

> If I wanted to go to the toilet, the cubicles were very small; I had to go to the teachers' room. They knew and I had someone outside the door just in case they'd come. It wasn't too bad.

There may be a level of comfort with the facts of human biology in this image, but it primarily depicts dependency-driven personal exposure, and as such it again indicates skewed peer relationships. The cumbersome arrangement must also limit access to classrooms and curricular activities. But as will be seen, this speaker's stoicism ('It wasn't too bad') was a feature of several participants' management strategies.

Happily, some participants went to schools that were well prepared to offer inclusion: flexibility in the built environment is possible, and as is clear in the next excerpt, access to the built environment and to the academic process were often almost synonymous:

> There were girls in wheelchairs and they got round easily and everything was at a level where they could do everything.

The note of social independence is also clear: students who can 'get around easily' and 'do everything' are free to relate as equals with their peers, and can leave their disability in the background.

But the dominant experience was of oversight to the point of virtual denial of the disabled student's existence. The following statements are shocking indicators of how able-bodied students were learning to treat the variety of human capability:

> One girl had spina bifida. She couldn't handle the crowds; there were 1200 in the school. She left.

> I had to go up four flights of stairs to get to my classroom and I had to come down before the rest. If I came down at the same time as them they'd just push; once they basically knocked me down one flight.

In this physical/social context, it hardly needs saying that it would be hard for a disabled student to trust in the possibility of developing mutually respectful peer relations.

**Actors or watchers**

Level three in physical access is being able to use the 'tools' of school work, to the level of each student's personal competence. The diverse list of tools could be paralleled by an equally diverse list of supports and adaptations needed, so that students with disabilities have equitable access to use of home economics and science instruments, PE equipment and means of transport for field studies, as well as oral instructions (hearing aids or lip-reading) and written text (reading aids or substitutes) in almost all arenas. But focus on diversity of needs could distract from the commonality in the social impact of access difficulties. This level of access also became a disability-focused social issue, and talk of this impact was threaded through the accounts of all participants.

Teacher–student relations are not part of the topic of this paper, but the following quote highlights the impact on peer relationships where supportive teachers are not resourced within overall school provision:

> A few teachers took me aside and went through things with me. But we had to work in the canteen; there was nowhere else. Classmates were astonished at me — spending time with a teacher! If they knew what they were talking about they'd know I needed the extra help.

The same pattern emerged often in their talk, of exclusion arising from lack of supports, and inclusion being only possible through friendly help. And in the following extracts from a participant with dyslexia, the helpful peer is an example of respectful discretion:

> She took the notes and I copied them. It was never discussed, it just happened. She was everything to me; she was a brilliant, brilliant friend.

She felt she could not turn to others in her class:

> I wouldn't ask for help. You might not be actually told you're stupid,

but you're getting the hidden messages so you're not going to go 'I'm stupid, can I have help?' Like writing down homework from the blackboard was a nightmare for me — I always went home with half sentences or with the same sentence down three times.

For people with physical disabilities, this struggle against slipping from actor to audience status in the learning situation is particularly clear in subjects that require physical work. Again, schools varied, as the following selection of remarks bears out:

In science, using things on the bench, I just sat down and watched.

We'd pair up and my partner used to do all the physical work. I just couldn't do it. I couldn't hold a glass of water.

I think most of us were excluded especially in sports — the school wasn't equipped to cope. They tried, but the majority of times you had to stay out.

I wasn't excluded from any sports. Actually they pushed me into things more than taking me out — 'you are going into this, no questions asked!'

But the dominant order can seem natural, even invisible, even to a student with a disability:

The PE teacher let me watch. There was no discrimination.
*[Q: Did they include exercises suited to you?]*
Oh no, no. But he was very good.

Demonstrating how the two-phase interview structure opened possibilities for evaluation for participants, this speaker had come to a different viewpoint by the second interview:

> The nearest I got was inside the hall… He could have let me
> referee, there's nothing wrong with my mouth.

So, school custom and practice could seem immutable, not just to able-bodied professionals and peers, but also to the very students who were disadvantaged by system rigidity. The hidden curriculum of the able-ist environment must be made visible and questionable to all, if the social fabric of the school is to become truly inclusive. This becomes even clearer in relation to extra-curricular outings.

> I would listen to them when they came back — 'You missed a great
> couple of days, we'd great fun.' Even sitting beside them hearing
> them laughing, it was laughing at something you didn't understand.
> I didn't like that.

This is a dramatic illustration of how true it is that 'to take no stand is to take a stand'. System oversight delivers a powerful lesson about the legitimacy of the status quo, to the included and the excluded alike.

The culture of silence about disabilities affected peer interactions: students with 'hidden' disabilities could encounter insensitivity born of general ignorance:

> [A] lad in my class said something about computers and I said I
> have a problem with remembering everything, I have to write them
> down ever since I got sick like. He said, 'Being sick wouldn't have
> anything to do with your brain,' and I said, 'I think it might'. He
> didn't realise what is wrong with me. Which is hard to cope with in
> some ways. I feel like I have to put it out in the open when I see
> people.

It is difficult to see how this speaker could have avoided having to explain her disability, but the unthinking 'able-ist' social ethos of some second-level schools (as noted above) would both increase the need for her to explain, and discourage her from doing so.

To conclude this section, a return to what is generally assumed to be the core work of the school will serve to highlight what participants wanted from their second level experience. System oversight and priorities lead to escalating stress:

> In second level it was stress just to get the academic first, to be the same as everyone else. Then it started to be the stress — to stop you being different, in social life and academic.

In this compacted statement, the speaker depicts herself moving from a common assumption that second level school is about academics, to the realisation that the social is also significant. At the same time she moved from trying to be 'the same as everybody else', to the greater struggle to 'stop you being [made] different'. She had had to struggle hard to get ability-matched placement in a streamed school. The key to freedom from such escalating stress and exclusion is an inclusive school environment and ethos, one that recognises the student right to have what he or she needs to fly free, as the next speaker did in college:

> I have the technology now, which is my wings, that's the biggest difference. I can overcome people's attitudes now, I can, I'm independent, I can read on my own, I can type on my own. I haven't come up against exams yet so I will see how that goes.

Participants wanted normality, but the school system reflects and endorses the 'normal' exclusionary ethos of society unless the issues involved in making normality inclusive are specifically addressed.

## Life after school: social and personal

This section expands on how participants' unsupported struggle distorted their general social relations with their peers, in and out of school. In effect, the topic of socialising was opened up in their talk about events like school trips. The curriculum and broader social life feather off into each other: socialising during school activities and socialising in and out of school are marked in similar ways by thoughtlessness born of ignorance, and by lack of supports.

In the previous section, the ignorance of able-bodied peers was highlighted. The next remark suggests that this ignorance may well be born of unfamiliarity:

> If one of my friends walked in here [centre for further education for people with disabilities], they would be frightened to talk to someone and that is horrible to say, I think … They would be frightened of the unknown really, like I was when I first got sick.

The majority 'suffer' from ignorance, the minority with disabilities pay the price. Given their de facto marginalisation in putatively integrated education and work settings, it is not surprising that many young people with disabilities have skewed peer group relationships. Participants expressed anger and depression as their efforts not to be 'different' were frustrated. As noted in the talk of school above, many of them were developing stoic acceptance of the status quo ('it was alright', 'there was no discrimination'). Given the absence of emancipatory supports in mainstream schools, it is not surprising that many of them welcomed the 'level playing pitch' of specialised provision and were happy to work with disabled people while at the same time holding on to other able-bodied friends. Not surprisingly also, de facto exclusion resulted for many in a thin and erratic presence in the social scene. Participants' talk about socialising (a heartfelt need in adolescence) was so powerfully clear, it requires little comment. The following excerpts illustrate how the wider social environment and the classroom realities intertwine:

> I have a very select few friends. It takes me a long time before I'd trust them with certain aspects of my life, and I think the fact that I couldn't do as much as other people meant I was excluded from going out with the class — I think they were nearly afraid I would hurt myself.

It was unreal the slagging and it can be at disabled people. They're just doing it for a joke; they don't know what the person feels.

The following interaction shows how damaging the outcomes of inappropriate school provision can be:

*S1:* I suppose I excluded myself. I didn't feel I was worth anything. I wasn't the type of child that would burst into a room bubbly. I was just too caught up, I hated school, I hated everything about it. I spent my whole life trying to be sick — you know, the ear aches and stomach aches, that was me. I just went in and tried to survive the day. I wasn't bullied or picked on, I just switched off for an awful lot of years.

*S2:* It happened to me for a year as well … there was no purpose in transition year, it's just bang in the middle and they give you work and they don't care if you do it or not and I got depressed for the whole year. And you're going through puberty whatever it is and I was drinking. I had a major drinking problem … ah, I don't know why, I just lost all my confidence. I just didn't know how to find a friend. It was all going through my head, OK, these people they weren't paying enough attention.

In an environment that didn't 'expect' them, they became invisible. This continued on into wider social activities. The following account shows how a young woman's friends learned, but not before they had unthinkingly left her in deepest personal isolation:

[When] I got sick all my friends were just starting to go out to night clubs … I told them I didn't want to hang around with them anymore … I just put the phone down and cried because none of them had a clue … Three and a half years later, I went out with them a couple of weeks ago and I remember thinking to myself they were really looking out for me. Everyone was upstairs, all the young people dancing away and one of my friends [said] 'We'll go downstairs, there are no seats'. She was thinking of me and that never happened before ... They are only realising now. Better late than never.

One young man tentatively identified the rejection he encountered as akin to racism:

If someone talks to me and I go sorry, I'm deaf, I lip-read, and if they walk away, fine, but I'm not going to talk to them again. I don't know, 'racist' might be the word, it might be too strong. But I'm in a club and some people don't accept it. They might think I'm talking very loud and drunk out of my head and I'm talking a load of rubbish. Girls stand back, they seem to have really big problems with my being there. I don't know why. If they have a problem it's not my problem. I have to be straightforward, I can't hide it, can't go saying 'I'm not deaf, I know exactly what you're saying'. I *don't* know.

It hardly needs saying that these extracts pose a challenge to schools: how to prepare majority and minority to build an inclusive society. The next speaker expands on the school agenda:

Underlying the school really in second level it is the exam in the end. But it is also how you relate to each other ... you know life does not go kindly, life just throws bad deals at some people and I think there should be a support group in every school and college to deal with it — specialised people, their job should be to help people ... and teachers should be trained to spot these signs at their early stage.

This young man was speaking about second level provision for all. When it comes to building a social life, many if not most adolescents experience insecurity and feelings of isolation. What is significant about the experience of young people with disabilities is that their pain could so clearly be reduced if they could engage in their adolescent struggles within an inclusive society that supplied them as a matter of course with the resources they need for independent living and learning. Obviously, in such a society, in which diversity of capabilities was accepted as normal, life for all young people would be vastly improved.

## Concluding comments

Access to the curriculum is a social achievement. Participants' opinions about the 'work' of school, about attending classes, doing assignments, participating in activities relating to areas such as home economics, PE, science, and school trips — all this talk was saturated with how the struggle to engage, conducted under the gaze of their peers and without appropriate supports, was also a struggle against skewing their social self-presentation and peer relations towards an omnipresent disability focus.

Underpinning inadequate educational responses is a simplistic perception of students with disabilities. The system lacks ambition for them; indeed at times it is even suspicious of their right to recognition as young people with highly varied potential and needs. Often, in the absence of system commitment to providing adequate and appropriate supports, participants had to rely on the kindness of individual peers and teachers.

It is worth noting what happened when participants negotiated the two 'moments' of entrance and exit (choice of school, and — though it was not strictly part of the topic of this chapter — applications for supports for examinations). These moments are relatively private, in that they need involve only the student, guardians and professionals. At this point, system unpreparedness and even suspicion culminated for many of them in a struggle to access examination supports. In both these moments, many students with disabilities start all over again to reach for normality, to push open the doors of academic ambition and social involvement for themselves. This is probably true for all young people, but it has particular significance in relation to those with disabilities. Thus, the restrictions of primary level are shed in transition to second level, and likewise, ambition for normal life informs many students' approaches to third level, despite their struggles and failures, and ensuing chronic focus on their disability and how to surmount it, during their years in second level. Such resilience and ambition demand an equally ambitious response from the system.

Happily, most of the participants had at some time met good teachers; some of them were fortunate enough to have found good schools. However, ad hoc responses are grossly inadequate. Development of an inclusive ethos and provision of adequate supports are ethical imperatives above all because they are a human right and necessity — as is proven by the drastic impact of their absence on the social lives of these young people. Whatever their academic status, people with disabilities live in society and are entitled to be full members of it, especially of their peer group.

In their engagement with learning and living within any level, most participants continued to display great resilience. For instance, the young woman with dyslexia persisted until she found her technology, then flew joyfully into her course reading and could look the world right in the eye. There was some bitterness, as in the case of a participant who perceived the whole world as being opposed to her (she summarised college as 'me against 799'). It is surprising that far more of them were not bitter, especially given the intense pain in their social experiences. Rather, there was a lot of talk about how people are basically decent. But in the accounts of depression, anger and defeated struggles there is a clear indicator of the need for counselling supports as well as learning aids and physical needs assistance. Those who opted for specialised provision were undoubtedly most articulate about their disabilities, most actively engaged in identifying their rights, and critiquing the able-ist agenda informing all our social structures. One measure of truly inclusive education will be when such reflection can be engaged with openly in mainstream.

This focus on the social dimension of the participants' experience powerfully highlights the ethical urgency of the task of transforming our overall education system, schools ethos, built environment, and pedagogic resources and procedures to ensure inclusive education, informed by ambition for all students. Young people with disabilities want normality, and in school terms this means the freedom to spread their wings academically and socially, in the company of their peers, in an educational context that expects them all to aim for the stars.

## References

Atkinson, D., and Williams, F. (eds) (1990) *Know me as I am: an anthology of prose, poetry and art by people with learning difficulties.* London: Hodder and Stoughton.

Beresford, B. (1997) *Personal accounts: involving disabled children in research.* Norwich: Social Policy Research Unit.

Booth, T., and Ainscow, M. (1998) 'Ireland response: limited resources for inclusion?' In T. Booth and M. Ainscow (eds), *From them to us: an international study of inclusion in education.* London: Routledge.

Colgan, A. (1998) *Access to mainstream classrooms: a review of current practice and policy towards enabling students with special educational needs to have access to their local mainstream school.* Dublin: Disability Federation of Ireland.

Department of Education (1993) *Report of the Special Education Review Committee.* Dublin: Stationery Office.

Department of Education (1995) *Charting our educational future: white paper on education.* Dublin: Stationery Office.

Department of Justice, Equality and Law Reform (1996) *A strategy for equality: Report of the Commission on the Status of People with Disabilities.* Dublin: Stationery Office.

Government of Ireland (1998) *Education Act.* Dublin: Stationery Office.

Government of Ireland (1998) *Employment Equality Act.* Dublin: Stationery Office.

Government of Ireland (2000) *Equal Status Act.* Dublin: Stationery Office.

Kenny, M., McNeela, E., Shevlin, M., and Daly, T. (2000) *Hidden voices: young people with disabilities speak about their second-level schooling.* Cork: Bradshaw Books.

Kenny, M., McNeela, E., and Shevlin, M. (2001) *Access to third level education for people with physical and sensory disabilities, and specific learning difficulties (dyslexia)*. Dublin: AHEAD (Association for Higher Education access and Disability).

Kitchin, R., and Mulcahy, P. (1999) *Disability, access to education and future opportunities*. Dublin: Combat Poverty Agency.

Lewis, A. (1995) *Children's understanding of disability*. London: Routledge.

Lewis, A., and Lindsay, G. (2000) 'Emerging issues'. In A. Lewis and G. Lindsay (eds), *Researching children's perspectives*. Buckingham: Open University Press.

Lynch, P. (1995) 'Integration in Ireland: policy and practice'. In C. O'Hanlon (ed.), *Inclusive education in Europe*. London: David Fulton.

National Council for Curriculum and Assessment (1999) *Special educational needs: curriculum issues*. Dublin: NCCA.

OECD (1994) *The integration of disabled children into mainstream education: ambitions, theories and practices*. Paris: OECD (Organisation for Economic Cooperation and Development).

O' Keeffe, M. (1997) 'Charting developments in educational provision for visually impaired students in Ireland (1970–1997)'. Unpublished M.Ed. Thesis. NUI, Maynooth.

Oliver, M. (1990) *The politics of disablement*. Basingstoke, Hampshire: Macmillan Education Ltd.

Potter, J. and Wetherell, M. (1989) *Discourse and social psychology*. London: Sage Publications.

Stukat, K.G. (1993) 'Integration of physically disabled students'. *European Journal of Special Needs Education* 8 (3), 249–68.

van Dijk, T.A. (1998) 'Critical discourse analysis'. Second draft, January 1998. In D. Tannen, D. Schiffrin and H. Hamilton (eds.) (forthcoming) *Handbook of discourse analysis*. Oxford: Blackwell. http://www.hum.uva.nl/~teun/cda.htm.

# 10

## CREATING A CULTURE OF CHANGE: EXPLORING THE PERSPECTIVES OF YOUNG PEOPLE WITH HEARING IMPAIRMENTS

### NATALIE ROONEY

Schools are social institutions and should provide opportunities for all students to develop the skills of interaction necessary to equip them for life in the wider community. In this chapter Natalie Rooney explores the particular challenges encountered by pupils with hearing impairments as they attempt to establish themselves within the mainstream school environment. The fine balance between providing the ethos of a mainstream school while recognising the need to retain teaching approaches that are sympathetic to specific pupil needs, is explored from the perspectives of both the researcher and the young people involved in the study. A theme that runs through the paper is the need to encourage and support the teachers to adopt positive attitudes and high expectations.

## Introduction

> Among the boys I was for a while a curiosity, interesting because of
> my deafness, then the novelty wore off and I found my friends and
> enemies like anybody else. (Wright, 1969, p. 40)

Children and young people with hearing impairments were among the first
recipients of special education in Ireland, which began in the late nineteenth
century. However, education for deaf girls and boys was at that time a
qualitatively different experience than for students with hearing impairments in
Ireland today. In contrast to the early residential special schools, modern
educational provision for students with hearing impairments is based on a
continuum of needs, whereby special units and integrated programmes within
the ordinary school system, as well as the special schools, serve to meet the
needs of deaf students. Grounded on the empirical findings of psychological
and educational research that demonstrated the capacities of pupils with
disabilities, government legislation during the 1980s led to a pedagogical shift
in special education, with an increased focus on the needs of the individual.

The principle of integration has become firmly entrenched within the
political framework of the Irish educational system, and significant advances
have been made since the early 1990s regarding the implementation of
integrated programmes and link schemes in mainstream schools. Numerous
governmental policies, such as the White Paper *Charting Our Education Future*
(1995), and discussion documents, including the Report of the Special
Education Review Committee (SERC) (Department of Education, 1993), the
Report of the National Educational Convention (Department of Education,
1994) and the Report of the Commission on the Status of People with
Disabilities (Department of Justice, 1996), have identified the ordinary school
system as being the most appropriate educational provision for children with
special needs. Moreover, these papers called for an appraisal system to be
implemented whereby the special schools and the special units within
ordinary schools would be continually evaluated in terms of the extent to
which they are meeting the intellectual needs of pupils. This focus on the

academic needs of children with special needs reflects the extent to which special educators have been concerned with planning and evaluating the effects of integration on the academic performance of children with hearing impairments. Yet, in order to meet adequately the needs of the whole person, the mainstream school system is required to plan and evaluate the effects of integration on social interaction between hearing and hearing-impaired pupils. In order to assess sufficiently the quality and purpose of the social interactions between pupils with and without disabilities, it is crucial that the perspectives of the children themselves are sought.

Since the implementation of the UN Convention on the Rights of the Child (1989), consulting with children and young people and ascertaining their views on their educational needs has become an integral part of policy development. By offering a forum in research and professional practice where children can articulate their attitudes and perceptions, it is hoped that policies and services will be more responsive to their wide range of needs and abilities (Lewis and Lindsay, 2000, p. 25) Indeed, recent Irish legislation such as the National Children's Strategy (Department of Health and Children, 2000) has highlighted the value of children's perspectives in educational reform and affords priority to the voice of the child in research. In this way, children, and particularly those with disabilities, are not perceived merely as passive recipients of events impinging on their lives, but as active participants in shaping their social worlds.

## Overview of findings

Participants in this study discussed their experiences of being in an integrated educational setting. The themes that emerged related mainly to the social context of school. Issues such as the pupil's feelings about school, their relationship with teachers, their friendships, and their overall feelings of inclusion were discussed. Those with hearing impairments felt most included when they were engaged in structured activities within the classroom setting. Outside of this structured setting, the majority of the hearing-impaired pupils perceived their disability as being a hindrance to social interaction with their teenage peers. Yet, by and large, the hearing pupils perceived their hearing-impaired peers as being equal members of their class, capable of participating fully in all activities and being completely accepted as individuals. This disparity in perceptions between the two groups raises questions as to how effectively the existing integrated programmes and link schemes are catering for the educational and social needs of pupils with disabilities. Or perhaps it is the 'disability' label itself that hinders the pupils' full participation in social situations and interactions and it is this perception that is a barrier to full inclusion.

This discrepancy between the perceptions of the pupils with hearing impairments and the perceptions of their hearing peers as to the quality of their inclusion will be the main focus of this chapter.

## Survey procedures

The primary aim of this study was to ascertain the subjective experiences of pupils with hearing impairments in an integrated classroom. As with any sub-group in society, 'disabled children' are not a homogenous population, as each child differs in age, family background, economic and material security, health, education, etc. It is essential that researchers do not fall prey to the stereotypes of children with disabilities but rather strive to grasp and highlight their individualism. Therefore, ethical considerations in conducting research with young people with disabilities were accorded due attention in order to ensure that while the research grants children with disabilities a voice, it does so through ethically and methodologically sound work (Beresford, 1997).

A secondary aim of the study was to seek the perspectives of the hearing pupils in order to ascertain the degree of social inclusion that the pupils with hearing impairments were experiencing. This aspect of peer support can be crucial in facilitating the integration of pupils with hearing impairments, and research has shown that the attitudes of the hearing group can often determine the success or failure of integrated programmes (McConkey and James, 1998).

Focus group interviews were conducted with fifteen hearing-impaired students who were attending six of the seven 'designated' mainstream schools in the Republic of Ireland.[1] There were eight males and seven females, of whom ten were in the Junior Cycle (aged twelve to fourteen) and five were in the Senior Cycle (aged fifteen to eighteen). The interview questions for pupils with hearing impairments were based on four broad topics: *feelings about school, relationship with teachers, friendships,* and *feelings about being included.* Focus* group interviews were also conducted with twenty-four hearing pupils, and the questions sought to ascertain how they perceived their peers generally; whether or not they perceived their hearing impairments as presenting a barrier to social inclusion; and whether or not they considered that the appropriate resources were in place to facilitate the integration of their hearing-impaired peers within the ordinary school system.

The following summary of research findings presents the students' experiences in the context most pertinent to their lives — the social dimension to school.

## Feelings about school

Participants in the study discussed their general feelings about school in the context of their choice of school. The pupils essentially evaluated their options in terms of their friends' choices, school facilities and teaching standards. For pupils with less severe hearing losses, it was simply a matter of going to the 'follow-on' school: 'I don't really know what the kind of special schools is like.' Going to an ordinary school with their primary school friends had been such an integral part of their life experience that it had been taken for granted that they would attend their local secondary school. 'Yeah, I have everything, I can see my friends from school and from where I live.'

A sixteen-year-old participant with a moderate to severe hearing impairment preferred the mainstream option owing to its array of learning opportunities:

> Well, I'd actually feel very uncomfortable going there, as in a special school, you work much more slowly, and learning in a special school would take much more time, while in a school like this, you're expected to move with the rest of the class. It's more of a challenge.

However, the level of hearing impairment influenced the choice of school to a certain extent, as it was vital to the hearing-impaired students that the school would not become 'too ordinary', meaning that the mainstream teachers should be cognisant of the issues related to a hearing disability and able to provide the appropriate resources:

> Definitely, if you don't want to go to a school where it's all people with hearing disabilities, then at least a school that has come this far [i.e. special classes, facilities] I think is the way to go, instead of just going into a school that knows nothing about it and thinks 'Ah sure, you're just another student, or whatever.'

## Relationship with teachers

The interview question on pupils' relationships with their teachers evoked a lively discussion that centred on the importance of teacher–pupil relationships in settling into their new school. The interview transcripts indicate that the pupils with hearing impairments were comfortable not only in approaching the special needs teachers, but also the mainstream teachers when expressing their needs and requesting certain practical arrangements such as asking the teachers to speak slowly and clearly in the class situation.

> They're very helpful; if I don't understand what they are talking about, they'll stay behind with me after class and they'll explain it to me rather than rushing through it myself afterwards. And sometimes, I come into school early the following day, around 8.30 a.m., and they explain it in more detail.

However, although the mainstream teachers were accommodating in providing additional resources when requested by individual students, the teachers were not proactive in identifying these students' educational needs, so pupils felt embarrassed when expressing their particular difficulties as it made them feel different to their hearing classmates:

> I feel really awkward, so I do, I don't like making myself look different.

If teachers ask you and you didn't hear the question and they just happen to repeat the question for you, you know you'd hear some of the rest of the students at the back of the class making comments on it ... you feel really embarrassed because of it, you feel like the teachers should stand up for you.

Although the teachers and the mainstream pupils responded willingly to the pupils' requests, such a *laissez-faire* tracking system can be detrimental to the inclusion of students with hearing impairments, as it militates against their full participation in the class.

Oh no, I wouldn't really, I find it hard to talk to her about it, I find it hard. Sometimes, I want to tell her a few of my problems but I find it hard to.

It is therefore essential that class teachers regularly track and monitor the pupils' progress in terms of whether their learning needs are being met.

## Teachers' expectations

Generally, the hearing-impaired participants felt that their class teachers expected them to perform as well as their hearing peers. The majority of them maintained that once they used their technical aids, such as the hearing and the radio-aids, and took ownership for their work, they were as equal and capable as their hearing peers.

I'm no different from other students in my class, so I don't think they expect anything less.

Moreover, they strongly felt that this was reflected in the teachers' expectations of them, as they were treated with the same respect as the hearing students.

Basically, I try to be as independent as I can and I don't go out of my way to, you know, make it all, you know, 'look at me, I have a hearing aid so treat me different; and I think they respect me for that as well, which is a good thing.

The views of the hearing peers concurred generally with the perceptions of the pupils with hearing impairments in relation to teachers' expectations. They felt that the teachers treated everyone equally, not granting their disabled peers special treatment, since they felt that their hearing-impaired peers were just as academically capable, and in some cases more so:

> He even like, he probably does even better at stuff, actually he did do better at stuff than I did in my exams.

## Friendships

*The importance of friendships*
A common theme that emerged from the focus groups was the importance of developing friendships and gaining the trust of their peers. For the pupils with hearing impairments, friendships were valued highly. One sixteen-year-old girl talked about the joy she felt when she fitted in well with her peer group:

> I was the only girl with a hearing problem there [primary school], so it was all right, like you know, all the people that were in [primary] school came up here [post-primary school] with me, they all knew about me and that was it, there was no odd one out or anything! So that was nice.

Another pupil stressed the importance of being accepted by her immediate and close friends:

> My friends, they're always, you know, 'cos I think if you have the attitude, just get on with life, then you get on with life, do you know what I mean? I've made friends and they've accepted me for who I am and I've accepted them for whatever they have, you know, so it's

grand, I don't see myself as much different to anyone else. I try not to anyway!

Although the hearing-impaired pupils seem to enjoy integrating with hearing pupils within an ordinary school environment, for a significant number of the pupils this need for acceptance has not been met. These pupils maintain that lack of hearing-impaired pupils in the school has militated against their full inclusion within the school. They identify the need to have a stronger presence of their hearing-impaired peers:

> Well, I like this setting, but sometimes I would be a lot happier if there were a few more people around with hearing difficulties other than myself and Andrew. When I was in first year, there were five people, I prefer it that way, it is more relaxed because people would know how you have the disability and know where you are coming from.

Due to an increase in the uptake of pupils with disabilities into local mainstream schools, it is not feasible to guarantee the enrolment of a proportional amount of disabled peers within the mainstream classroom. The onus, therefore, lies with the respective schools to implement programmes that effectively include children with disabilities. For example, the teachers involved in the integrated programmes can ensure that the mainstream pupils understand the type of difficulties that students with disabilities encounter by specifically teaching about a disability prior to the pupil commencing at the school. Such an initiative could serve to avoid stares and curiosity that, while natural, can be upsetting to the pupil with special educational needs.

*Difficulty in making friends*
Participants discussed that often they had to make a tremendous effort to communicate with their hearing peers. Yet, in spite of these efforts ('sometimes I try to make people laugh to try to make friends with people and that'), they often do not lead to lasting friendships.

The views of the hearing pupils suggest that there are difficulties in effectively communicating with their hearing-impaired peers. The pupils with the more severe hearing losses tended to stick together, and this exclusiveness appeared to hinder the hearing pupils in initiating contact with their hearing-impaired peers. Although efforts do seem to be made on the part of the hearing students, they are perceived as being rebuffed and refuted: 'If you go up to them, they walk away, sometimes'. Social interaction in any meaningful sense between the hearing-impaired students and their hearing classmates is therefore hindered by a lack of mutual understanding of their communication abilities.

However, if the aim of inclusive education is to be achieved, that is, to create an attitude and philosophy that accepts and welcomes diversity, the onus lies with the schools to implement measures that will facilitate such a culture of acceptance.

The positive social interaction that occurs between the hearing-impaired pupils and their hearing classmates impacts significantly on the lives of the hearing pupils. Friendships between these groups have enriched the lives of all concerned, and the anecdotes shared with the researcher offer promising peer–peer relationships in the future:

> I'd say that, I wouldn't know because I'm a girl but I'd say for a boy like he's really a good friend, very honest and all. He's really honest, that's what he is. Like, one time he said something rude to one of the teachers in primary school, and our teacher goes, 'Now, I'm not going on until someone owns up,' and he owned up immediately and then she let him off because she knows that Matthew hasn't got the best hearing.

According to such perceptions of the hearing pupils, interactions between the pupils with and without hearing impairments can certainly be a rewarding experience.

**Feelings of inclusion**

*Academic inclusion*

By and large, the pupils with hearing impairments felt included in all classroom activities. They perceived themselves as just as hard-working as their classmates. They did not perceive their disability as being an obstacle to academic performance and therefore perceived their contribution to the class as being valuable.

> You know, just because you have a hearing aid doesn't mean that you don't know anything ... it's nothing, you know, I can still read and I can still, whatever, it's just you can't hear as well.

The views of the hearing pupils concur with the perspectives of the hearing-impaired pupils. They perceive their hearing-impaired peers as being academically capable in all the subject areas and maintain that the hearing loss of their peers is not a hindrance to their academic inclusion in the class.

> Well, he gets involved with a lot of things, Mrs M. helps him a lot with the tutoring and loads, but he goes to all of the classes and stuff. In history class, he's always asking questions and that. He doesn't struggle or anything.

*Social inclusion*

Much of the discourse with both groups of students focused on the centrality of communication skills for social inclusion. The participants with hearing difficulties maintained that speaking clearly and having good lip-reading skills are essential for effective social interaction with their hearing peers. They consider that the ability to speak clearly is a prerequisite for acceptance into their peer group. The participants talked openly and directly about the reactions from their hearing peers. At times they were met with passivity and apathy and at other times their peers completely avoided interacting with them at a social level. One thirteen-year-old felt that inadequate lip-reading skills can often hinder effective communication with his hearing classmates:

> Wow! They think, well I think they think that if I, if they talk to me I
> won't be able to understand them, right? So when they ask a
> question, I just guess and say yes or no and they just think that I
> don't want to continue in the conversation, so that's a problem. I
> only once said 'pardon' and they would go away.

Yet the hearing pupils generally do not perceive significant difficulties in
communicating with their hearing-impaired peers:

> You don't have to talk to him slowly, because he reads your lips real
> quick.

The perception of being rejected by one's peers prevents the majority of the
pupils with hearing impairments from initiating contact with their classmates
in social situations. The study findings indicate that they generally depend on
their hearing classmates to initiate conversations in the social setting, as they
feel unsure of their communication skills. As a result of the apathy and
indifference on the part of the hearing classmates, this can further compound
the communication barrier. One of the hearing-impaired participants expressed
her frustration about this lack of openness on the part of her hearing peers.

> Sometimes, you'd wish they would just come out and say it, rather
> than looking at you for a half an hour going, 'What's that, what's
> that?' Because sometimes you wish you could just say, 'Look, it's a
> hearing aid, okay? People wear them.' But sometimes then people
> just kind of look and notice, and then they don't say anything else
> and that is just it, they understand, and other people just tend to
> kind of look and stare.

In contrast, the peer group of this student did not notice these so-called overt
signs of disability. The following girl comments that she was not aware of her

classmate's disability until she was told about it:

> In first year she used to wear two [hearing aids]. I thought it was a walkman at first before I even knew she had a hearing problem and I asked her what she was listening to! That's when I found out that she had a hearing problem.

In adolescence, the need for acceptance from one's peers is of pivotal importance, and sensitivity to peer reaction is heightened. A negative social interaction of any kind will be interpreted by the hearing-impaired student as a rejection. One of the students in the study related how he had experienced a negative interaction with his hearing peers.

> Sometimes a few people tell me to go away and all of that, but sometimes they don't mean it or whatever, I don't know. Then I find that hard.

Through the discussion, it became apparent that this young person attributed the rejection to wearing his hearing aid. He felt that since the aid made him look different, it therefore impeded his ability to interact with and be accepted by his social peers. Consequently, the participants generally avoided wearing their hearing aids in an attempt to fit in with the dominant peer group. They were more reluctant to wear their hearing aids as they began their secondary schooling, although they unequivocally wore them at primary school.

> In first year it was like, you're young and you get over it anyway, but now if people say it to you, you take it more to heart as well, because they should know better ...

The discrepancy between the pupils with and without hearing impairments relates to how each group perceives the disability. In the same situation, both groups of students are interpreting it in completely different ways and this affects the quality of the social exchange. If integrated schools are to serve as micro-inclusive societies, acceptance of diversity must be an integral part of their social fabric. Therefore, integrated schools have a responsibility to plan extra-curricular activities and programmes that will facilitate the students to interact with ease, and also to harness the willingness of the mainstream pupils to initiate and strengthen social interaction with their hearing-impaired peers.

## Integrating people with disabilities into mainstream schools

Perhaps the most positive finding arising from the focus groups with hearing pupils relates to the degree of acceptance for their peers with hearing impairments. Overall, the pupils embrace the concept of inclusion and maintain that the integration of students with disabilities into the mainstream school system benefits all concerned. For example, one sixteen-year-old boy recognised how integration would enrich his school experience and prepare him for participation in an inclusive society:

> Yeah, it's a good thing like, because when you go for a job and there's somebody there with the same difficulty, you're able to understand him, a bit more than other people that work there.

Others viewed it from a more humanitarian framework: 'It helps us to see that we're all the same really.'

Generally, the hearing pupils maintained that the philosophy and practice of including students with disabilities into mainstream schools is a worthwhile endeavour. However, the students were divided in their perceptions regarding the extent to which principles of inclusiveness should inform inclusive educational practices. While some pupils maintained that the responsibility rests with the institution in providing appropriate resources for effective inclusion, others argued that the onus lies with the pupil with disabilities to adapt to his new social and learning environment.

> No, just because one person uses sign language, doesn't mean that we all have to learn sign language to talk to him. If you were good friends with them, maybe then, yeah, but I wouldn't expect

everyone to learn sign language ... If one of your friends had a hearing difficulty, you'd learn sign language, but you'd probably learn it anyway by picking it up.

The majority of the pupils believed that since they were all entitled to equal opportunities in education, they themselves are required to make every effort, including learning the basics of sign language and adopting positive attitudes, to ensure that their peers become active members of their class.

## Discussion

The hearing-impaired participants in this study maintain that they perceive themselves as individuals first and foremost and therefore prefer others to view them in this way also. They perceive themselves as striving to become involved in the social life of the school community. Their attitudes and perceptions indicate that in order to facilitate their full inclusion, it is necessary for professionals and mainstream teachers alike to re-evaluate their attitudes towards pupils with disabilities. Moreover, both mainstream and special needs teachers need to revise their understanding of pupils' abilities and to err on the high rather than on the low side of academic expectation. It therefore seems that regardless of innovative measures that may be implemented, listening to the views of the pupils themselves will be instrumental in the provision of an appropriate education for all pupils with special educational needs.

According to the special education literature, mainstream schools are required to construct a coherent system incorporating adequate resources and effective curricula and pedagogical strategies of intervention to provide an appropriate education for all. However, translating this principle into practice has proved difficult for the mainstream school system, as few practical guidelines exist to direct individual initiatives in ordinary schools that serve to include children and adolescents with disabilities. In relation to pupils with hearing impairments, certain measures have been implemented within the mainstream and special school system that have enabled these pupils to achieve their academic potential. For example, the Department of Education and Science has facilitated the provision of specialised resources and coordinated a support service that has been instrumental in meeting the intellectual needs of the pupils with hearing impairments. For this reason, hearing-impaired children in ordinary schools perform academically on a par to their hearing peers. However, research has shown that the social and psychological needs of the pupils with hearing impairments are not being sufficiently met, and this is consistent with the findings of the current research.

Providing for the social and psychological needs of pupils with hearing impairments necessitates specific organisational changes to the current integrated programmes. By implementing certain teaching methodologies, the integrated classroom can facilitate learning while also enhancing the quality of peer-peer relationships. For example, the pupils in this study with severe to profound hearing impairments tended to feel insecure in the company of their hearing peers, as they felt intellectually inadequate to significantly contribute to group work. However, by ensuring that the organisation of classroom activities provides opportunities for positive relationships between pupils with and without hearing impairments, as in mixed-ability grouping, collaboration and cooperation between peers can be encouraged, thereby providing preliminary social interaction. This reciprocal working together can be actively applied in all areas of the curriculum. Collaborative and co-operative learning in classrooms can be achieved through sensitive pairing of pupils for certain tasks, such as 'pairing' or 'buddy' systems, where both parties can contribute and learn from each other.

While the mainstream teachers appeared to be sensitive to the educational needs of the pupils in this study, the pupils with hearing impairments contended that encouragement and support from their teachers was essential to feeling included within the classroom setting. It is therefore essential that the work the pupils produce is publicly valued and that the students' achievements are celebrated. This overt acceptance by teachers of students with disabilities as class members with full entitlement provides a positive role model for the mainstream students.

Although the hearing-impaired pupils in this study regarded the mainstream teachers' expectations of their academic performance to be as high as their hearing peers, it is nonetheless crucial that the teachers continue to be positively encouraging and to plan lessons that are non-restrictive in terms of content and breadth in order that these students are enabled to strive to their full potential.

Many of the pupils in this study perceived their sensory disability as a deficit, and they saw this as a major reason for their peers disliking them. For example, the majority of the pupils with hearing impairments maintained that good communication skills, speaking clearly and effectively lip-reading others, are prerequisites for being accepted by their peers. Due to a perceived lack of similarities, the pupils were by and large deterred from initiating and maintaining contact with their hearing peers. Taking into consideration the sensitive perceptions and feelings of the pupils with hearing impairments, it is imperative that the school does not reinforce these perceptions, but rather tries to raise self-esteem. By incorporating certain strategies such as providing opportunities for the pupils to share games and activities with mainstream pupils, opportunities to demonstrate their own expertise and even providing opportunities for pupils to take responsibilities in the classroom and the school, their feelings of inadequacy can be overcome. By providing such opportunities, the pupils with hearing difficulties are enabled to engage effectively in the life of the whole school community.

## Conclusion

The research findings from this study indicate that generally the pupils with hearing impairments are socially accepted among their hearing peers. For the students who do not feel as included, specific measures and initiatives to be undertaken by the integrated schools have been put forward by the researcher. However, the efficacy of the integrated programmes in meeting the social and psychological needs of pupils with hearing impairments is dependent on the implementation of an inclusive whole school policy. Policies that validate the perspectives of the pupils and seek to provide equal opportunities to enhance their educational and social progress ensure commitment and delivery.

Addressing the individual needs of pupils with disabilities fundamentally challenges the conventional education system, as this requires changes to the existing organisation, curriculum and pedagogy. The presence of children who are not suited to the existing 'menu' of the mainstream schools lends impetus to general educational change, as it provides encouragement to explore a more inclusive philosophy within which teachers are supported in experimenting with new methodological approaches. Therefore, research into special needs education serves the whole school system. By identifying the particular needs of pupils with disabilities, as Hart (1992) contends, insights are provided into possibilities for improvements in the education system that might otherwise have passed unnoticed.

## References

Ainscow, M. (1996) 'Towards inclusive schooling'. *REACH Journal of Special Needs Education in Ireland* 9 (2), 67–75.

Beresford, B. (1997) *Personal accounts: involving disabled children in research.* Norwich: Social Policy Research Unit.

Department of Education (1993) *Report of the Special Education Review Committee* (SERC). Dublin: Stationery Office.

Department of Education (1994) *Report of the National Education Convention.* Dublin: Stationery Office.

Department of Education (1995) *White Paper: Charting our Education Future.* Dublin: Stationery Office.

Department of Education and Science (1998) *The Education Act.* Dublin: The Stationery Office.

Department of Health and Children (2000) *National Children's Strategy.* Dublin: Stationery Office.

Department of Justice, Equality and Law Reform (1996) *A Strategy for Equality: report of the commission on the status of people with disabilities.* Dublin: Stationery Office.

Hart, S. (1992) 'Differentiation: part of the problem or part of the solution?' *The Curriculum Journal* 3 (2), 131–42.

Lewis, A., and Lindsay, G. (eds) (2000) *Researching children's perspectives.* Buckingham: Open University Press.

McConkey, A., and James, T. (1998) 'Secondary school children's attitudes to disability: a comparison in integrated and non-integrated schools'. *REACH*

*Journal of Special Needs Education in Ireland* 12 (1), 35–44.

Wright, David (1969) *Deafness: a personal account.* London: The Penguin Press.

**Note**

1  The status of 'designated' mainstream school, assigned by the Department of Education and Science, qualifies the school for the provision of additional resources in order to implement specific facilities (such as resource room, sign interpreter, radio-aids, etc.) for the pupils with hearing impairments.

# between
# two worlds

# 11

## TOWARDS AN ADULTHOOD WITH A DIFFERENCE

### DORA BJARNASON

Dora Bjarnason's paper introduces an international dimension to the discussion on encouraging voices from marginalised groups. The insights from this Icelandic study illustrate that the issues explored within an Irish/UK context are equally relevant elsewhere. In this paper, Dora describes the effects of mainstream and special placements on the lives of a number of young people with learning difficulties. These young people and their families reflect on the impact of a variety of placements, including special, special/mainstream and mainstream, on their ability to develop reciprocal relationships with their peers. It was agreed that achieving adulthood is the ultimate goal of education. The young people with learning difficulties and their families discuss how each type of placement contributed to or hindered the process of achieving an interdependent adulthood.

## Introduction

This paper focuses on the findings of a qualitative study of thirty-six young Icelandic adults with disabilities, aged from sixteen to twenty-four, as well as their parents and some of their friends and teachers. The study explores the circumstances and experiences of disabled individuals that lead to social discrimination, how they see themselves, and how they are perceived by parents, friends and teachers. The study also looks at what young people with very different disability labels have in common, how they experience their situations differently, and how such differences may be related to different social situations and decisions made by their parents.

All the young people have significant disabilities, but their disability labels vary across most disability categories. Their backgrounds are also as varied as possible across socio-economic categories, and they represent both urban and rural sectors. These young people can be described as the first integration generation in Iceland, because they were the first disabled people to grow up with inclusion and normalisation as the law of the land.

## Overview

This study used qualitative methods largely influenced by grounded theory and hermeneutics (Glaser and Strauss, 1967) and placed the work within the interpretivist paradigm (Ferguson and Ferguson, 1995). The primary method for collecting data was interviews. This author's professional and personal experience over the past twenty years as a university teacher and researcher of sociology and disability studies, and also as a single mother of a son with a significant impairment, informs and focuses the research. Additional information was gained from workers within the local and state welfare services, from statutory laws and regulations, from high school principals, from staff at the Ministry of Education and the Ministry of Social Services, and from various publications.

## Three portraits

The interpretation of the data gives rise to a metaphor for the young disabled people of the study, which helps frame the interpretation. There are three groups of young disabled people, travelling along two roads, or wandering about like nomads in the wasteland in between. Group A, comprising fourteen people, are seen to travel on the highway alongside the rest of us, a few in the express lane, more along the middle of the road, but most at a slow pace. Group C, comprising fifteen people, are seen to travel on a much narrower special road. Group B comprises seven nomads, who are seen to wander about in the wilderness between these two roads, sometimes aiming for the highway and sometimes the slower road, but belonging with neither.

## On the highway

Ólafía is twenty-three years old, small and skinny. She has thin, dark hair, and is letting it grow long. She lives with her mother, a semi-skilled worker, in a small town. Her older siblings have moved away from home. Her mother describes Ólafía thus:

> She is sometimes uncomfortably frank, 'calls a spade a spade' without concern for … We all do that in my family … we all say straight what we mean … She is fully aware of the fact that she is retarded … I have always taught her that, but also that that is OK.

She has the label 'cognitively disabled'. She attends the special education class at the local upper secondary school part time, even though she graduated last year. She works part time as a volunteer at a local firm; goes to 'disabled sport', uses summer camp for disabled children and youth, and also the local respite service. Now she has a support family with whom she stays every other weekend. She has a paid support person to help her participate in social activities a few hours a month, and a few typical friends with whom she loves to spend time. She has been included in general education from pre-school until upper secondary school, where she attends the special class, and has been fully included in her local community from birth. She has benefited greatly from the efforts of her iron-willed mother, who picked from available special and general services what she thought might be of use to her and her daughter, and paved the way for the inclusion of other kids with cognitive disability labels in mainstream school and in her community.

Ólafía likes to talk. Her mother says that 'when she is happy, she talks all the time if you let her; she is like the rest of the family in that. But she can also sulk or be quiet as a mouse'. Ólafía has a big vocabulary and appears to love to be the centre of attention. She laughed when she told me that she has a temper, which sometimes gets her into trouble. Ólafía denied being an adult: 'I'm not a grown-up, not yet', but she expected to become a grown-up very soon. Her mother is teaching her to deal with practical things such as housework and paying the bills.

When Ólafía was little, her mother, backed by her friends and family, was determined that Ólafía should grow up knowing both disabled and typical children. Her mother managed to persuade the local community to provide Ólafía with some therapy at the local pre-school.

For her first years at school, she attended mainstream school in the morning and went to her old pre-school in the afternoons while her mother worked. After her first years at school, where she repeated the beginner's class twice, she was moved to a different school. There she was enrolled in a mainstream class, but with children two years her junior. She was pulled out into special education on a regular basis to the point that some days each week, she spent more time in the one-on-one special education than in her class. She liked her school and loved her special education teacher, a woman who worked with her for most of her compulsory school years. She also said she liked all her class teachers in the compulsory education schools. Ólafía learned to read at the age of nine and count, but it took her much longer to learn to write. Now she uses a computer. Her mother explained that as Ólafía learned to control herself better, she got to accompany her classmates more. She changed schools yet again and went to a small compulsory education school instead of entering a much bigger school with her former classmates after sixth class. Ólafía liked her new school and found new friends there. She said that she liked studying Icelandic language, cooking and woodwork, but hated geology. 'It is stupid, I have to go out in the rain and pick up stones on the beach.'

Ólafía was confirmed with her classmates at the local church and invited family and friends to a party.[1] In her early teens she developed her first deep friendship. Her best friend, who was also labelled cognitively disabled, had a life-threatening illness. They used to watch videos and TV together and hang out in each other's homes. The friend died when they were both in their teens. The sorrow touched Ólafía to the core, but, supported by her mother, she learned to grieve and heal.

A string of support persons — paid companions a little older than Ólafía — went through her life. She befriended some of them, but not others. These young people went with Ólafía to the cinema, bowling, to Pizza Hut, and to a number of events for disabled youth. In her early teens, Ólafía became almost fully included in all classes and school activities. Four of her typical classmates became her very special friends; they phoned each other, they included her with other friends, and looked out for her. This opened new social possibilities for Ólafía.

Ólafía expected to join her friends and classmates at upper secondary school, but the special education teacher at the upper secondary school had other plans. He did not believe in inclusion and liked to have a firm structure in his work. This was a big disappointment to all of them. Ólafía asked:

> I am the same [as I was], I have not changed, so why can't I be with my friends?

Her mother said:

> The teacher tells me she [Ólafía] is happy at school, but when she is at home she protests strongly against going there. I also feel the change ... This teacher treats me as if it [her schooling] is not my business. I am told that it is he who is the teacher, not me ... I asked if she could not occasionally attend a class with her old classmates. The teacher refused on the grounds that my Ólafía is not about to take the exams with those classes ... He wants to structure his teaching like that and he believes that 'they fit best with others like them'.

Ólafía explained her special class and the upper secondary school like this:

> I find the class fun, good to get to know more friends … but I know these kids, we were always at camp [summer camp for cognitively disabled children and adults] in the summer, but the boys are boring, they are always teasing me, and one boy hits me all the time. He has always hated me.

She had no friends in the special class. When I asked her about school friends, she said that Gunnar was her best friend [her best friend from the compulsory school]. Then she said that it was really difficult at the upper secondary school to meet with him and the others from her old class.

> They are here, but I never see them … when I see them, they must go. This is not right. I miss them.

Gunnar said he missed her too, and that he is unhappy that he is drifting more and more out of her life. He said that 'Ólafía has become more of an outsider since we started upper secondary school'. Still, Ólafía finds things to do at home and in the town during the days. She participates little in the evening activities of her age peers since she joined the special class.

She, her mother and friend all agree that her upper secondary school graduation was one of the highlights in her life. She went with all the other graduates up on a big stage at the school. She was dressed in an expensive and elegant black dress, high-heeled shoes and wore a beautiful gold pendant around her neck. Ólafía confessed that she was nervous and shy, but after she had received her certificate and shaken hands with the headmaster, she turned and gave her mother a triumphant 'thumbs up'.

Her dream is to move away from home and get into a general college for a year (which she did a year later). In the future, she said, 'I hope to live by myself, in a house that is all mine'. I asked if she might get lonely in such a house all by herself. Did she want to live with someone, a man or a woman? She said that she does not want to live with another woman 'because that is not possible', and she doubts if she wants to live with a man.

She wants to carry on working at the place where she is now volunteering. Later she wants to move to the city, go to the bank and pay her bills, be near her sisters, uncles and aunts. She wants go to the National Theatre, dine at good restaurants and have pizzas. Ólafía follows national politics on TV. She voted at the last national election for a political leader, 'because he is sweet … but my mother says he is a jerk'. Like most people, Ólafía hopes to live a long time.

> I don't want to be old, I never want to die, I am so healthy. You see I
> am not handicapped, I am just retarded. … It is not fun to be
> handicapped, there are too many handicapped in my school.[2]

Ólafía is firmly embedded in her local community even though her adult status is somewhat in the margin of the highway. Her mother is proud of her. She said:

> I have always said that Ólafía is the best I have had … and I think
> that everyone who gets to know her discovers that she has an
> unusually strong self-image…

Ólafía's mother plans to get her a flat, but she also dreads the separation. Ólafía has become a source of support for her mother.

## Nomad in the wilderness

Margrét is twenty-one years old, an upper secondary school student. She is tall and slim and could be mistaken for a model. She is deaf, speaks fluent sign language and is also able to lip-read and talk (somewhat unclearly) with her voice. Because of her parents' work, she has lived abroad. She has a younger sister, and an older brother who has left home. Margrét lives in a little apartment in her parents' house.

She was a year and a half old when her parents discovered that she was deaf. This 'changed everything' for them. They set out, as soon as possible, to learn what they could about deafness. Her mother enrolled in a course to learn sign language and mastered the basics. Margrét's father had much greater trouble with learning the language. He felt really uncomfortable trying to make his daughter understand him. The result was that even now he gets his wife to interpret what he needs to say. Margrét talks to him and when he does not understand, she writes to him. Shortly after Margrét's diagnosis her father took on more responsibility at work to improve his prospects and pay. Her mother's opinions and superior knowledge mostly prevail in matters to do with the education and support for Margrét.

Margrét started in a general day care centre when she was two years old and had a pedagogue with her who spoke sign language. She was a lonely child. There were no deaf children her age anywhere near her. She went both to the school for the deaf and for a few hours each week to her local school for hearing learners. She was not very happy in those years, she said: 'It was hard. I belonged nowhere ...'

There were problems in the family due to the fact that Margrét and her father could not communicate properly, and misunderstandings and mistrust grew between them. The family was moved abroad for a while when Margrét was in her early teens. There she went to a special deaf class in a mainstream school. The deaf students spent much of their time in the special class and some time in general class. Her classmates in the special deaf class had been together in that class from when they started school. It was hard to get into the group. She was rejected.

> I was looking forward so much to this school and then I had problems in my new class. The kids called me names and laughed at the Eskimos in Iceland. I felt ashamed, I felt really bad, I wanted to die.

Finally, she got a boyfriend and that changed a lot for a while. She wanted to move away from home at the age of sixteen, and she took a job as an au pair with a deaf family in a different town. She felt unhappy and left her job.

She started to smoke and drink alcohol and tried to fit in with a group of hearing kids that were a little older than her. Next, her parents sent her to a foreign boarding school for deaf students. Here, at the age of almost seventeen, she found herself accepted by students and teachers. All the teaching was in sign language and many of the teachers were deaf.

> I was excited and scared when I started [school]. I had a kind of shock, I had never seen so many deaf people before and I did not know if I could manage. I waited outside my classroom, was afraid to go in … then I opened the door and saw all these hands swaying in the air. I met a deaf teacher. This was a new experience and it made me so very happy.

At the end of the school year Margrét returned home. The situation between herself and her father had not improved. Margrét said she became filled with anger at her father. She asked:

> Why could he not bother to learn sign language, why did he talk to my sister on the phone all the time and tell me to study, when there were just the two of us…?

She felt lonely and terrible. She got involved with kids who used dope, began to drink a lot and used hash and other substances. After a time, she became very depressed and tried to commit suicide. Two years later she stopped using drugs. She began to think more about her life and realised that 'I needed bigger and bigger doses of dope to function. I got scared.'

After working at this and that she started school once again. She is now studying with hearing students. She said that she 'quite likes it'. She uses an interpreter in class. She worries that 'the interpreter may disturb the other students'. She also complained that the interpreters sometimes 'get it all wrong'. Margrét is not optimistic that she will graduate.

> Time and time again, I do not understand what the interpreters are signing.

Margrét is still very alone. On the one hand, she said she wants to be with hearing people, 'because I want to get to know new people and hear new points of view'. On the other hand, she said she feels herself drawn to the deaf group because 'we all talk sign language, a beautiful language, our mother tongue'. She complained about some of her deaf companions:

> I have travelled and seen things. I want to have my own opinions. Many deaf people are very narrow-minded … prejudiced and judgmental … but not all. Some listen …

She has some acquaintances who are hearing. She said she enjoys going out with them, but:

> Some of them think I am too lazy to try to understand what they are saying. Some cannot understand me when I speak with my voice because I do not speak clearly. This can breed horrid misunderstandings.

Margrét's dream is to see more of the world. Later she hopes that she can get into a university for the deaf. She is not over-optimistic that she will get there, but she is hopeful that her life is improving. Margrét and her parents talk about having had a rough ride. The parents feel that they have fought every inch of the way to help Margrét.

Margrét ended the interview by telling me:

> I am glad I have experienced all types of schooling, for the deaf and for the hearing. I know that the deaf are often prejudiced against the hearing and vice versa. I find this really sad. Prejudice comes at us from all different directions. But in the Icelandic effort to modernise and create a better life for everyone, people always forget us. It is real hard to be strong sometimes.

**Traveller in the special lane**

Björg is eighteen years old. She and her brother, Magnús, who is a year older, live with their parents in a comfortable villa in one of the suburbs of Reykjavík. Another older sibling has moved from home. Björg, who has cognitive impairment, is the youngest in her family. Since her birth, according to her parents, she has been the centre of the family's love and attention. Björg is small and delicately proportioned. Her parents have wanted the best available professional help for her; therefore, they have chosen special services when available. She attended special school, special sports, has had the same support family for ten years, and she has gone to summer camp for disabled children and youth. She has also travelled, both in Iceland and abroad, with her parents and siblings. Björg is now in a special class in upper secondary school.

When she was born, her impairment was immediately clear to her mother, who described it as 'a crisis'. The couple supported each other through the shock and felt that they got extremely good help from the professionals from the beginning, but not from their own social network. Björg almost immediately received special services for therapy.

Björg's father worked hard at building his business. He stayed abroad from time to time. Her mother did almost all the work. She looked after the children and the home and drove Björg to treatment five times a week.

At the age of two, Björg started at a general day care centre. There she had a special teacher who supported her and taught her 'one-on-one' for a part of each day. Her parents were relieved:

> The services were excellent. This just happened, happened without our doing anything to bring it about. They found a woman to train her and she learned total communication, so as to be able to help Björg. Even after we moved [to a villa in a different part of town] they came for her, picked her up by bus. The special teacher decided what to teach her and worked with her alone for two hours each day. They used a programme from the Assessment Centre.

They moved to a bigger house, Björg started at the general day care centre in her new neighbourhood and things changed. Björg was now supported by a person who was not qualified in special education. She wanted to include her with ordinary kids and drop the total communication approach. Björg's mother said that the teacher accused her of delaying Björg's language development. This hurt and she 'felt completely alone and angry'. She complained to the principal and to the central office of the special education services. Finally a new support person was found and things calmed down.

When Björg was six years old she went to a special school. Magnús told me that Björg had wanted to go with him to his school. He said that it felt odd that when he walked to school in the morning, a bus came for his little sister and took her to a different school, 'but this was just the way it was'. The parents praised the special school. The mother said:

> This is an excellent school. I did not want her in general school. I was so afraid that the professionals would treat her like a little doll. She was so small and delicate, you see. And I knew my local school and did not want her pulled out of class for special education all the time. I wanted her in a classroom with her equals. This is why we chose the special school and we were very pleased with the school.

Björg herself did not quite agree with her parents' enthusiasm for the special school. She said:

> It was fun and not fun. Some of my teachers there talked so much, I stopped wanting to learn ... they told me to learn but I did not want to until after the teacher stopped talking ... The teachers there were OK. My friends were there. I felt sometimes good and sometimes bad.

She was confirmed with her brother and his classmates, but got religious preparation for the event with the kids in her special school.

From the age of fourteen to sixteen, Björg, like many Reykjavík teenagers, had a paid gardening job in the city parks. She joined a workgroup of disabled teenagers and had a support person on the job. This job programme stops when the teenagers become sixteen. However, disabled young people are invited to work on, but for fewer hours and much less pay. Magnús told me that Björg was only allowed to work four hours a day this summer, and only three hours on Fridays, but she had worked eight hours a day the previous summer.

Friendships and interests changed as the siblings grew older. Magnús had 'a legion of friends', his mother said. His little sister did not fit into this. She had other interests and pursued these with her own friends. She went to dances, parties and other activities at her special school. Sometimes Magnús would accompany her there. He said:

> We spend less time together now, but she is still the best sister in the world, wonderful, always smiling and positive. I love to see her smile ... We are moving in two different directions. I think my life will be very different from hers ...

Björg is very happy in the special class in the upper secondary school. The special class is in the school, but the disabled students only mix with the general students at break time, if they mix at all.

> My teachers are good and they are fun. I have learned a lot there. I did not want to go to the same upper secondary school as my brother. I know kids in his school, but my best friends are here [in the special class at the upper secondary school] ... My boyfriend, my love, he is there, and my girlfriends.

Her parents confirmed Björg's happiness at the upper secondary school, but they had concerns about that school. Her mother said:

> She is really on Cloud 9, she is so happy at the special class in the upper secondary school. While that is so, we should feel at ease. She really looks forward to going to school each morning and that is just great ... But ... we are worried about her future, what comes after this?

They said that the teaching was really good and that their daughter did 'not have the intelligence to part take in more complex lessons'.

Björg has a very full life. She has friends, interests and goes to sport regularly. She loves to spend time with her boyfriend, playing music and watching videos. She enjoys being at home with her family. She likes it when she can go out with her brother and drive in his car. She said that she sometimes thinks about why she is disabled but not him. She told me that 'If I become a grown-up, I want to move away from home, live with my love, and work at home.' For her, adulthood was a very long way away. But her hopes for that future are to get a job 'somewhere indoors'. When I asked her if she wanted to have children of her own, she said:

> I am not sure if I want that. I am disabled. I don't think I want … I will not be very good [mother].

Her mother explained, smiling:

> She has a crush one of her classmates. She calls him her boyfriend. She asks me to phone him … She brings him home sometimes and we drive him home. They play together, watch videos … she says she plans to marry him and move. She keeps reading the property announcements in the newspaper [laughter].

The father added:

> … nothing happens unless we phone, fetch him and return him home. It is the same with her girlfriends. Nothing happens unless we arrange it. Her social life depends upon our ability to keep it moving. She is great at sports, but even here we have to organise it. [Otherwise] she will simply sit at home and watch videos all day long. We drive, fetch, wait …

Björg's parents are proud of their daughter, of her abilities and her politeness, but as she gets older they find fewer options for her. They said that it was as if 'the society put a price on her special needs as she got older, and found it all too expensive'.

The parents have a dream for their daughter. They want her to live 'where she could receive visits from her family and friends without intrusion ... but', said her mother, 'she is still very young'.

## The social construction of young adulthood

Adulthood is described as a social construction taking its meaning and content from the culture and the socio-economic structure of society. Arnet made the point that transition to adulthood as perceived by young Americans is individualistic and emphasises qualities of character, primarily accepting responsibility for oneself, making independent decisions, and financial independence (Arnet, 1994). These points tie in with the Fergusons' three dimensions of adulthood, *the personal dimension*, *the cultural dimension*, and *the familial dimension* (Ferguson and Ferguson, 1993; 1996). The personal dimension of adulthood implies gaining personal autonomy. The cultural dimension of adulthood involves a more symbolic focus. It goes beyond the personal circumstances to citizenship with its legal, political and social rights and obligations (see also Marshall, 1973), with membership and reciprocity of the 'good citizens' and 'responsible adults', as framed by cultural values. The familial dimension of adulthood is a simultaneous translation and merger of the personal and the cultural dimensions into a family definition of adulthood. That involves a process of gradual change in the relationship between that person and his or her parents and family, which results in increased independence and self-determination for the individual and less daily responsibilities and involvement for the parents.

There is a difference between coming of age and achieving adult status. Symbolic communication certifies that a person has been endowed with the status of adulthood. Bates (1976, cited in Ferguson and Ferguson, 1996) defines adulthood thus:

The status of adulthood is most often correctly assumed as part of a tacit exchange of complex information through the interactive elements of language, social context and cognitive interpretations of relevant information about age (e.g. the appearance, voice, size and so forth).

Bates's definition involves a communication process via symbols (language, social context and cognitive interpretations). It suggests that typical Icelandic young people are enabled to start that communication in their early or mid-teens, while not officially obtaining the legal status of adulthood until eighteen years of age. This communication process is woven into the webs of the young persons' relationships (Coleman, 1961; Nielsen, 1991; Edelstein, 1988). Even though most people get through adolescence and young adulthood prepared to take on the rights and duties of adult life, for some, the pursuit of adolescence and young adulthood can become tricky, and sometimes painful, problematic and lonely. But most of us get to become adults and are recognised as such by others.

## The social construction of disabled adulthood

In what way does the social construction of young adulthood differ for young disabled people? The broad picture, as painted by this research, suggests some important differences in all three dimensions of adulthood. The individual (medical) model of disability dominates both professional and lay people's perceptions of the problems facing children and young people with disabilities. That approach depicts them as lacking, sick, pathetic, incomplete beings in need of care and kindness, to be trained, mended or cured by professionals, and as a source of sorrow, stress and toil to their families (Barnes, Mercer and Shakespeare, 1999). The welfare state, its special schools and special classes in mainstream schools, and its leisure and work establishments for disabled people are organised from within that paradigm (Oliver, 1990). Disabled children and young people are consequently stigmatised and often (more or less) barred from normative participation in general settings, paternalistically 'for their own good' (Högsbro, *et al.*, 1999). Normative adulthood and normative adult status based on independence in Arnet's sense — full responsibility for self, for one's own decisions and finances (Arnet, 1994) — may not be fully within the reach of many disabled persons (Booth and Booth, 1996; Sigurjónsdóttir and Traustadóttir, 2000).

### The personal dimension of adulthood

The personal dimension of adulthood implies gaining personal autonomy and the ability to make significant choices about one's personal life (Ferguson and Ferguson, 1996). It has also got to do with personal identity — the sense of who we believe we are.

Due to the formidable challenges facing disabled young people within society, and because of the vulnerability of many of these young people, it is an uphill struggle to support each and every one to forge a toolbox of symbols for the communication of their adulthood (Bates, 1976, cited in Ferguson and Ferguson, 1996; Ferguson, 2001a). It takes work opportunities and wages, access to mainstream schools and typical peers (or an empowering disability subculture), and technical supports, for young disabled people to be able, in accordance with the personal meaning of adulthood, to claim full personal autonomy. My data suggests, for example, that most of the disabled young people were likely to graduate with few marketable skills into low-paying jobs, sometimes in a sheltered workshop with token pay, or to no work. That and the low disability pension do not hold much of a promise for full financial independence, in a country where the cost of living is among the highest in the world.

Further, in the case of young people labeled with significant cognitive disabilities, it takes supportive non-paternalistic relationships to bring and sustain the relevant symbols of adulthood to the individual (Ferguson and Ferguson, 1996, Ferguson, 2001a).

### The cultural dimension of adulthood

The cultural dimension of normative adulthood may not be fully within the reach of most persons with significant disabilities of any type, and certainly not without supportive, empowering relationships and access to social goods and symbols of an adult status. For a few of my research participants, joining a disability subculture was one option, but very few of the young people in the sample had accepted that option so far.

Joining an all-engulfing subculture based on acceptance, in a society that has excluded its members for whatever reasons, has both positive and negative aspects. One the one hand, the need for mutual supports and the celebration of difference is likely to empower individuals and groups that have been rejected by mainstream society. But on the other hand, it can be argued that if people learn to accept and respect each other's differences, a foundation is built for a more tolerant and a culturally richer society. Perhaps the answer could be that labeled people need *both* membership and acceptance within a disability culture of their own making *and* within the culture of mainstream society.

Many disabled people join subcultures by choice. For persons with cognitive disabilities, such choices have been made by others in the individual's social network, such as parents, professionals, staff or advocates. Ferguson (2001a) describes the congregation of persons with cognitive disabilities as placing them in 'a professional or bureaucratic subculture that engulfs people with mental retardation'. Furthermore, he argues that, at worst, such segregated settings for persons with cognitive disabilities may result in what he calls a 'ghettoization' of people with the most significant cognitive disabilities on the margins of both the disability community and mainstream culture.

Ólafía was one of the young participants in the study who can be seen as moving along the highway. Her story suggests that, despite her impairment, she managed with support from friends, family and paid staff, to engage in culturally ascribed age-appropriate but somewhat fragile adulthood. She did many of the things other young women engage in, but less often and only with support. She reached what the Fergusons call 'fragile assimilation into dominant culture' (Ferguson and Ferguson, 1996).

Björg, on the other hand, moved along in the special lane. Despite her age and her vitality, she was getting more and more locked into a special world for disabled people, dominated by professional bureaucratic structures that were none of her making. Within that structure she had found friends and companions (see Gustavsson 1999), The fact that she could only see them at organised activities for special people, or when parents were available to drive her, irritated her somewhat, but she accepted that as a fact of life.

The young disabled people referred to as nomads had a much harder time fitting into the culturally prescribed dimension of adulthood, but for different reasons. Margrét (and her parents) had made a number of different choices that sometimes directed her towards the highway and sometimes away from it. Margrét's personality and her thirst for trying all kinds of new things and testing new boundaries, made it difficult for her at the time of the interview to settle on her journey on the highway. Due to her very different experiences from that of many deaf children and young people in Iceland, and because she did not identify with the deaf culture, it was also hard for her to find acceptance there.

It is sometimes difficult to distinguish between what can be rightfully described as joining a subculture by choice, and joining a 'bureaucratic' or 'professional' subculture populated by professional staff and the group of disabled clients. Some of the young participants in the study who came from segregated schools or classes, like Björg for example, said that they chose special settings rather than general settings with which they did not have much experience, because that is where their friends were. Can it be said that they made their choice in full knowledge of what the alternatives might be? Or sometimes such a choice was the only available option, a choice between some service and no service.

Most of the disabled young people with cognitive disabilities in the study found themselves, at least at upper secondary school level, more or less engulfed within the 'bureaucratic' or 'professional' and 'family/advocate' subcultures, but created small groups of very important friendships and activities within those parameters. However, the parameters for the creation of such *gemeinschaft* were narrowly focused, and were largely provided by staff or parents (Gustavsson, 1999; Grue, 1998; 1999).

*The familial dimension of adulthood*
Finally, the familial dimension of adulthood takes on distinctly different forms and processes in families of most disabled youth than it does for typical children and youth and their families. Different families deal differently with disability (Turnbull and Turnbull, 1997; Sætersdal, 1985; 1994, Ferguson, 2001b;

Gallimore *et al.*, 1989). However, at least two things seem to impact the relationship between parents and their disabled children, and distinguish them from most typical parent–child relationships.

First, there is the physical work involved in caring for children and youth with disabilities, the bulk of which is done by mothers (Traustadóttir, 1992), and the resulting dependency and interdependency between the parent(s) and the child, that is built into such family settings. Parental responsibilities change over time but they seldom diminish with the disabled child coming of age. Some of the work can be farmed out to paid or non-paid helpers, but the parent(s) continue to feel responsible (Ferguson and Ferguson, 1996; Traustadóttir, 1992; Sætersdal, 1994).

Second, the gradual change in typical parent–child relationships, with a shift towards increased independence and self-determination for the child and a reduced level of daily responsibility for the parents, negotiated as the young person moves towards adulthood, can become difficult to achieve in families with disabled children. Parental love and concern and the routines built into family settings (Gallimore *et al.*, 1989), so necessary in the disabled child's childhood, can lock both the parents and the person with a disability into a harmful paternalistic mode of interaction and interdependence (Bjarnason, 2002).

Parents like Ólafía's mother, who managed to build negotiations into their relationship with their disabled children, inviting both 'dignity of risk' and the gradual increase of independence and self-determination, could support their child's transition to adulthood, and equip them with access to the symbols of an adult status. This involves encouraging and rewarding choice, empowering the disabled child to advocate for his or her own needs, attention to age-appropriate interactions, and respect for the person's coming of age. In the case of persons with cognitive disabilities, a support person close to the young person's age can be brought in to help with such negotiations, and some of the parents' daily tasks can be given to others, including paid helpers or friends.

In Björg's case, parental supervision appeared to have changed much less than it had for Ólafía. For Björg, and for many of the other disabled young people in the special lane, parents, in consultation with professionals, made many important and relevant decisions on their child's behalf. That suggests that the negotiations in the parent–child relationship, so important for the development and reconstruction of parent–child interaction, may have been less prevalent than in the case of the young people on the highway. As mentioned before, Björg described herself, and was described by her significant others, as a 'very good girl'.

Margrét's situation regarding the family dimension of adulthood was different. She felt that both her parents were not equally supportive of her. This had created problems in her home, spurring Margrét on to test her boundaries within her family. All the participants that were categorised as nomads expressed that they had been a burden to one or both parents, or in one case that the parents had failed them. No such views were expressed by the young disabled people on the two roads.

## Conclusion

The social construction of disabled adulthood appears to be different to that of typical adulthood along the three dimensions, personal, cultural and familial, in the relational aspects of each of these dimensions. All of the participants in the study needed support to embrace interdependence (rather than independence) and to access and adopt personal and cultural symbols of adulthood. Such support must be relationally anchored to membership of mainstream society and/or in a disability culture of their own free choice. The young people with physical or sensory disabilities need access to non-patronising supports, social, educational and economic resources, and technical aids in order to embrace their interdependent adult status. The young people labeled with cognitive disabilities, need *in addition* to have the symbols of adult status brought to them in an age-appropriate and culturally appropriate way through interpretation and reinterpretation.

In short, a socially constructed adulthood with a difference is within the reach of each and every one of the study participants, but not everyone had the relational supports at the time of the study to access that status, in the personal, cultural or familial dimensions of adulthood. Consequently, a fully normative autonomous adulthood may only be within the reach of a few people with significant impairment, but a culturally appropriate status of adulthood involving the symbols of citizenship, membership and reciprocity could be opened up to most disabled people. Adulthood with a difference in this sense builds on interdependence, rather than independence, on appropriate interpretation of the person as an adult, and on community membership. Hopefully, such adulthood with a difference can bring these young people an acceptable quality of adult life with a caring circle of friends and relations in inclusive settings.

## References

Arnet, J.J. (1994) 'Are college students adults? Their conceptions of the transition to adulthood'. *Journal of Adult Development* 1, 154–68.

Barnes, C., Mercer, G., and Shakespeare, T. (1999) *Exploring disability: a sociological introduction.* Cambridge: Polity Press.

Bjarnason, D.S. (2002) 'New voices in Iceland: parents and adult children: Juggling supports and choices in time and space'. *Disability and Society* 17 (3), 307–26.

Booth, T., and Booth, W. (1996) 'Supported parenting for people with learning difficulties: lessons from Wisconsin'. *Representing Children* 9 (2), 99–107.

Coleman, J.S. (1961) *The adolescent society: the social life of the teenager and its impact on education.* New York: Free Press of Glencoe.

Edelstein, W. (1988) *Skóli, nám, samfélag* (School, learning and society). Reykjavík: Idunn.

Ferguson, D.L., and Ferguson, P.M. (1993) *The promise of adulthood: instruction of students with severe disabilities.* Columbus OH: Macmillan.

Ferguson, D.L., and Ferguson, P.M. (1995) 'The interpretivist view of special education and disability: the value of telling stories'. In T.M. Skrtic, *Disability and democracy: reconstructing special education for postmodernity.* New York: Teachers College Press.

Ferguson, D.L., and Ferguson, P.M. (1996) 'Communicating adulthood'. *Topics in Language Disorders* 16 (3), 52–67.

Ferguson, P.M. (2001a) 'Winks, blinks, squints and twitches: looking for disability and culture through my son's left eye'. *Nordic Journal of Disability Research.*

NNDR Conference, Copenhagen.

Ferguson, P.M. (2001b). 'Mapping the family. Disabilities studies and the exploration of parental reponses to disability'. In G.L. Albreckt, K.D. Seelman and M. Bury (eds), *Handbook of disability studies*. London: Sage Publications.

Gallimore, R., Weisner, T.S., Kaufman, S.Z., and Bernheimer, L.P. (1989) 'The social construction of ecocultural niches: family accommodation of developmentally delayed children'. *American Journal of Mental Retardation* 94, 216–30.

Glaser, B., and Strauss, A.L. (1967) *The discovery of grounded theory: strategies for qualitative research*. Chicago: Aldine.

Grue, L. (1998). *Paterskelen: En undersökelse av funksjonshemmet ungdoms sosiale tilhorighet, selvbilde og livskvalitet* (On the threshold). Oslo: University of Oslo.

Grue, L. (1999) *Funksjonshemmet ungdom og livskvalitet* (Disabled youth and the quality of life). Oslo: Noyam, Gyldendahl.

Gustavsson, A. (1999) *Inifrån utanförskapet: Oma at vara annorlunda och delaktig* (Inside the outsiders' group: on being different and participating). Stockholm: Johansson and Skyttmo förlag.

Högsbro, K., Kirkebæk, B., Blom, S.V., and Danö, E. (1999) *Ungdom, utvikling og handicap* (Youth, development and disability). Copenhagen: Samfundsliteratur.

Marshall, T.H. (1973) *Class, citizenship and social development*. Westport: Greenwood Press.

Nielsen, L. (1991) *Adolescence: a contemporary view*. Florida: Holt, Rinehart and Winston Inc.

Oliver, M. (1990) *The politics of disablement*. Basingstoke: Macmillan.

Sætersdal, B. (1985) *Når veiene skilles: samtaler med foreldre som har utviklingshemmede barn på institusjon* (When the paths divide: conversations with parents of disabled children who live in institutions). Oslo: Universitetsforlaget.

Sætersdal, B. (1994) *Menneskekeskjehner i HVPU-reformens tid: Livshistorier og sosiale forandringer* (Human destinies in a period of service reformation: Life histories and social change). Oslo: Universitetsforlaget.

Sigurjónsdóttir, H.B., and Traustadóttir, R. (2000) 'Motherhood, family and community life. In R. Traustadóttir and K. Johnson (eds), *Women with intellectual disabilities: finding a place in the world*. London: Jessica Kingsley Publishers.

Traustadóttir, R. (1992) *Disability reform and the social role of women: community inclusion and caring work*. New York State: Syracuse University.

Turnbull, A.P., and Turnbull, H.R. (1997) *Families, professionals and exceptionality: a special partnership*. Upper Saddle River, NJ: Merrill.

## Notes

1 Confirmation in the Icelandic Lutheran Church is both a religious event and a rite of passage from childhood to young adulthood. Children get presents that signify their new status and hold a party for family and friends, where many are the centre of attention for the first time in their lives.

2 The word 'handicapped' is here used to refer to people who use wheelchairs. Other young people in my sample use the word in a similar manner.

# 12

## THE EXPERIENCES AND PERCEPTIONS OF GYPSY TRAVELLER PUPILS IN ENGLISH SECONDARY SCHOOLS

### CHRIS DERRINGTON AND SALLY KENDALL

The marginalisation of Gypsy Traveller students within the education system has been characterised by low expectations of academic performance and stereotyped images of a largely misunderstood section of the school population. In this paper Chris Derrington and Sally Kendall explore some of the preconceptions held by teachers and also consider the ways in which Gypsy Traveller students regard secondary education. By listening to the views of students, the authors provide insights through which we can begin to understand some of the barriers that are being faced both by these students and also by teachers who have a commitment to inclusion.

## Introduction

Although developments concerning the education of Traveller children in England have accelerated significantly over the past ten years, issues relating to access and achievement remain matters of concern. The situation is particularly serious for secondary age Gypsy Traveller pupils. While increasing numbers of Gypsy Traveller pupils are registered in the primary phase, this pattern is not maintained in the secondary sector. Evidence suggests that where Traveller pupils do transfer successfully to secondary school, they are unlikely to complete Key Stage 3. Between 1992 and 1995, a survey of forty-five Traveller Education Services was conducted by HMI, and the subsequent report (Office for Standards in Education (OFSTED), 1996) described the situation for Traveller children of secondary school age as 'a matter of grave concern'. It was estimated that only 15 to 20 per cent of secondary age Traveller children were enrolled at schools in England and, of those Traveller pupils who did transfer to the secondary phase, a disproportionate number were excluded from school, 'despite the general assessment that the behaviour of Traveller pupils is good'.

Moreover, Department for Education and Employment (DfEE) statistics (for the periods 1996/7 and 1997/8) revealed a further decline in the number of secondary age Traveller pupils enrolled at school, although primary enrolments were on the increase. The OFSTED report, *Raising the attainment of minority ethnic pupils* (OFSTED, 1999), found that Gypsy Traveller pupils were 'the group most at risk in the education system'. In half of the schools surveyed, no Gypsy Traveller child had ever taken a GCSE exam, and many had opted out of education by the end of Key Stage 3. It concluded that 'raising the expectations of Gypsy Traveller pupils among secondary teachers is probably the most urgent priority'.

Recent studies of attitudes and actions that may affect the engagement of Gypsy Traveller children in secondary education have included those by Clay (1999), Jordan (1996; 2001), Kiddle (1999), Lloyd *et al.* (1999) and OFSTED (1996). Although it should be emphasised here that Travellers do not constitute a single, homogenous group, a number of common and significant cultural influences have been identified in the literature. Adolescence is traditionally the time when young Traveller people are expected to help generate income or take on a wider range of domestic responsibilities. Some parents may hold the conviction that secondary education has little value or relevance to the Traveller lifestyle. Many Traveller parents express anxieties about their children's moral, emotional and physical welfare in what they perceive to be a strange and hostile environment. A study of Travellers in Scottish secondary schools found that conflict with teachers often led to non-attendance and that much of what schools saw as a lack of discipline, in the form of violent behaviour for example, may have been in response to racist name-calling from other pupils (Lloyd *et al.*, 1999). Additionally, there may be practical difficulties relating to homework and uniform policies, which create further barriers to access.

In view of the above findings, the authors gained sponsorship from the Nuffield Foundation and the National Foundation for Educational Research (NFER) to conduct a major longitudinal study of a cross-section of Gypsy Traveller pupils in England. The three-year research project aimed to chart and record the educational progress, engagement and experiences of a sample of Traveller pupils as they approached and advanced through Key Stage 3. It aimed to gather and report upon the personal reflections, accounts, expectations and aspirations of the pupils, their families and teachers, and to identify and examine the factors that may affect attitudes, levels of achievement, and continued involvement in secondary education. The study was conducted in collaboration with thirteen Traveller Education Services, from fifteen Local Education Authorities (LEAs) across England. The sample of forty-four pupils identified by Traveller Education Service coordinators during their last term in Key Stage 2 (aged eleven) reflected a balance of gender and ability. It included pupils with and without a family history of secondary attendance, living in a range of accommodation (private, local authority and roadside sites and housing in both rural and urban areas), and from families with a range of attitudes and expectations about secondary education. All the children who agreed to take part in the study had been engaged in primary school education for at least the preceding two years. Data were collected twice a year throughout the duration of the study via in-depth interviews involving all relevant groups of participants, informal reviews with pupils and families, and supplementary postal surveys to schools and Traveller Education Services.

At the time of writing, the project is still in progress and the pupils have just commenced their final year in Key Stage 3. The forty-four children are now aged between thirteen and fourteen, and, to date, less than half the original sample have been retained in the school system. A full report on this study by Derrington and Kendall is due to be published by NFER at the end of 2003.

This chapter offers some preliminary insights into the attitudes and experiences of Gypsy Traveller pupils with regard to secondary education, as described in their own words to the researchers. It also highlights the significance of the underpinning socio/psycho-cultural pressures and influences that permeate the secondary school experience, culminating in a climate of cultural dissonance.

## Cultural dissonance

As early as 1975, Adams *et al.* found that even pre-school Traveller children demonstrated an awareness of the existence of two contrasting 'worlds' within which they would operate. This is compounded as Traveller children move through the education system and are increasingly exposed to the norms and values of the majority culture and the influence of peers as 'significant others'. Thus, Traveller children often find themselves operating in a state of cultural dissonance, responding as 'a pupil one minute, a Romani chavi [child] the next' (Clay, 1999). The impact of such culturally based role demands and the often conflicting expectations of these two contrasting worlds is perhaps most apparent when Traveller pupils progress to secondary school. This is particularly significant given that most theories of self and identity (for example, Erikson, 1968) suggest that it is precisely around this stage of development that young people need to achieve a strong sense of ego identity in order to avoid role confusion and identity crisis.

This paper highlights some examples of cultural dissonance that were revealed during the course of the current research. However, the views and perceptions of the young Travellers and their parents reflect not only the challenges that present themselves in terms of psycho-cultural pressures, but also the cultural boundaries that are maintained and negotiated. Different people react in different ways to cultural dissonance and it is important to note that these boundaries can be fluid and may be mediated and/or shifted by both Travellers and non-Travellers.

## Engagement in formal education

In related studies, hypotheses surrounding Traveller children's non-attendance or irregular attendance at school, in particular secondary school, are well documented (for example, Hawes and Perez, 1995; Jordan, 1996). It has been suggested that too much formal learning is considered to be a threat to the Romani way of life. Thus, the longer the period of schooling, the greater the likelihood for young Travellers to yield to the influences of the majority culture. Clay (1999) postulates that factors such as the values of predominately white, middle-class teachers and the increased opportunities to mix socially with members of the opposite sex and with non-Traveller peers generally, all represent pervasive forces that threaten to draw young Travellers away from their own community and traditional way of life. Significantly, the opting-out of young adolescents from school may relate to and facilitate their adult role and status within their own community. Both Kiddle (1999) and Jordan (2001) highlight the importance attached to, and the benefits associated with, a 'Traveller' education, particularly family-based learning and the family economy. However, both Kiddle and Jordan suggest that the formal education system tends to devalue the skills that Traveller children learn within the home and that these are often at best ignored or dismissed, and at worst vilified.

In examining home/school relationships, Jordan (2001) suggests that the importance attached to Traveller children's interdependence and independence within the home often conflicts with relationships in school, which tend to be based on dependency, and an awareness of Traveller children's interdependence is not reflected in school practice. She argues that educational strategies that focus solely on ethnicity and anti-racist approaches to support Traveller pupils have not led to a commensurate increase in participation and/or attainment. She contends that there is a need to raise Traveller children's attainment and participation by challenging institutional exclusion within a school system 'designed for an academically aspiring group within the local settled population'.

Above all, it is important to remember that the Traveller way of life is a dynamic one that has always adapted to constantly changing demands and circumstances. Jordan (2001) suggests that 'the pathologising of Travellers as a victim group with little choice in the face of racism in service providers does little to reflect the reality of their strengths in making balanced choices between acceptance and rejection of what is freely available' in the education system. Many Traveller adults do recognise the need and have a desire for their children to access secondary education and gain the skills and knowledge that will equip them for adult life in the twenty-first century.

Acton (1974) described four types of Traveller response in relation to this dichotomy:

> Conservative: opposed to change and resistant to schooling.
> Culturally adapting: accepting of the advantages of schooling and
>     wanting access.
> Culturally disintegrating: acquiescent but lacking in commitment
>     to schooling.
> Passing: hiding identity in order to compete with non-Travellers.

Examples of each response type can be identified from interviews in the current study. In this project, we have come across examples of culturally adapting families who welcome the opportunities that secondary education can offer their children in a world where Traveller lifestyles are constantly shifting and adapting. The research has uncovered how and why some children attempt to hide their cultural identity in school, and there are several examples of what might be described as 'disinclined acquiescence' to the expectations of the education system. By the very nature of the research, families that agreed to take part in the study were perhaps less likely to present 'conservative responses', although some Traveller fathers were apparently more resistant to the prospect of secondary education than their wives. An earlier study by Littlewood (1996) concluded that the factor most likely to influence educational take-up was the attitude of the mother. Moreover, the current research found evidence to suggest that some mothers were acting as gatekeepers and managing a delicate balancing act — even withholding certain information from their husbands that might jeopardise the continued engagement of their children in school.

## Cultural identity, disclosure and racism

The research team asked the young people in the study whether the teachers and other pupils at their secondary schools *knew* that they were Travellers, and, if so, *how* did they know? We were interested in finding out about the pupils' experiences of these attitudes and whether or not the pupils themselves felt able to be open about their cultural identity in school, and with whom. This phase of questioning induced some reflective responses. Significantly, the pupils' responses highlighted the extent of trust and mistrust within their relationships with peers and staff in school. Although parallel interviews with parents generally suggested that their children were encouraged at home to be proud of their cultural identity (even despite parents' own anxieties about bullying and racism), this sense of pride was only articulated emphatically and consistently by one female pupil during the course of the project:

> When we go to the fairs like Stow or Appleby or Cambridge, I always tell my friends all about it. They are quite jealous I think and they say they want to come too. (Female: Year 6)

> I am proud of what I am! (Same pupil: Year 8)

According to her teachers, this pupil actively challenged and positively raised the profile of Travellers through her written and oral contributions in class: 'I like writing about Travellers and people who are prejudiced.' This pupil's confidence was, however, not representative of the sample, although some children in the study who attended schools where there were several other Traveller pupils, or where there was an established pattern of having Traveller pupils on the roll, appeared to be relatively relaxed about whether or not people knew. They were quite open with their friends, but they suspected that not everyone knew.

Most of the pupils in the study transferred to secondary schools where there were few other Traveller pupils, and therefore they were quite isolated culturally. Consequently, a number of pupils appeared more guarded about their cultural identity in secondary school than they had been in primary school. In order to explore how the young people felt generally about their minority status within school, pupils in the study were asked to reflect on this. First, we asked the pupils: 'Are there many other Traveller pupils at your school?' and then we asked them: 'How do you feel about that — is it a good thing or not?'

Apart from a small number (who tended to be at the schools with larger numbers of Traveller pupils) who said that it didn't make much difference either way, several (particularly girls) believed that having other Traveller pupils in the school was beneficial. One boy articulated that it was advantageous for all because it helped to raise awareness among non-Traveller pupils and created a more culturally diverse learning environment, 'everyone just mixes in', but responses were more often related to social, emotional, and even physical security:

> I think it's a good thing. I don't know why really … it just is. To have something in common with other kids. (Female: Year 8)

> I'd like it if there were more Travellers in school 'cos it'd be more people to hang around with. (Female: Year 8)

> It's better when there are other Travellers 'cos if anything happens you know that someone else is there for you. (Female: Year 8)

Interviews with parents identified a strong pressure on Traveller pupils to protect or 'look out for' their younger siblings and cousins in school. Parents who had older children already at secondary school often appeared reassured that younger siblings would be taken care of and expressed less anxiety because of this. Pupils themselves recognised this:

> It helps having [older sister] there. She sticks up for me. (Male Year 8)

Interviews with teachers confirmed that older siblings would often take the responsibility of reporting instances of bullying or racial harassment or, alternatively, would take matters into their own hands and deal with the perpetrator directly.

However, these perceived advantages were tempered with a commonly expressed concern about stereotyping. A number of pupils told researchers that their experiences in school were, to some extent, reliant upon the conduct of other Traveller pupils.

> Sometimes people do think that we are all like the same. Say, if a Traveller has been in trouble, then people might think that we are all like that. (Male: Year 8)

> I think it helps if there are a few others [Traveller pupils] but if you get too many, you might get some naughty ones and then the teachers just lump you all together and you get the blame for everything. (Male: Year 6)

> No [it isn't a good thing] the boys just get us all into trouble! They are rude. [Name of boy] was excluded because he kept making trouble. I think things have got better since they went. (Female: Year 6)

> I think it's better that there aren't any other Travellers. At [name of primary school] the other Traveller children used to get us all into trouble and encourage you to do things. (Female: Year 6)

> They'd only come across one other Traveller — and he was a bully so they thought I'd be the same. (Male: Year 8)

> It's better to be the only Traveller, 'cos I'm the best boxer! (Male: Year 8)

This last reference to the physical pecking order could be significant in that the majority of pupils in the study claimed that they had been subjected to racial harassment or bullying by non-Traveller pupils at school. The first days and weeks after secondary transfer seemed to be particularly difficult, and pupils who had transferred with a group of loyal friends appeared to have an easier time during the induction period. Where there had been instances of bullying, or altercations between pupils in the early days after secondary transfer, this almost always involved pupils who came from different feeder primary schools, possibly where there were no Travellers. One boy explained how this lack of awareness made it difficult for him to extend his friendship group in the first few weeks of term:

> I had friends and that ... it's just that when I went to make other friends they just didn't want to know. If you know what I mean ... like, say my friend now ... before he was my friend, he would just turn and walk away from me because he knew what I was.

> Researcher: You mean a Traveller?

> Yeah. And that really hurt me ... None of the trouble I had came from people who went to my primary school. It was the ones who went to primary schools where there were no Traveller children ... so they thought ... [pulls a disgusted face to depict their reaction]. (Male: Year 8)

Strategies for coping with racism ranged from presenting a 'tough' persona, to hiding or even denying their cultural identity. A few pupils suffered prolonged bullying and even physical assault in silence, and one young Year 6 girl demonstrated the confidence and assurance to respond in this assertive way:

> Some people call me 'gyppo' but I say 'Yes, and I'm proud of it!' My mum told me to say that.

Several children (girls as well as boys) believed that they were perceived as 'hard', and although this offered some protection against bullying, it also generated unwanted challenges from peers who needed to clarify their own position in the 'pecking order'. Although their schools promoted rigorous anti-bullying policies, Traveller pupils claimed that many teachers were unlikely to take their reports of racism seriously and were, therefore, much more likely to respond in the way that their parents had impressed upon them.

> My people say if someone hits you, you must hit back. I think I would probably give them a warning first. (Female: Year 6)

> When I first started in reception I got beaten up so I hit back like my dad told me to but I broke his nose! (Male: Year 6)

> In Year 3 I got into trouble 'cos a boy picked on me and I told my cousin to hit him. (Female: Year 6)

> If anybody says anything to me they get a punch in the face. They don't say anything, but if they did, they'd get a punch in the face. (Male: Year 8)

> I am not the sort of person to go telling a teacher every time. I like to settle it myself, but if it gets out of hand I'd tell a teacher or I might hit them … but would apologise for it. (Female: Year 6)

Some pupils highlighted individual teachers who they felt had better cultural awareness and who could be trusted to take effective and appropriate measures against racial harassment or bullying. However, the consensus was that Travellers were much more likely to end up in trouble (for retaliating) than the pupil who made racial taunts.

Other pupils guarded or hid their cultural identity in order to protect themselves emotionally (and perhaps physically). This response was found to be more common in the case of boys than girls. However, one young eleven-year-old girl hid her identity in Year 6 after a bad experience of being bullied at another primary school and told the researcher:

> At my old school I used to get bullied. This girl used to call me a 'dirty, stinking gyppo'. I wanted to change schools to get away from that. No one knows I'm a Traveller and that's the way I want it. It can be tricky! Say, if someone says 'can I come round your house?' I have to say something like 'I'm going round my nan's tonight'. I do wish I could invite friends round to play. I am always having to make things up and it's very hard for me. It would be much easier if I could tell my friends the truth and I have thought about it but when I ask them 'would you still be my friend if I was a Traveller?' they say 'Ooh no, I *hate* Travellers!' (Female: Year 6)

The same pupil (one of the few who did not achieve secondary transfer) also told us how she agonised when the Traveller Education Services teachers came into school to work with her:

> I always feel worried when they [TES personnel] are in school in case they forget and say something about Travellers. Sometimes other children ask why I am going out and I have to just say something quick. It is usually on my own but a few times there has been a little group of us. That's when I worried the most — in case anything slipped out.

Another girl who felt the need to disguise her Traveller identity felt betrayed by people she thought she could trust:

> I told [name of girl] something … a secret of mine …'cos I told her I lived in a caravan, 'cos she was going to find out sooner or later … I thought *she* lived in a caravan but she don't … she lives in a house. So I told her and she spread it around. She's still my friend though, but not the kind of friend that I wanted.

Me friend thought it was alright 'cos there was loads of land to it. I brought her brother to my caravan as well but he's blabbed. He's told everyone on the [name of village] bus and it's got out into school! People call me 'slag'. (Female: Year 8)

Some of the boys admitted to keeping a low profile during their early days in secondary school and even denying their cultural background until they felt more secure in their relationships.

For the first couple of days I pretended I wasn't a Traveller. I said I didn't live in a trailer and that ... and then gradually I came straight. (Male: Year 8)

When you get talking to people and they ask where you live, sometimes I tell them and they are OK, sometimes they go off you when they know and sometimes I don't bother telling them about who I really am ...'cos it's better not to. (Male: Year 8)

Where pupils were not universally open about their ethnicity, it could lead to situations where they found themselves being included in conversations containing racist comments. One boy (Year 8) gave the following example:

I was sitting next to this girl the other day and she was saying, 'I hate Travellers, don't you?' I said 'Not really'. And she said 'Oh I do! They stink and they're all thieves!' I said 'Not all of them are,' and she said, 'What do you know about it anyway?' I had a little smile to myself and thought, 'If only she knew!' I thought it was quite funny.

A young female in the study (when asked about name-calling) explained:

I used to get called names but it's kind of stopped now. It's just the odd pupil talking about Travellers and not being aware of me. They just need to understand about Travellers and then probably they'll stop.

A few other pupils or their parents told the researchers about siblings who continued to hide their identities at school or denied they were Travellers. One girl was told by her older brother that he did not want her attending the same secondary school in case she 'blew his cover' there. Her mother went on to describe how her son played for the school football team and when he received a lift home after matches, he would ask to be dropped off somewhere near houses and then ask his parents to pick him up from there. He had even hidden his cultural identity from his closest friends.

Finally, an eleven-year-old girl explained the impact of racism on her self-esteem in this way:

> You can get very depressed when you are being bullied for [being] a Gypsy. You get all excited if someone says that they don't mind about it. You start feeling good about yourself. I am not ashamed of what I am though. Some of my cousins are ashamed and they pretend they aren't Gypsies.

## Language

Although it is not widely known, many English Gypsy Travellers retain the use of a largely stigmatised language (Anglo-Romani) and are adept at code switching. Language can be seen as a positive force within communities and may be used by minority groups to emphasise their distinctiveness in order to reinforce a sense of group identity. The languages and dialects of the Travelling communities can be seen as positive cultural markers and at times may prove useful in countering or subverting the discrimination of the non-Traveller community. Thus, knowledge of Romani may be used to create and maintain boundaries and to reinforce the concept of a separate cultural identity. Courthiade (1993) has suggested that, even for those Travellers who do not speak Romani, the language remains a cultural reference point and an affirmation of shared identities. Conversely, the incorporation of Romani words into the English language also reflects the level of interaction with and influence on the non-Travelling community and its culture. Within the school environment the knowledge that Traveller pupils have their own language may be a source of pride and support for Traveller children. However, there is little formal recognition in schools that Traveller children may be bilingual, and the value of Travellers using or having their own language tends to be negated.

In order to explore some of the issues surrounding the use of language, the research team asked the young people in the study whether:

- they spoke Romani at home;
- they used Traveller words in school that other people did not understand;
- they found it difficult understanding non-Travellers when they spoke.

Most pupils said they spoke some Romani at home, even if it was only 'odd words' (Male: Year 8), although the parent of one youngster who said she only knew odd words actually said that the use of Romani was 'second nature' to her. For others, Romani was an intrinsic part of their home environment: 'We speak at home just the way Travellers do' (Female: Year 8).

When youngsters were asked about their use of Romani at school, responses were mixed, but a significant number said that they did openly use it within school. In some instances, the language or the use of Romani words had achieved an almost cult-like status among their non-Traveller peers. Thus, a degree of credibility was attached to the use of Romani and Traveller pupils' knowledge of the language:

Yeah — all our friends want to learn it too! I think that's so funny! They [the teachers] don't understand some of the words we use! (Female: Year 8)

All our mates that ain't Travellers try to pick it up and start to say some of the words. They say: 'What does that mean? … How do you say this…?' (Female: Year 8)

Yeah. They ask me what I mean. Then they say it back to me. (Male: Year 8)

All the kids round here want to learn it. So I teach 'em. One of the little boys says he wants to go into business with me when we are older. I have taught non-Travellers lots of our words so lots of us use them! (Male Year 8)

I've learnt my mates what some of the words mean because I'm always saying them. (Female: Year 8)

Quite a lot of the words are used by Gauje children like: 'Kushti', 'chor' and 'mush'. (Female: Year 8)

The above comments highlight that Traveller pupils having their own language can be a source of pride for them, and sharing that language may be seen as a way of seeking acceptance among their non-Traveller peers. Thus, some Traveller pupils saw benefits associated with letting non-Travellers have some limited insights into 'their cultural world'. In other instances, Romani was used as a source of support between Traveller pupils, as an affirmation of shared identities and also as a form of protection, allowing Traveller pupils to mark the cultural boundaries between themselves and non-Travellers. Students were using language to maintain a positive ethnic boundary and/or to act as a form of cultural security within school:

Sometimes we do [use Romani] … when we don't want someone to know something. (Male: Year 8)

It's like a language but it ain't a language, it's like words we [Travellers] all know but some people wouldn't understand. (Male: Year 8)

Sometimes I use words that they don't understand and they look at me funny and I say 'sorry' and I speak it how it should be said. But when I'm talking to other Travellers I always talk like that.

Researcher: Do you ever find it difficult to understand when 'Gaujes' speak?

No. I just know what they're saying, but they don't know what I'm saying. (Female: Year 8)

Generally, adults within schools appeared not to have shared the credibility and value attached to Romani by some non-Traveller pupils. Pupils made a number of comments about how their use of Romani was misunderstood or was even seen as threatening by adults within school. Their comments also show a lack of awareness/understanding regarding the language, which could lead to misunderstanding and conflict:

The dinner lady moans when we use Traveller language. (Female: Year 8)

At primary school we had a supply teacher who thought I was swearing once! I was talking in Traveller's language to [name of friend] and she thought I was swearing. I walked out of class and sat in the playground!' (Male: Year 6)

The latter comment highlights how a lack of understanding was interpreted by the staff as negative behaviour on the part of the Traveller pupil. However, one girl interviewed in Year 6 said that the Traveller pupils were compiling a 'Traveller dictionary':

We put our word in and then a slash and then the meaning of it. All the Travellers are doing it. It's good to do because if we say stuff people know what we're saying and we don't feel different.

### Cultural and family commitments
Gypsy Travellers in England today are predominantly settled, in the geographical sense (due largely to political and legal restraints that have

curtailed the nomadic lifestyle). However, cultural traditions, family commitments and symbolically significant events such as traditional horse fairs and, in some cases, Christian conventions, were found to impact on the school attendance of some pupils. Cultural dissonance was identified when schools did not recognise the significance of such activity and where Traveller pupils themselves were torn between school and family expectations. This mismatch of expectations could also impair home–school relationships. One girl in Year 6 described how the head teacher got angry if they asked for time off to visit fairs so 'it is just easier to say I'm poorly'. Her mother explained, using the following example:

> Last year I went to tell the head teacher about going to Appleby and he went mad. He said, 'She isn't going to learn much by sitting round campfires listening to stories!' What a cheek! He's like something out of the ark! He hasn't got a clue. I suppose he thinks we sit there making pegs and eating hedgehogs too! (Mother of Year 6 Female).

In this case, cultural dissonance led to an erroneous interpretation by the head teacher and perceived disrespect, which significantly damaged home–school relations. Further, the great value placed on family loyalty and support is something that schools do not always recognise, including the culturally significant expectation that family members will attend funerals, weddings, christenings and celebrations, as well as providing support to relatives in need or those who are sick.

> We don't go off because we want to go off, we go off for a reason, like somebody's died or something. (Male: Year 8)

> When I came back to school there was someone else sitting in my place and [name of teacher] said, 'Well, it's your own fault — you shouldn't have been away, should you?' (Female: Year 6)

I don't come to school if I have to go visiting. (Female: Year 8)

Sometimes we have to go to a funeral. My mum will send me if she can get back in time but sometimes she can't get back in time. People live all over the place and it's hard to get back. (Male: Year 8)

Researcher: Have you missed very much school due to travelling?
Pupil: Yeah … London.
Mum: That wasn't for travelling — we were going down to see my mother.
Researcher: Did the teachers mind?
Pupil: You have to bring a letter — but what's the point of bringing in a letter when you have to go again the next week?
Mum: [Incredulously] It was granddad's birthday party! (Male: Year 8)

## Aspirations and continuing education

At each stage of the research, participants' views about future engagement in education and vocational aspirations were collected and compared over time. We asked the young people (and their parents) to predict what they would be doing at the age of fourteen and as young adults. Some pupils, supported by their parents, held high expectations and envisaged themselves going on to further or higher education in pursuit of a 'good' career. Two girls were determined to become teachers, another wanted to become a midwife and had researched the career route she would need to take to fulfil this ambition. Some of the boys recognised that they would need to gain qualifications and spoke positively about further education after the age of sixteen.

I've been thinking that I would like to go to college and learn how to do woodwork and that properly. I'd like to do that I think and then I could help me dad build the wagons. There's money in that! (Male: Year 8)

> If you don't go to secondary — you ain't going to have no exams
> — when you get a job. You'll be stuck in some field all your life.
> There's no future in that! You need at least two GCSEs to get into
> college. (Male: Year 8)

However, a number of Year 8 pupils who were still attending school predicted (and often correctly) that the following year they would be out of school. The boys in this category said they would be out earning a living with their male relatives, and this reiterated what they had said in Year 6. The girls said they would be at home helping their mothers. Most of the boys had been working with their fathers and/or other male relatives since they were in Year 6 while still attending school, but as they grew older, working in the Traveller economy became more important. They also emphasised the irrelevance of gaining qualifications because their economic role within the Traveller economy was already mapped out for them.

> Next year I'll be at home learning how to clean up and do things
> like that, helping me mum ... We don't really get jobs and that or do
> GCSEs or anything. We usually stay at home until we're eighteen,
> nineteen, and then usually get married and then be a housewife ...
> I think if you can read and write it's all you need to learn, that's all
> I want to learn and I can read and write ... They [people at school]
> don't understand why we've got to leave school early [young] and
> that. (Female: Year 8)

Interestingly, this girl's mother had told researchers two years earlier:

> As long as our children can read and write, that's all we can ask for.
> Boys go with their dads and girls goes with their mam. I don't want
> them to go to college because we don't use them. I'll be happy as
> long as my children can read and write.

This pupil was also described by her teachers as expressing 'a longing to leave and attend to domestic duties' and had not attended during the latter part of Year 8.

> Pupil: I'd like to be a mechanic — a motor mechanic.
> Researcher: Do you know anybody who does that kind of work?
> Pupil: No.
> Mother: I think uncle [name] is hoping you'll go and work for him!
> Pupil: Oh well, that's my job out the window then!
> Researcher: Is he a mechanic?
> Mother: No, he's got a gardening business. (Male: Year 8)

## Conclusion

The need to raise the achievement levels of secondary age Gypsy Traveller pupils has been identified as a matter of urgency (OFSTED, 1999). The research undertaken by the authors would suggest that even when pupils are settled geographically and have accessed primary school and transferred at the appropriate time to secondary school, their continued engagement in formal education remains highly vulnerable.

The research described in this paper highlights some of the key issues that need to be addressed to enable Traveller children to successfully access and continue to engage in secondary education. Fundamentally, socio/psycho-cultural factors will shape pupils' identity as learners and will influence their educational experiences. Individuals that feel isolated, socially and culturally, are unlikely to reach their full potential. Models of 'inclusive schooling', therefore, need to take account of all the ways in which pupils can be disenfranchised, and recognise that some pupils are negotiating competing cultural norms and values within a primarily ethnocentric school culture (Markus *et al.*, 1997).

Theories of cultural dissonance and boundary maintenance have been used here to highlight the nature of the barriers that Traveller pupils continue to face within the educational system. These barriers were particularly apparent in relation to issues of racism and the need that some pupils felt to guard or hide their cultural identity. However, Traveller pupils' ability to confront these issues within the school setting and to successfully mediate and shift cultural boundaries also needs to be acknowledged. The development of bi-cultural or multiple identities by young Traveller pupils may equip them to adapt and respond more effectively to fluid role demands and to succeed in the dominant culture while retaining their cultural roots and loyalties (LaFrombie *et al.*, 1993).

Greater awareness of, and emphasis on, Traveller pupils' ability to successfully operate within different cultural contexts is part of the process that schools need to address. Inclusive schools will also acknowledge the potential effects of ethnocentrism that permeate policy and practice, and encourage all pupils to achieve without stereotyping or pathologising behaviour that is inconsistent with the sanctioned dominant culture (Yeh and Drost, 2002).

## References

Acton, T.A. (1974) *Gypsy politics and social change*. London and Boston: Routledge and Kegan Paul.

Adams, B., Okely, J., Morgan, D., and Smith, D. (1975) *Gypsies and government policy in England*. London: Heinemann.

Clay, S. (1999) 'Traveller children's schooling'. Unpublished Ph.D. Thesis. Cardiff: University of Wales.

Courthiade, M. (1993) 'The work of research and action group on Romani linguistics'. *Interface* 9, 3–7.

Erikson, E. (1968) *Identity: youth and crisis*. New York: W.W. Norton and Co.

Hawes, D., and Perez, B. (1995) *The Gypsy and the State: the ethnic cleansing of British society*. Bristol: SAUS.

Jordan, E. (ed.) (1996) *Inclusive education for secondary age travellers*. Edinburgh: STEP at Moray House Institute of Education.

Jordan, E. (2001) 'From interdependence to dependence and independence: home and school learning for Traveller children'. *Childhood* 8 (1), 57–74.

Kiddle, K. (1999) *Traveller children: a voice for themselves*. London: Jessica Kingsley.

LaFrombie, T., Coleman, H., and Gerton, J. (1993) 'Psychological impact of bi-culturalism'. *Psychological Bulletin* 114 (3), 395–412.

Littlewood, J. (1996) 'Gypsy challenge'. *Project Newsletter* 2.

Lloyd, G., Stead, J., Jordan, E., and Norris, C. (1999) 'Teachers and Gypsy Travellers'. *Scottish Educational Review* 31, 48–65.

Markus, H.R., Mullally, P.R., and Kitayama, S. (1997) 'Selfways: diversity in models of cultural participation'. In U. Neisser and D.A. Jopling (eds), *The conceptual self in context: culture, experience and self-understanding*. New York: Cambridge University Press.

Office for Standards in Education (1996) *The education of Travelling children*. London: OFSTED Publications.

Office for Standards in Education (1999) *Raising the attainment of minority ethnic pupils: school and LEA responses*. London: OFSTED Publications.

Yeh, C.J., and Drost, C. (2002) 'Bridging identities among ethnic minority youth in schools'. *ERIC Digest* 173 (February), 1–2. Columbia University.

# 13

## TRANSFER FROM SPECIAL TO MAINSTREAM: THE VOICE OF THE PUPIL

### *MARGARET O'DONNELL*

The transfer of pupils from special to mainstream schools should provide an ideal opportunity to gauge how moves towards a more inclusive education system may be achieved. Margaret O'Donnell suggests that a rich source of evidence about the efficacy of such transfer has far too often been overlooked. Drawing on the opinions and ideas of twenty-eight pupils who have experienced transfer from special to mainstream schools, she provides insights into some of the emotional as well as the practical aspects of such moves. It is clear from this research that inadequate attention has been given to seeking the views of individual pupils and that, while consideration is given to the likely academic outcomes of school transfer, important matters such as the retention of friendships have received only limited attention.

## Introduction

While both legislation and research highlight the right of pupils with disability to inclusion in mainstream schools, there is a distinct paucity of knowledge as to what the reality of inclusion is from the pupils' perspective. My interest in their opinions arose from my own teaching experience in a special school for pupils with physical disabilities. Over the years many pupils transferred to mainstream schools, and once the initial reports were furnished there was little or no communication links between the special school and the receiving mainstream school. As no follow-up had ever been done on the progress of such pupils, I deemed it prudent and timely to explore the pupils' perception of transfer in order to aid policy-making and to provide a guide for future practice on the transfer of pupils.

Transfer from a special school to a mainstream school presents many new experiences for pupils with disabilities. These experiences present physical, intellectual, social and emotional challenges as they leave their existing peer group and join a completely new group in a radically different environment. The sheer size of the new class group, the differences in the organisation of the school day and the lack of support networks for their parents and themselves are but a few of the experiences that await them. How pupils relate and respond to these new demands is critical to the success, in terms of integration, of the transfer.

## The voices of pupils with disabilities

While much research exists with regard to the inclusion of pupils with disabilities into mainstream schools, there is a clear dearth of consultation with these pupils themselves (Shakespeare and Watson, 1998; Beresford, 1997). This oversight can be explained primarily in terms of the cultural stereotypes that we associate with disability, which influence our perception of the pupils' ability to contribute to the research process. We fail to understand the normality of disability and we see people with disability as deviant. There is also a belief that such pupils lack the maturity necessary to make judgements or to give opinions, that they are unable to express themselves, and that they are both suggestible and unreliable. There are also ethical objections to using these pupils for research purposes, based on the power relationship between pupil and adult, which could leave the pupil feeling vulnerable, unable to refuse consent and having little or no power to control and influence the research process. There is a need for strict adherence to a code of ethical conduct when engaging children in the research process (Alderson, 1995). In this study every effort was made to obtain informed valid consent and to ensure that the pupils were meaningfully involved in the decision-making process. The principles of empowerment and reciprocity guided the study at all times and the findings were furnished to all the participants on completion of the study. There was clearly no evidence that these pupils lacked maturity to make judgements or to give opinions.

## Why should we explore the pupils' experience of mainstream schooling?

To date, much research has looked at the education of pupils with disability in mainstream schools using a psychological-educational framework. The primary focus of such studies was the academic performance of pupils with disabilities versus able-bodied pupils (Whelan, 1988; O'Moore, 1977; Anderson, 1973). Other studies examined the attitudes of teachers and able-bodied pupils towards having pupils with disability in their class (O'Connell, 1987; Feerick, 1996; Gash and Coffey, 1995).

Due to the heterogeneity inherent in pupils with a disability, researchers have highlighted the difficulties encountered in research involving them (Kurtz, 1997; Moore, Beasley and Maelzer, 1998; Stukat, 1993). Attempts to make comparative analysis between pupils with disabilities and able-bodied pupils have been difficult due to the wide range of variables involved. It is totally unethical and flies in the face of social justice to compare two totally different groups against a norm that pertains to only one of those groups — the able-bodied (Moore, Beazley and Maelzer, 1998).

Education and learning are generic social processes and are intrinsically bound up with the rich interpersonal, social and emotional lives of the pupils themselves. Pupils with a disability have many different life experiences compared with their able-bodied peers. Integral to their learning process is their relationship with their parents, friends and significant others, and how positively or negatively these relationships shape their self-concept. Learning cannot be assessed in isolation from these factors.

The presentation of the self by disabled pupils in the adjustment process is clearly of crucial importance to the integration process. Pupils appear instinctively to choose which aspects of themselves they will present to others. If they are sensitive to a particular aspect of their disability, this will undoubtedly affect their presentation of themselves to others and perhaps crucially affect the process of integration (Goffman, 1963).

Pupils with spina bifida and cerebral palsy may also experience a number of educational difficulties associated with their condition. Perceptual, attention, memory, visual-spatial, auditory and information processing difficulties are some of the characteristics that may affect reading and mathematical achievement (Stakes and Hornby, 1996; Whelan, 1988).

Much has been written about the effect of attitudes of significant others in helping or hindering pupils with disability in the inclusion process (Feerick, 1996; Gash and Coffey, 1995). While conducting the research reported on in this chapter, it was interesting to explore the pupils' perceptions of these factors as they related positively or negatively to their inclusion.

## Have children anything to contribute: Is it worth seeking their views?

In recent years researchers from different disciplines have acknowledged the lack of consultation with children and have sought to correct this deficit in research (Lewis and Lindsay, 2000; Wade and Moore, 1993; Jacklin, 1996).

Sheldon (1991) examined the perception of pupils with disability who transferred from special to mainstream schools and found that pupils' success or failure was very much an individual matter. Pupils who succeed are able to form reciprocal relationships with their peers and are able to endure a modicum of teasing which pupils normally engage in.

Jacklin (1996) reports that we must examine the transfer at two levels. The first level concerns the support structures within the school. This was found to be necessary but insufficient on its own to maintain the pupil successfully within the school. School factors such as size and organisation, as well as prior presence of pupils with disability, affects the attitude towards the incoming pupils. These were important factors in the transfer and adjustment process. The second level concerned the adjustment process and the building of friendships and relationships after transfer. This proved to be the crucial factor in the transfer process.

Jacklin examined the transfer process from the pupils' own perspectives and developed a 'Pathways Model' to illustrate the adjustments required of pupils at key stages of the transfer process. How pupils view a new school depends on the comparisons they are able to draw with their old school. Their ability to compare is based on a set of cultural expectations of their 'outgoing' school and of their 'incoming' school. Some pupils saw their special school as a place where they did very little work or saw themselves as being too clever for a special school. Pupils' perceptions of the mainstream schools are reported as strange, unfamiliar, big and confusing.

Following transfer, pupils need to be able to pick up new cues fairly quickly in order to adapt to their new environment. This ability to pick up cues also defines the individual in the eyes of the other pupils, who often tease or bully pupils seen as slow in cueing in. This is a very important skill in developing new friendships. There is a difference between being able to cope with curricular demands and being able to adjust socially. Having friends and being accepted was shown to be more important than any relationship with teachers. This has implications for helping pupils develop friendships and promote sociability on transfer, perhaps through a 'buddy' system.

Bennett and Cass (1989) outlined the case studies of five pupils who transferred from special to mainstream school and found that those transferring at a younger age made better academic progress and were better able to keep up with work than those who transferred at an older age. While the study showed that a high proportion of tasks given to high achievers underestimated their ability, conversely an equally high proportion of tasks for low achievers over-estimated them. It also highlighted the fact that it is not the child alone who determines whether or not the transfer is successful, but the relationship between the pupil and his or her environment. What a child has to cope with and how they pick up cues and respond to new demands are crucial factors in the transfer process.

Research by Wade and Moore (1993) examined pupils' perspectives following transfer on a wide range of personal and interpersonal relationships, both within school and in the community. Their research shows that pupils can give reliable and valid insights into their needs through describing their experiences and outlining their opinions on a wide variety of topics. They highlight that while case conferences, assessment and debate take place in the pupil's interest, the  views of the pupils are not ascertained. They claim that pupils' views have an untapped potential, which can aid educational provision and teacher understanding. In order to properly provide for pupils with special needs who transfer to mainstream schools, we must take notice of their views, as their perspective adds a dimension of understanding that we cannot afford to ignore.

**Research design and procedure**

In identifying pupils' perspectives on transfer from special school to mainstream school, research was conducted with twenty-eight pupils — seventeen boys and eleven girls, age range 6.5–20 years. This return rate represented 62% of the original sample of forty-five, chosen unobtrusively from school records that showed the number of pupils who transferred to mainstream primary schools in the north Dublin area over a fifteen- year period from 1984–1999.

The study comprised thirteen pupils who had cerebral palsy, ten pupils with spina bifida, four pupils with osteogenus imperfecta, and one pupil with sensory motor neuropathy. All pupils transferred to local schools in their area, with eighteen going to mixed schools and ten going to single sex schools All of the pupils had been assessed as having special educational needs and all had a physical disability that necessitated different arrangements being made in the receiving schools.

An approach combining qualitative and quantitative research methods was used. Eight pupils were interviewed using a qualitative approach and the remaining twenty were surveyed using a structured questionnaire approach. Purposive sampling was used to select the eight pupils in order to represent a variance in age and in disabilities. The qualitative method was deemed suitable, as the research pertained to pupils with special educational needs and as such would allow greater in-depth expression of the multiple realities experienced by the pupils, which quantitative methods would not permit (Schindele, 1985; Eisner, 1991; Jackson, 1968; Peck and Furman, 1992).

Quantitative methods in the form of questionnaires were used with twenty pupils to help triangulate the findings from the qualitative data and to extend the veracity of the study by examining if the wider group endorsed the views expressed by the interviewees. The questionnaire content was closely aligned to that of the interview schedule in that it explored the academic, social and emotional experiences of pupils following transfer from special to mainstream school. Because of the anonymity of the respondents, the risk of bias by response effects in the interview process was reduced (Selltiz, Jahoda, Deutsch and Cook, 1962, cited in Bell, 1993).

## Themes explored with pupils

The topics explored the academic, emotional and social challenges experienced by pupils following transfer from a special school to a mainstream school. Attitudes of friends, parents, teachers and principals were explored. Pupils' opinions on inclusion were explored in relation to themselves and to other prospective pupils who might transfer to mainstream school. Should the receiving class be given information regarding the nature of their disability by themselves or by the class teacher? What are the best and worst aspects of school? What are their aspirations for the future? Finally they were asked to consider whether it is right and proper to seek pupils' opinions in the first instance.

From the areas explored I have chosen topics that reflect the reality for pupils with disability following transfer to mainstream schools, in order to help us glean a better understanding of the inclusion process from their perspective.

## Pupils' perspectives on changing schools

'Changing Schools' explored pupils' perception of the special school and their understanding of the reasons for transfer. It explored the emotional impact of changing schools and the support structures within the receiving schools to facilitate their inclusion.

The majority of students saw academic ability and the need to develop friendships in their local communities as the primary reason for their transfer. Others highlighted the need for a wider curriculum and the desire to be educated with able-bodied peers. Pupils generally had not been included in the decision-making process regarding their transfer and many were ill-prepared for their new school:

> No, I didn't visit but I saw it, I knew where it was. (Michael, 15)

> Yes, I did, but I only saw it on the outside — I didn't go inside. (James, 11)

Younger pupils had clearly confused ideas as to the reasons for transfer:

> Because I was getting older. (Colm, 8)

Older pupils saw their academic progress as the main determining factor for their transfer:

> Well, I was the highest in my class and I needed more tuition like, I didn't get enough education in the special school. They didn't teach you a lot. They didn't teach you very much. I didn't do Irish. (Peter, 12)

Some saw the necessity of attending a special school for a short period:

> Well, yes, in the beginning but when I started to get smarter than all my other classmates it was time for some decent education, but I never knew that I'd have to change schools, I just came home one day and Mum and Dad said that was your last day at the — because you're changing to a new school. (Thomas, 12)

## New beginnings

While the necessary structural changes were made in the receiving schools through the provision of ramps, accessible toilets and adjustable tables, there was no monitoring of the suitability of these facilities by therapists following transfer. No further communication occurred between the special and mainstream schools after the initial transfer.

Leaving the familiar environment of the special school and transferring into schools where the disabled pupils were now in the minority was a time filled with mixed emotions:

> At the start I felt a bit shy and stuff. It took me a while to mix with the others but after a while it got fine and that. (Paul, 14)

> Weird, and different because nobody was in a wheelchair except myself. (Peter, 12)

> I remember coming into class and when we were coming into class and seeing everybody walking, that's the only thing I remember. (Matthew, 10)

> The building was different. It looked real big. (Michael, 15)

Sadness at the loss of friends was another emotion frequently mentioned:

> I was kind of sad really leaving all the friends that I made in the special school.

> I'll never forget him, I knew him through for six years. He was my best friend.

> Yes, I felt a bit nervous leaving this school and I didn't know what the teacher would be like. (Thomas, 12)

I was very nervous. Well, I didn't know anyone and it was all different. (James, 11)

The curiosity of the other pupils at the new arrival to their school was often difficult to endure:

Well, you know how hard it is for us, they all stared at us and I felt what are they staring at, we're just in a wheelchair. (Peter, 12)

I didn't feel good. I told them not to look at me. (Colm, 8)

Parents coming to the school to toilet them were a source of annoyance:

When I started off in the school my ma had to come down and change me in the wheelchair toilet and my brother and sister had to come down as well and it wasn't really fair on them. (Paul, 14)

Well I could move around the class but the toilet was too high. I had to use a bit of invention here and there. (Matthew, 10)

## Schoolwork

The importance of adequate information on the implications of physical disabilities such as spina bifida and cerebral palsy on the learning process is essential for effective teaching. These potential areas of difficulty in the area of attention, memory, visual-spatial, auditory and information processing all impinge on the pupil's acquisition of number concepts (Miller and Mercer, 1997; Stakes and Hornby, 1996).

The theme 'Schoolwork' examined the pupils' perceived ability to cope academically with the mainstream curriculum. It looked at their attitudes to assessment and their overall inclusion in school activities.

In relation to academic achievement, mathematics and the volume of homework caused the most difficulties for the majority of the group:

Well, I know that I wouldn't be able to do it, so I just wouldn't do it. (Michael, 15)

The teacher used to give us a whole chapter in maths, which were about thirty sums. (Peter, 12)

Well, maths was a bit hard but I managed most of it. It took me longer to do the maths than any other subject. (Deirdre, 13)

At the start it was hard to keep up, I had to get grinds and stuff. I'm still getting grinds in maths. (Paul, 14)

Well, the one I hate the most is maths because I haven't been doing very well over the last week. He jumped to something new like percentages, I don't understand it very well. (Thomas, 12)

I just hate it [maths], it takes too much time. (Colm, 8)

Because of their learning difficulties, assessment for pupils with disabilities can be a daunting task. When asked how they did in tests and how they would rate their performance in relation to other pupils, some of those interviewed felt that they did well in tests, but the majority felt that they sometimes got low marks and generally didn't perform well in tests.

Mostly I do well, I'm at the middle. (James, 11)

Well, I'm the best at reading. (Peter, 12)

Yesterday I got 20 out of 20 for my spelling. (Matthew, 10)

One boy stated, 'I get A's and B's, mostly A's'. On being told 'You must be a brain box', he replied, 'No, I hate school as much as the next fellow' (Matthew, 10). Another boy who was awarded a yearly medal for the highest achievement in spelling tests stated, 'Well, I'd be near the top of the class'. On being congratulated on his achievement, he replied, 'Well, I'm not one of the nerds now, I'm not that smart.' When pressed to explain what nerds do, he said, 'They don't laugh, they read books all the time' (Thomas, 12).

While the majority of pupils felt that they were treated the same as other pupils, less than half of the group felt that they were always as capable as their peers, and more than half reported that they found it hard to complete class work in time, and they sometimes felt left out of things at school.

Pupils were often excluded from physical education and from school outings due to the lack of suitable transport. Using transport provided by parents was not a popular option for students, as they missed sharing in the fun and experience of school trips.

> Well, they play football and running and things like that and I can't do those things. (James, 11)

> The writing and the studying and all that I'm included in, but I'm not always included in physical education and sport, like in third and fourth class when everyone went to physical education I had to stay back in class and that was really boring. (Peter, 12)

> I just sat there and watched them. (Michael, 15)

Feeling left out of sport was sometimes due to lack of access to equipment:

> The worst thing about school is when you go to get a football they're usually all gone, that's the baddest thing, because everybody there, there's big crowds and you can't get to the footballs. There are hurleys and everything but by the time I get to them they're all gone).

> Well, there are a lot of footballs and all that and I was thinking if they could do more games that wheelchairs would be allowed join

> in, like say dodgeball or something, netball, baseball, you know, anything that wheelchairs can be included in. (Matthew, 10)

The worst aspect of school for another pupil was, 'being incontinent and not being able to play tennis or football (Paul, 14).

Factors associated with the pupils' disability also made them feel different. The desire to be accepted as normal made one boy decide to stop wearing splints, claiming that none of his classmates knew of his disability.

> I did it for a year but after that I didn't wear them at all in school, you'd be tripping and falling all over the place when I have them on. I'd rather wear them at night. (Michael, 15)

Positioning in class and seating arrangements was another factor that made pupils feel different:

> The worst thing about school was being put up in front of my class on my own because there was no room for my table and wheelchair. I have a bit bigger table because I'm higher, everyone is sitting on little chairs and I'm huge. (Matthew, 10)

Pupils who felt that they were not given the same treatment as their peers also highlighted class tours:

> Yeah, we'd get to go but we couldn't go on the bus, we'd have to be dropped there. (Thomas, 12)

> They wouldn't let me go on one of the tours when I was in sixth class. There was a tour to a factory and they wouldn't bring me, they had no wheelchair facilities in the plant. I felt bad as I'd be at home and they'd be out having fun. (Paul, 14)

However, for one pupil with minimum physical disability for whom school was boring, going on school tours was the most memorable and enjoyable thing:

> Going on school tours. The school tour was the best thing. Going to
> Mosney. (Michael, 15)

## Teachers

Overall pupils reported that teachers were positive, encouraging and receptive
to their needs. Hard work was encouraged, although some pupils felt that
teachers gave low marks and didn't understand their problems.

Few pupils reported negative attitudes from teachers and principals. One
pupil with sensory motor neuropathy, which had implications for the speed at
which he was able to walk, got continuously angered by the attitude of the
teachers and the principal when they would shout at him to quicken his
pace.

> Well, if I was out in the yard he'd say, 'Come on, come on, hurry up
> and get in there in that line,' and I'd be taking my time to get in line
> because of my legs, you know the way. (Michael, 15)

This pupil presented continuously with behavioural problems as, in his own
words, teachers didn't understand his needs.

> They just didn't know what to do. They didn't understand not to
> push me around, 'cos I couldn't be pushed around.

He also felt that this lack of understanding pertained to other areas: 'In English
and maths I needed more help too.'
The personalities of the teachers were also highlighted:

> Well, Mrs B., she wasn't nice, she was real narky. (Peter, 12)

> The senior principal, she was a bit narky. (Paul, 14)

> Yeah, she's nice when she's not obviously giving out, but she totally loses the head, not really to me but to this guy Paul in my class. (Thomas, 12)

The kindness of teachers was highlighted by many, including one pupil who said:

> ... the teachers would help me with a lot of stuff, you know, if I'm doing a maths problem and I get confused, they help me, and if I need to get out of my wheelchair, they'd hold on to it while I climb up, because the thing could topple over on me. (Matthew, 10)

Much has been written on the attitudes of able-bodied pupils towards pupils with disabilities (Gash, 1996; Feerick, 1996; O'Connell, 1987). It was interesting to explore the pupils' views on whether information on their disability should be given to the class by the teacher. Opinions were equally divided on this issue.

> No, I didn't want them to know I'm like this. They know I'm in a wheelchair. Because I don't want to be known as 'Oh don't do that, that will hurt him'. (Peter, 12)

> I feel it's not for other people who don't like me; it's not their business. It's kind of my dark secret so I only tell my best friend that. (Thomas, 12)

> I told my close friends. I had to explain it in a way that they'd understand what it was like. (Deirdre, 13)

> 'Cos if you let more know that I'm not a weirdo or anything, I'm not different from anyone else, 'cos some kids might think he's a dope and all that. (Paul, 14)

### Friendship

For the majority of pupils, having friends was the most important thing about attending mainstream school.

> The most important thing for me is having friends, because if you have friends you are happy. (James, 11)

Very positive attitudes towards friends and friendships were revealed. Friends were kind, considerate and also liked to be with them. Pupils were rarely ignored, made fun of or seen as different because of their disability. The caring quality of friendship shown by other pupils was widely reported:

> Yeah, they were all nice, well if I had any problems they'd help me. (Deirdre, 13)

> I'd say my friends would help me a lot. (Matthew, 10)

> This guy from third class, he'd bring me down to the toilet and wait outside with my chair as well and stuff and he's still my helper now. (Paul, 14)

Most pupils reported that they made friends easily. Only two pupils stated that they did not have a best friend:

> Yeah, I have a load of friends. (Peter, 12)

> Oh God, I've got a ton. Yeah, most of them are here on the road [where I live] and then I've got a load of friends in sixth, fifth all the way from third to sixth. (Matthew, 10)

Name-calling and 'slagging' were reported by many pupils interviewed. Pupils rationalised the slagging through reasons relating to poor home background and lack of understanding. However, this seemed to diminish after the early stages of adjustment, and friendships were formed:

> Perhaps the pupils who slag just grow up. (Michael, 15)

> They used to slag me and my Dad had to go up to them and everything because they were slagging me in school and all that, and we had to warn the school and tell the school about the fellas who were slagging me. Up the top of the road people used to slag me, it's a rough part. They came from a wild family. In the primary school they were only young kids and they didn't know right from wrong and all this and they were slagging me and all, but in secondary school they're brilliant. It took me only a week to get used to the school. (Paul, 14)

> Sometimes I'd tell the teacher if it's really bad 'cos they call you a rat if you tell without having a really good reason. Well, I've been slagged quite a few times, but I seem to be able to put up with it, I don't know how though. (Peter, 12)

Pupils were included in activities with friends in school and in after-school activities. Break-time was sometimes fun and sometimes scary:

> Sometimes I like to pretend I'm chasing people and they all run away, they think I'm a car or something. (Matthew, 10)

> There were a few times when things got a bit scary. Well, a guy fell on top of me. Occasionally it was unsafe for someone in my condition if fights broke out. (Peter, 12)

Does friendship in school lead to inclusion in friendships after school? This study revealed that many pupils actively engaged in a wide range of activities with school friends after school:

There's a club over there for swimming. I go there every Wednesday. (Michael, 15)

Just last year I joined An Óige club for people around the area. It's great fun, we go on trips, play games and that. (Deirdre, 13)

Well I have a bike, I go out on my bike or I play football on my crutches. (Paul, 14)

## Inclusion of other pupils with disabilities into mainstream schools

It was interesting to explore pupils' opinions on how they would advise other students who were considering transferring, and what they would consider to be the best and worst aspects of school. The majority of pupils felt that inclusion in the mainstream school would be dependent on the pupil's academic ability, their level of disability and the degree of help needed in order to access the curriculum:

Well, people in a wheelchair like me and no other disability should go. They might need to go to the special school at first but if they're getting over-smart, then they should change to the ordinary school. (Matthew, 10)

Well, to go to the school I'm in now you'd have to be smart. (Thomas, 12)

Well, some should go. Well, I only went because I was getting above average then and I was moving on to the E-books and they ran out of books. (Peter, 12)

Well, if you need a bit of help, just a bit more help than I need, then maybe they should stay in the special school but anyone like, if they can get around and don't seem to have any problems, yeah they should go. (Matthew, 10)

> Yeah, if they're like me or in a wheelchair and not really bad, that'd be OK. Yeah, able to write, able to speak and everything. (Colm, 8)

> Some of them maybe, because some of them wouldn't feel comfortable going, some of them might want to stay in the special school. (James, 11)

> If they had the help in school, well they should go to their local school. (Michael, 15)

On initial questioning one boy replied, 'Yeah, everyone should be treated the same, we're no different than anyone else', but then on reflection he stated:

> Yeah, it depends, there could be people worse than me, they might need a bit of help. Not everyone in a wheelchair should go to a special school; some of them are well able. It's actually better to go to their normal school. It'll help them a bit. They might need a bit of remedial and stuff. If they have the help they should go. If they're bad at subjects they should get remedial and stuff like that to boost them up a bit. Apart from that they should be fine. I'd say the school tours would be a problem I think. (Paul, 14)

> Well, I'd say you can only go there if you're really smart and they know that. The work is really heavy there. You have to be smart, you have to study, learn spellings and all that. (Peter, 12)

Advice on how to cope with the initial 'slagging' was frequently given:

> Well, I'd probably say try not to resort to violence when they're slagged. (Thomas, 12)

> Well, if people call them names just ignore them. (Deirdre, 13)

All pupils thought that it was a good idea that their views were being sought on their experiences of transferring to mainstream schools, summarised in the following statements:

Yes it is, as I'm the one who has done the things. (Deirdre, 13)

Yeah, because if you don't ask you'll have no idea what we think of things. (Michael, 15)

Yeah, people will learn — it's good. People don't ask their opinions because they think they're thick, they're not though. It's a brilliant idea; it'll make life a lot better if they did, to facilitate them and all that. (Paul, 14)

Yes, it's the only way you'll get to know if they liked transferring and how they're getting on. (Peter, 12)

Just to see how it turns out and all that. (Matthew, 10)

**Best and worst aspects of school**

For the majority of pupils in this study the two most important factors relating to mainstream schooling were having friends and mixing with their able-bodied peers.

The fact that it was just regular, mixing with people not disabled.

Being treated like everyone else.

Going to school with normal children.

Meeting normal kids and having a normal life.

Being near home and being nearly normal.

The worst aspects for those attending mainstream primary school were identified as relating to personal and academic pressures:

Lots more work and being stuck in a classroom all day.

For other pupils it was feeling different, being stared at or being 'slagged':

People stared at me at first but grew to like me.

Being incontinent and not being able to play tennis, football or anything else in PE.

Not being listened to.

Put up the front of my class because there was no room for my table and wheelchair.

For one boy it was his first teacher who:

... did not want me in her class so I had to move to another school.

Pupils were questioned as to their future aspirations. Two pupils had already chosen: one is presently studying Commerce at university level and another is in full-time employment in customer service.

While many younger pupils stated that they had not decided on their future, some older pupils saw themselves as attaining a wide range of occupations. These ranged from teaching (3), computers and animation (5), architect (1), journalism (2), actor/singer (1), artist (1), hospital work (1), librarian (1), printer (1). For some, their aspirations were a mixture of work and achievement:

Get a good job and be the holder of the 100 metres in wheelchair racing. Do the weather on RTE or read the news. (Paul, 14)

Oh, I'd like to be a businessman. (Peter, 12)

I asked my teacher about jobs and he says that you need high points in your exams for some jobs and I said what do you need to make video games — to design video games and put them in a video shop — and everyone laughed at me. (Thomas, 12)

To work with disabled people or children. (Deirdre, 13)

A bank manager with loads of money. (Colm, 8)

The range of occupations indicated that these pupils had normal aspirations for their future.

## Conclusion

Transfer of pupils from special schools to mainstream schools involves by its very nature a change of focus. Pupils who for some part of their lives have been seen as special and in need of segregated provision become pupils in need of inclusion. The concepts of specialness, educational need and educational provision are not always fully understood. The pupils in this study were designated as having special educational needs coupled with disability.

Much has been written on the importance of preparation for transfer and the impact of such a change on the pupil (Jacklin, 1996; Bennett and Cass, 1989; Wade and Moore, 1993). The government White Paper *Charting Our Education Future* ((1995) states that equal access for these pupils will need positive intervention to make it happen. However, the findings of this study reveal that despite these recommendations, there is no infrastructure in place to facilitate the transfer of pupils from special to mainstream school. Pupils are ill-prepared for the transfer, lack the knowledge regarding the reasons for transfer and experience confusion surrounding the transfer process.

While the necessary structural changes were made in the receiving schools, there was a distinct lack of coordination, consultation and cooperation between the various providers of special services. The continuum of communication as recommended by the Report of the Special Education Review Committee (SERC) (Department of Education, 1993) is far from being realised. The view expressed by the National Council for Curriculum and Assessment (1999) is more accurate: 'at present there is little or no contact between mainstream and special schools in the sharing of resources and expertise' (p. 1).

While most teachers were kind and supportive, adequate provision was not made for the pupils' specific difficulties, both academically and physically. Although half the group reported experiencing difficulties in mathematics, which supports the existing research, learning support was customarily not provided in this area. The volume of homework was the worst aspect of school for the majority of pupils. Exclusion from involvement in physical education and class outings supports the literature that inclusive education means more than integration. The fundamental principles of equality and inclusion were not being implemented with regard to these pupils.

The pupils in the study initially experienced the effect of stigma as outlined by Goffman (1963). Gash (1996) tells us that attitudinal change takes place at different levels. The majority of pupils stated that it would be helpful if the teacher explained to other pupils about disability, not by highlighting their deficits as in the medical model, but by explaining their normality as in the social model of disability.

Pupils' perception of mainstream school reflects an opinion that only the more able-bodied pupils, both physically and academically, should transfer from special schools. It could be argued that these pupils have an elitist view of themselves as being smarter and more able-bodied than those remaining in special schools. On the other hand, it could also be argued that from their experience of both special and mainstream systems, the pupils' opinions are based on the level of accommodation provided in the mainstream school. Their constant reference to the extent of help needed by pupils would support the latter opinion.

Integration leads to friendships and inclusion in community activities. This in turn affects the pupils' self-concept as reflected in their aspirations. Pupils' opinions on their future indicated a normal range of expectations and occupations. Some pupils were already on their way to achieving these. For others, their strong beliefs and ideals will surely carry them forward.

The ability of pupils in this study to express their views on a wide range of relevant topics pertinent to their learning and schooling experience will hopefully heighten the awareness of all educationalists to listen and provide a forum for pupils to take an active part in the education process. If inclusion is to have any real meaning, then it must include the voice of the pupil.

In Paul's words, when questioned if it was a good idea to seek pupils' opinions: 'Yeah, people will learn — it's good. People don't ask their opinions because they think they're thick, they're not though. It's a brilliant idea; it'll make life a lot better if they did, to facilitate them and all that.'

### References

Alderson, P. (1995) *Listening to children.* London: Barnardos.

Anderson, E.M. (1973) *The disabled school child: a study of integration in primary schools.* London: Methuen.

Bell, J. (1993) *Doing your own research project: a guide for the first time researcher in education and social science* (2nd edition.). Buckingham: Open University Press.

Bennett, N., and Cass, A. (1989) *From special to ordinary schools: case studies in integration.* London: Cassell.

Department of Education (1993) *Report of the Special Education Review Committee* (SERC). Dublin: Stationery Office.

Department of Education (1995) *Charting our Education Future: White Paper on Education.* Dublin: Stationery Office.

Eisner, E. (1991) *The enlightened eye: qualitative inquiry and the enhancement of educational practice.* New York: Macmillan.

Feerick, A. (1996) 'Integration: attitudes of children in mainstream education towards their peers in special classes'. *REACH Journal of Special Needs Education in Ireland* 10, 1–16.

Gash, H., and Coffey, D. (1995) 'Influences and attitudes towards children with mental handicap'. *European Journal of Special Needs Education* 10, 1–16.

Gash, H. (1996) 'Changing attitudes towards children with special needs'. *European Journal of Special Needs Education* 11 (3), 286–97.

Goffman, E. (1963) *Stigma: notes on the management of special identity*. New Jersey: Prentice Hall.

Jacklin, A. (1996) 'The transfer process between special and mainstream schools'. (Doctoral dissertation, Sussex University). Dissertation Abstracts International (DAI): (University Microfilms No DX202O94).

Jackson, P.W. (1968) *Life in classrooms*. London: Holt, Rinehart & Winson, Inc.

Kurtz, L.A. (1997) 'Cerebral palsy'. In M.D. Batshaw and Y.M. Perret (eds), *Children with disabilities*. Baltimore: Paul H. Brookes.

Lewis, A., and Lindsay, G. (2000) *Researching children's perspectives*. Buckingham: Open University Press.

Miller, S.P., and Mercer, D.C. (1997) 'Teaching maths concepts to students with disabilities'. *REACH Journal of Special Needs Education in Ireland* 10 (2), 100–113.

Moore, M., Beazley, S., and Maelzer, J. (1998) *Researching disability issues*. Buckingham: Open University Press.

National Council for Curriculum and Assessment (NCCA), 1999. 'Special Educational Needs: Curriculum Issues'. Discussion Paper, Dublin: National Council for Curriculum and Assessment.

O'Connell, T. (1987) 'Attitudes to integration'. *REACH Journal of Special Needs Education in Ireland* 1 (2), 51–8.

O'Moore, M. (1977) 'Social acceptance of the physically handicapped child in the ordinary school'. *Child: Care, Health and Development* (6), 317–38.

Peck, C., and Furman, G. (1992) 'Qualitative research in special education: an evaluative review'. In R. Gaylord-Ross (ed.), *Issues and research in special education*. 2nd edition). New York: Teachers College Press.

Schindele, R. (1985) 'Research methodology in special education: a framework approach to special problems and solutions'. In S. Hegarty and P. Evans (eds.), *Research and evaluation methods in special education*. Philadelphia: NFER Nelson.

Shakespeare, T., and Watson, N. (1998) 'Theoretical perspectives on research with disabled children'. In C. Robinson and K. Stalker (eds), *Growing up with disability.* London: Kingsley.

Sheldon, D. (1991) 'How was it for you? Parents' and teachers' perspectives on integration'. *British Journal of Special Education* 18 (3), 107–110.

National Council for Curriculum and Assessment (1999) *Special Educational Needs Curriculum Issues.* Dublin: National Council for Curriculum and Assessment.

Stakes, R., and Hornby, G. (1996) *Meeting special needs in mainstream school: a practical guide for teachers.* London: Fulton.

Stukat, K.G. (1993) 'Integration of physically disabled pupils'. *European Journal of Special Needs* 8 (3), 249–68.

Wade, B., and Moore, M. (1993) *Experiencing special education: what young people with special educational needs can tell us.* Buckingham: Open University Press.

Whelan, P. (1988) 'Spina bifida children in ordinary schools'. *REACH Journal of Special Needs Education in Ireland* 2 (1), 14–17.

# 14

## CRITICAL VOICES: REFUGEES, EXCLUSION AND SCHOOLING

### *KEVIN MYERS*

The plight of refugee children has been a topical issue for many years, but has been heightened by recent tensions and global conflicts that have brought greater attention to the needs of this population. Kevin Myers considers the ways in which refugees have been regarded throughout the twentieth century and in so doing emphasises the failure by policy makers and practitioners to learn important lessons that can enable the children of refugees to play a full part within our education system. Listening to the concerns of refugee children can not only provide us with a greater understanding of their personal experiences and concerns, but should also give us some clear indication of how we might best address their educational needs.

**Introduction**

Refugees are arguably the defining characteristic of the twentieth and early twenty-first centuries (Marrus, 1985). They can be seen as a kind of lamentable testimony to one of the most murderous and catastrophic periods in modern history, a century and more of war and persecution, genocide and torture, famine and natural disaster. All of this was framed by a growing divide between the rich and poor areas of the world and by 'global inequalities in income [that] increased in the twentieth century by orders of magnitude and out of proportion to anything experienced before' (United Nations, 2000). Such a world creates huge numbers of refugees; and some, but only a tiny proportion of them, have settled in Britain.

Attempting to trace the experiences of these refugees is, however, largely to search in vain (Kushner and Knox, 1999). Put simply, really very little is known about the experience of exile. This is not quite the same as claiming that there has not been a deluge of work concerned with refugees in Britain. The problem is that it tends to take two distinct but conservative forms. First, there are numerous studies whose starting point is some more or less explicit idea of the refugee problem that shares a close relationship to media agendas about the so-called 'asylum crisis'. Typically, these are studies that investigate bogus applications and asylum racketeering, describe the characteristics of particular groups, explore the 'racial' tensions allegedly provoked by refugee settlement, and analyse refugees' economic utility (Home Office, 2001). Amongst all this data the voice of the refugee is barely audible. There seems to be little interest in refugees as active subjects and agents who critically negotiate the complex processes of displacement, involuntary migration and settlement in a new country. And this is particularly true for women and children — suitably described by Charlotte Hardman (2001) as 'muted groups' — who account for over half of the world's refugee population of some 20 million people. They experience the multiple exclusions associated with being either a woman or a child and a refugee in cultures where to be an adult male with familial links in a home country is to maximise all the possibilities available within a given class structure.

The second form of writing about refugees in exile comes in the form of autobiography. Such work is undoubtedly interesting, and because there is at least some sense of agency, of active refugee participation in daily life, it is a potentially valuable resource. But it also needs to be treated with caution. Not least among its difficulties is that it inevitably tends to be written by individuals (especially males) and groups (in the case of collective autobiographies) who are widely considered to be model refugees. These success stories often have both the cultural resources that are a prerequisite of autobiographical publishing and the social sanction of teaching moral lessons. A significant case in point is the increasing amount of writing devoted to the experiences of child refugees from Nazi Germany in the 1930s. Alongside the individual and collective autobiographies of these children are studies of their subsequent achievements and, recently, a hagiographical film emphasising how British traditions of freedom and tolerance had effectively saved their lives (Snowman, 2002). All this makes for a comfortable rendering of refugee experiences in Britain — saved, welcomed and accepted by the British, role model refugees contributing to prosperity in the post-war period. By any standards this is a dangerously skewed account of what it is to exist as a refugee in modern Britain.

It would be tempting to dismiss these forms of writing about refugees as partial, incomplete or plain wrong and move swiftly on to an account that took seriously the perceptions of refugees themselves. Tempting, but mistaken. For in order to understand the importance of the 'refugee voice', and in order to make serious claims about its significance for future policy development, it is necessary to make quite explicit what is being challenged, why and how. It is to this end that the first section of this paper gives a very schematic account of refugee identity as it currently appears in both political and popular discourse. The aim is not only to partially explain the conservative forms of refugee writing that have already been sketched, but also to suggest something about the role that they play in contemporary social and political thought. Briefly, it is argued that highly prescribed ideas about asylum and refugees are an important if ambiguous element in powerful discourses about the nation, race and belonging. On one hand, they are frequently cited as evidence of the continuity in national character (a uniquely moral nation that continues to champion the underdog), but on the other hand they can be seen as a threat to an imagined community of racialised Britons (a threat to our identity and prosperity). Such discourses — or ways of seeing, knowing and talking — formulate their own subjects. They impose on these particular social beings a primary identity as a 'refugee' that serves not only to confine those people to particular locations in the social structure but also, in complex ways, to shape their subjectivity, their very sense of self. It will be important to keep this in mind when, in section two of this paper, the focus switches to a preliminary exploration of refugees' experiences in school.

Schools have long been understood as central to the reception and integration of immigrants and refugees in the UK. Widely regarded as centres for the promotion of national values and culture, schools have been consistently identified as an appropriate site for developing in immigrant and refugee children a sense of loyalty and a sense of belonging to the receiving society (Myers and Grosvenor, 2001). Again, however, such claims are nearly always made by policy makers and usually without reference to the children concerned. In fact, though claims about the integrative value of schooling for refugee (and immigrant) children are numerous, little empirical evidence exists to support them. Section two does not and cannot aim to address this significant lacuna. It does not claim to provide a comprehensive, representative or systematic guide to refugee experiences at school. Such a study requires both more resources and more space than were available for this paper, though it is hoped that a larger project, exploring both the historical and the contemporary experiences of refugee children in schools, will follow. Instead, by summarising some of the findings from existing literature in the field and complementing it with the results of numerous (semi-structured) conversations with refugee pupils, it simply aims to flesh out some issues. It seeks to give a voice to children who are usually not heard and to place their perceptions and experiences on the policy making table.

Such aims sound reassuringly democratic and humanistic, but expressed in these terms they are also naively empiricist. Implicitly, they depend on a notion of the transcendental subject who can be consulted to demonstrate the failings of current forms of schooling and to indicate a path for change. While the acuity of refugee children, and their ability to articulate (often in a second or third language) complex histories and experiences should not be underestimated, such an approach is to commit not only a serious epistemological mistake but a tactical one too. Empiricist research procedures have been extensively and decisively attacked elsewhere (Williams, 1998) and little needs to be added here. Tactically, empiricism is also a poor choice because it facilitates the dismissal of children's opinions in that they are supposedly pre-rational and lacking in adult powers of observation and understanding. It is for these reasons that this paper, as may already be clear, adopts what can be loosely called a realist position, one that takes seriously the structural conditioning of agency and subjectivity without falling into an uncritical relativism. And it is to that structural conditioning — to the ways in which wider structural relations condition but do not determine refugee voices — that attention now turns.

## The 'refugee crisis'

Judging by the portrayal of asylum issues in both political discourse and the popular press, there is a refugee crisis that threatens to destroy everything that is familiar and valued in Britain. Asylum seekers are arriving in 'floods' that apparently threaten the 'character' of England; they 'swamp' schools, hospitals and surgeries; they create unemployment and drain economic resources; they are implicated with crime waves and racketeering and they carry virulent diseases across national borders. They are 'crooks and dole cheats', 'criminals' and 'cadgers' (Greenslade, 2000).

While government ministers do not always employ the same kind of hyperbole to describe current issues around asylum, their basic message has not been substantially different to the one given by large sections of the popular press. Over the past decade and more, all governments, both Conservative and Labour, have spent considerable time and effort on the problems allegedly caused by asylum. In so far as there has been a persistent and coherent message, it has been that Britain is a small and overcrowded island with finite resources that cannot be disproportionately spent on 'bogus' asylum seekers. Such claims obviously cast doubt on the integrity of asylum seekers, but arguably their primary purpose is to establish a causal link between a certain level and character of refugee settlement and the economic prosperity of the nation. This message appears to be simple and rational; only a managed system of immigration and integration can ensure both continued economic competitiveness in the global market and control the 'community tensions' that arise as a result of migration (Home Office, 2001).

It is beyond the scope of this paper to deal in detail with this litany of complaints and assertions, but since they have a significant impact on the daily lives of refugee children in schools, it is appropriate to comment, however briefly, on the validity and accuracy of the claims being made. First, it is a repeated if vague claim that it is the sheer number of asylum seekers that is problematic. Yet in terms of asylum applications, Britain received 71,365 asylum applications in 2000, an 11 per cent fall on the figure for the previous year and a tiny proportion of all applications made worldwide (Home Office statistics, 2001). The effect was to contribute to an overall net migration of about 0.3 per cent of the total population (Hutton, 2002). Such migration should also be set against a profile of declining fertility and birth rates in Britain (and Europe) and a recognised need to recruit labour for economic reasons (United Nations, 2001). Second, the charge that these asylum seekers are overwhelmingly bogus and fraudulent is not supported by data that shows they consistently arrive from countries that are widely recognised as unsafe: Afghanistan, Iraq and Somalia among them. Even when their claims for asylum are rejected, this can be largely explained by the political drive to control the (invented) crisis, by a culture of disbelief among immigration officials, and by a general rhetoric of mistrust and deviancy where refugees are concerned (Pirouet, 2001). Third, the argument that tight controls on immigration and refugee settlement are necessary to ensure economic prosperity and good community relations is at best simplistic and very often misleading (Holmes, 1988). There has, for example, been no substantial research to support the claim that 'community tensions' will cease if strict controls are placed upon migration processes. The economic impact of immigration can be overwhelmingly positive, since it helps to fill shortages in the labour market, contributes positively to public finances and helps develop industries and jobs. It is no coincidence that London has a long history of refugee and immigrant settlement and it is one of the richest and most peaceful multi-cultural cities in the world (White, 2001). In fact, when bodies as diverse as Amnesty International and the Association of Chief Police Officers (along with a number of others) complain about misleading and negative media coverage of refugee issues, it seems safe to say that these have been substantially misrepresented in both political discourse and the popular press (Association of Chief Police Officers, 2001).

If it is accepted that contemporary coverage of refugee settlement in Britain is not a reasoned response to a calamitous situation, then the task becomes explaining such a reaction. In order to do so it is necessary to turn to history. For many of the assumptions that underpin the current debate on refugees have also been made about Irish, Jewish and black immigration in the past (Holmes, 1988). In the middle of the nineteenth century, for example, immigrant Irish communities in Britain — simultaneously feared and despised as feckless Fenians with an alien religion — were subjected to 'psychological terror, small-scale brawls, attacks on individuals and a routine diet of discrimination' (O'Day, 1996). For the first half of the twentieth century it was arguably the Jews — both immigrant and British — who were popularly thought to constitute the biggest danger to the British nation (Kushner, 1989). After 1945 Britain, argues Shyllon (1992), 'was disfigured by the naked and undisguised racism of the British authorities and the British people towards the Black communities'. Seen in this historical perspective, contemporary complaints against refugee settlement is simply the latest episode in a long history of what can be termed a discourse of exclusion that has been central to the development of British society, politics and culture over the past century or more.

The discourse of exclusion, similar to the tradition of anti-alienism that historian David Cesarani (1993) has identified, draws on a number of related themes around the nation. Newcomers are invariably seen as threats to the unity and stability of the nation because they are judged not to share the history, culture, language or the race identity of the British (or English) people. Over time these kinds of statements and beliefs were articulated not only in formal politics, but also in the processes and policies of dominant State institutions (through immigration legislation for example). In this way anti-alienism was employed to construct these relations between those who are like 'us' and belong, and those who are inferior and/or different. Moreover, these boundaries of inclusion and exclusion are not fixed but fluid, available to be taken up and deployed by social actors in different kinds of ways. Indeed, Alan Phillips (1997) has argued that, whereas in the past black immigration was the area in which ideas about national identity were articulated, 'many of the themes of ethnicity, belonging, nationality and xenophobia are now increasingly debated in the arena of refugees'. In other words, over the last fifteen years or so there has been a shift in the discourse of exclusion that has moved away from focusing on black immigration and towards the problems posed by asylum seekers and refugees. It is important to emphasise that this is a change in context, language and in the arena of debate rather than content.

All this clearly helps to explain the first form of refugee writing that was identified at the start of this paper. The centrality of the discourse of exclusion to contemporary British society, its crucial role in popular definitions of the nation and the patriot, go some way to explaining quite why relatively small numbers of refugees are likely to be viewed with suspicion and hostility. It also helps explain the high number of people who consistently report in polls that they feel hostile towards refugees, that they resent their arrival in Britain and feel threatened by migrant and refugee settlement (MORI, 2000). Such sentiments are a result of a history where immigrants and refugees have been presented in problematic terms, and a present where the same ideas continue to make sense of the world as it is experienced. It is these ideas that shape the horizons of thought through which the 'problem' of refugees is understood and the modes of action through which it is managed and controlled.

It is important to note, however, that the discourse of exclusion has never been completely dominant in British society. Instead, it has existed alongside a set of definite moral ideas about the integrity of the British nation and the decency of the British people, which can be used, even if only implicitly and in ways that can have ambiguous consequences, to challenge its dominance. In First World War Britain, for example, and particularly during the early months of the conflict, Belgian refugees were phenomenally popular and their presence lauded as a testimony to the superior morality of the British (Cahalan, 1982).

Both historically and today the presence of refugees can be a convenient resource for the development of popular patriotism and a method of reaffirming the traditional British commitment to freedom and democracy (Kushner and Knox, 1999). It is for precisely this reason that there is a significant genre of autobiographical writing in Britain by refugees from Nazi Germany. These are now universally recognised as 'genuine' refugees (though they were not at the time), and their subsequent achievements enter the popular and historical field as evidence of the goodness of the British. Essentially, they carry a valedictory message to the British public, reminding them of a valuable national tradition that saves lives. In this respect it is a valuable tactical resource for those who work to help refugees in British society, and it provides a space in which oppositional voices to the discourse of exclusion can be both articulated and understood. It does not follow, however, that this represents the authentic refugee voice in Britain. It is rather the only refugee identity that makes sense in the discourse of exclusion.

Inadequate though it is, this analysis of the construction of refugee identities in contemporary Britain must suffice. The central argument of this analysis is that such identities do not exist independently or neutrally in contemporary societies, but rather they are constituted through what has been termed a discourse of exclusion. Put simply, this discourse positions both refugees and members of the established community (though there is always the potential for social agents to intervene and transform it). In turning to the voices of refugee children it is important to remember that they are constituted in and through dominant forms of social relations.

## Refugee voices

In 1998 a report by the Refugee Council showed that many refugees and asylum seekers were being denied 'access to education' because their assumed examination results and their patterns of attendance were expected to lower the school's position in national league tables (*Times Educational Supplement*, 1998). There is also some anecdotal evidence to suggest that girls are disproportionately affected by these exclusions:

In my other country there were too many problems. I am happy here but I would like to go to school. I am fifteen and have not been to school yet ... social services said they might find me a school but that was ages ago. My mom said that we shall just have to find work now. I am forgotten now.[i] (Action Resource Development and Information Centre, Birmingham 2002)

Of the 69,000 refugee children who do attend schools, the majority are, as a result of their exclusion from those deemed to be successful, concentrated in inner-city areas in under-resourced schools. Moreover, though refugee children may be physically admitted to such schools, their experiences once there continue to be those of outsiders who are alienated or excluded by the routine practices of schooling.

One important area of schooling that contributes to the feelings of exclusion reported by refugee students is the curriculum. As part of the 1988 Education Reform Act, a centrally prescribed 'national curriculum' was introduced in schools across Britain. This national curriculum laid down a number of 'core' or 'foundation' subjects for all children to study whose selection was problematically underpinned by static notions of culture, community and national identity. David Gillborn (1990), for example, argues that the national curriculum was 'a nationalist curriculum, stressing "English" language, history and "culture"' that had little relevance to pupils from ethnic minority backgrounds. Moreover, recent changes to the national curriculum have failed to address the myth of cultural homogeneity that underpinned the original version (John, 1999).

In addition, there is also evidence to show that the 'hidden curriculum' of schools, their rules, practices and general ethos, also helps to shape the unequal educational opportunities offered to refugee children. To take just one example, a recent study of the experiences of refugee students found that

Among the many obstacles that they [refugee students] have to overcome are the negative attitudes of some teaching staff, attitudes which include ignorance from lack of awareness, and which range through low expectations to 'deficit model' assumptions about the learning capacities of bilingual students. (McDonald, 1998)

Students themselves sometime speak of the effects of these attitudes, of teachers who are not prepared to help refugees or who are perceived to treat them in a sub-standard manner (interview with Myers, 2002).

As well as highlighting the low expectations that teachers had of refugee pupils, one study also found that the attainment of refugee students was adversely affected by a lack of advice and guidance about pedagogical methods, educational opportunities and by inappropriate or inadequate initial assessment. It should also be recognised that for many refugee students verbal and physical abuse is a fact of daily life. The independent Glidewell Inquiry (cited in Alibhai-Brown, 1999) heard, for example, submissions from community workers who reported that children in playgrounds referred to refugees as 'bogus, scroungers, beggars, dirty and disgusting'. Other evidence suggests that this is a common experience and that refugees are singled out for abuse because of their identities as refugees:

> The children in the school batter me. They say 'go home' or we'll batter you. I hit them and the teacher blames me because I can't explain to him that it is their fault. (Action Resource Development and Information Centre Birmingham, 2002)

> I was so enthusiastic about starting school and learning English. I had been away from school for two years because we were travelling and did not have a permanent place to live … Nobody wanted to sit next to me in lessons and no one wanted me as their partner in PE. I was all alone … Once I even got beaten up by a group of students who used to bully everyone. They beat me up one evening when I was walking home alone. They said they couldn't stand me because I was a refugee who lived on the Government's money.[ii] (Quoted in Jones and Rutter, 1998)

Everybody kept staring at me. I was embarrassed, shy ... Most of the people in this country doesn't like refugees as well. So, even in dinnertime, I was scared to have my dinner ... They were talking about me. I know they were talking about me because they were calling my name in'it? So even though I didn't understand what they were saying, I understand that they were using my name. So they kept staring at me, talking about me, saying bad things about me, keep laughing at me so I was really upset then. (Mano Candappa, paper presented at Children 5–16 Conference, 2000)

These extracts also point towards two further common experiences for refugee children at school: involvement in physical violence (especially for boys) and a sense of isolation resulting not just from being a refugee but also from the difficulties of acquiring a competency in English. The extracts support a common research finding that suggests learning English is crucial in aiding refugees' social interaction (Jones and Rutter, 1998). Even here, however, the dominant social relations sketched in the first half of this paper intrude. Mano Candappa's work (2000) shows that refugee children have fewer friends both at school and among their neighbours than their non-refugee peers and it may also be that the friends they do have disproportionately come from refugee backgrounds. One refugee scholar suggested that the easiest way to improve schooling was for him to make more friends (interview with Myers, 2002). This kind of informal segregation seems also to make refugees a target of violence from their non-refugee peers and it is common for boys in particular to have been involved in fighting. Sometimes such violence is a rational response to racial harassment but at others it is certainly an indication of trauma resulting from persecution, migration and settlement in a new country. Too often, argues Candappa (2000), it is simply interpreted as bad behaviour with no recognition of underlying causes. In fact, the whole area of refugee children's mental health requires both more research and a greater dissemination of that which already exists. It should come as no surprise, however, that a recent study of refugee children's mental health found that interventions are more likely to be effective when they address the whole school culture, including the attitudes of staff, children and the wider community (Department of Health, 1999).

Despite these experiences, refugee children value schooling. They frequently recognise it as an important opportunity and, potentially at least, a place of safety and stability in turbulent lives. Attending primary school for one Kosovan refugee child 'was when my life here began, I was able to put the very frightening and horrible memories of what was happening in my country because school offered me so much'. And what schools can offer is an inclusive ethos, sadly lacking in wider society, which makes a serious attempt to understand the children's needs and respond to them in an appropriate fashion. This includes developing a clear induction policy that gives key information — on curriculum content, learning methods and so on — to both parents and children in an appropriate language. It includes preparing both the staff (through dissemination of information on student background and experiences) and the student body (through the development of a befriending system) for new refugee arrivals. It should also include an early assessment of children's learning needs and a review of progress after a short time. These are whole school issues requiring both policy development and resources, but there are a range of small tasks that can significantly aid refugee children in schools. Simply learning names, for example, is an important step, and providing opportunities for verbal contact with other students (through the distribution of equipment for example) encourages both social interaction and language acquisition. Since proficiency in English is a key concern of the children, any strategies that aid this are likely to be welcomed; short vocabulary lists can be provided in each lesson and the simple provision of a dual language dictionary to enable translation is highly valued. Rather than seeing refugee children as a burden, it is possible to see them as an asset, a resource that helps develop student knowledge about the world and encourages future citizens of a multi-cultural society. In fact, the critical voices of refugee children, presented here in a highly selective and mediated form, indicate much about what it is to live in a particularly marginal structural location in twenty-first-century Britain. They help pierce the easy and uncritical assumptions of contemporary popular and political discourse. They indicate a developed and critical consciousness in a society where the rhetoric of tolerant Britain and benevolent globalisation is deeply entrenched and difficult to challenge. In listening to such voices it may become possible not only to improve the experiences of young refugees in schools but also to develop more critical public attitudes in contemporary Britain.

## Acknowledgement

Action Resource Development and Information Centre (Birmingham) (2002), *Adolescent Refugee Team Newsletter* 1 (1) (April), 2. Thanks to Julie Stephenson for this reference and other material.

## References

Action Resource Development and Information Centre (Birmingham) (2002) *Adolescent Refugee Team Newsletter* 1 (1) (April), 2.

Alibhai-Brown, Y. (1999) *True colours: public attitudes to multiculturalism and the role of government.* London: Institute for Public Policy Research.

Association of Chief Police Officers (2001) *Guide to meeting the policing needs of asylum seekers and refugees.* London: ACPO.

Candappa, M. (2000) 'Building a new life: the role of the school in supporting refugee children'. Paper presented at the 'Children, 5–16' Final Conference.

Cahalan, P. (1982) *Belgian refugee relief during the Great War.* London: Garland.

Cesarani, D. (1993) 'An alien concept? The continuity of anti-alienism in British society before 1940'. In D. Cesarani and T. Kushner (eds), *The internment of aliens in twentieth-century Britain.* London: Cass.

Department of Education and Science (1988) *Education Reform Act.* HMSO: DES.

Department of Health (1999) *National Service Frameworks for Mental Health*, Appendix 4: Examples of good practice. London: HMSO.

Gillborn, D. (1990) *Race, ethnicity and education: teaching and learning in multiethnic schools.* London: Unwin Hyman.

Greenslade, R. (2000) 'We hate you'. *The Guardian* 20 March.

Hardman, C. (2001) 'Can there be an anthropology of children?' *Journal of the Anthropological Society of Oxford* 4 (1), 85–99.

Holmes, C. (1988) *John Bull's Island: immigration and British society, 1870–1971*. Basingstoke: Macmillan.

Home Office (2001) *Secure borders, safe haven: integration with diversity in modern Britain*. London: HMSO. (Cmnd. 5387).

Hutton, W. (2002) 'The unholy alliance against immigrants'. *The Observer*, 23 June.

Immigration Research and Statistics Service (2001) *Asylum statistics, United Kingdom 2001*. HOSB 9/2.

John, G. (1999) 'Paved with good intentions'. *Runnymede Trust Bulletin*, 9–10.

Jones, C., and Rutter, J. (1998) *Refugee education: mapping the field*. Stoke on Trent: Trentham Books.

Kushner, T. (1989) *The persistence of prejudice: anti-Semitism in British society during the Second World War*. Manchester: Manchester University Press.

Kushner, T., and Knox, K. (1999) *Refugees in an age of genocide: global, national and local perspectives during the twentieth century*. London: Frank Cass.

Marrus, M.R. (1985) *The unwanted: European refugees in the twentieth century*. Oxford: Oxford University Press.

McDonald, J. (1998) 'Refugee students' experiences of the UK education system'. In J. Rutter and C. Jones (eds), *Refugee education: mapping the field*. Stoke-on-Trent: Trentham Books.

MORI (2000) 'Britain today: are we an intolerant nation?' cited in *The Guardian* (2001), 'British most hostile to asylum', 21 February, p. 1.

Myers, K., and Grosvenor, I. (2001) 'Refugees, racism and educational policy: from the past to the future'. In D. Hill and M. Cole (eds), *Schooling and equality: fact, concept and policy*. London: Kogan Page.

K. Myers (2001) 'The hidden history of refugee schooling in Britain: the case of the Belgians, 1914–18'. *History of Education* 2001 30 (2), 153–62.

O' Day, A. (1996) 'Varieties of anti-Irish behaviour in Britain, 1846–1922'. In P. Panayi (ed.), *Racial violence in Britain in the nineteenth and twentieth centuries*. Leicester: Leicester University Press.

Phillips, A. (1997) Preface to D. Joly, L. Kelly and C. Nettleton (eds), *Refugees in Europe: the hostile new agenda*. London: Minority Rights Group International.

Pirouet, L. (2001) *Whatever happened to asylum in Britain? A tale of two walls*, Oxford: Berghahn Books.

Shyllon, F. (1992), 'The Black presence and experience in Britain: an analytical overview'. In J.S. Gundara and I. Duffield (eds), *Essays on the history of Blacks in Britain.* Aldershot: Avebury.

Snowman, D. (2002) *The Hitler emigrés: the cultural impact on Britain of refugees from Nazism.* London: Chatto & Windus.

*Times Educational Supplement* (1998) 'Audit Commission, Another Country: Implementing dispersal under the Immigration and Asylum Act'. 10 April.

United Nations (2000) *Human Development Report.* New York: United Nations Publications.

United Nations Population Division (2001) *World Population Prospects: the 2001 Revision,* Volume 3, *Analytical Report.* New York: United Nations Publications.

White, J. (2001), *London in the twentieth century: a city and its people.* Harmondsworth, Viking.

Williams, M. (1998) 'The social world as knowable'. In T. May and M. Williams (eds), *Knowing the social world.* Buckingham: Open University Press.

# common ground

# 15

## DIVERGENT VOICES

The Encouraging Voices project has elicited many responses from a variety of people, including those from traditionally marginalised communities and others involved in education policy and practice. A dialogue has ensued through a research symposium, a national conference and individual consultations. We believe this discussion provides a valuable opportunity to involve people from marginalised communities more centrally in a debate that crucially affects their lives. It is clear that common ground has been established in this debate between people from marginalised communities and those involved in education policy and practice. This debate must move forward and influence radical change in embracing an inclusive education policy and practice in our schools.

## Creating an inclusive school

**Thomas** *is a Year 8 student at Lodge Park Technology College (a mainstream school) in Corby. He has 'Asperger's Syndrome', which was diagnosed prior to transition. Transfer to secondary school was especially difficult for him because of the changes to the structure of his day. Currently, a team of Learning Support Assistants are working across several different subject areas to provide in-class support. A designated Learning Support Assistant is assigned to him, working on social skills and one-to-one withdrawal sessions twice a week.*

I have friends from school who live near me but Kerry [Kerry Noble, see Chapter 4] didn't have that. When she went to school, they should have taught her to read and write. It would have doubled her chance because her Mum was teaching her at home. My Mum and Dad help me with my education. Dad is an engineer and is very good for technical and factual information. They want me to have a good education — doesn't every parent want that? I don't think I should be treated any different because I have Asperger's Syndrome.

At university, Kerry's teacher was mean not to help her. I'm glad she had high expectations and did so well anyway. At my school I would definitely get help with work such as planning and good content. My teachers want the best for me and they encourage me. Sometimes when I misbehave they offer me help but I back away — Kerry never had a choice like that! If my parents aren't happy with anything at school they get it sorted. I have a special Learning Support Assistant (LSA) who helps me a lot. She's very patient; I like her. When I had difficulty joining in with others in Year 7, she worked with me and taught me how to do it. Now she's confident I can do that well so she's only working with me from time to time and on other areas. She taught me how to understand the ways in which my Asperger's will affect me in my school life. We made a personal profile on PowerPoint, then she used it to train the teachers and it helped them to understand me. This has made things a lot better. We're going to do this every year so that I can reflect back on how I've changed.

I know I've made good progress because in junior school my support worker was always beside me in class. I love being the same as everyone else now. The

LSAs give me more space in this school and the help I get is not forced on me anymore. Unlike Kerry my education has been well planned and I get individual help when I need it. If I didn't have this help I would never ever want to go to school!

Before I knew I had Asperger's my junior school teachers thought I was a bad boy. The other children teased and bullied me and it was a horrible time. Now I am more confident because more people understand me. Kerry had to wait until she was an adult to be accepted as herself. I've had problems with that too, but it's definitely getting better because more people take me as I am. That's because they have learned about me and know what to do for the best, and probably most important I am in a good school.

*Sally Sheils is principal of the North Dublin National School Project (NDNSP). She is a past president of the Irish National Teachers Organisation (INTO) and former chairperson of Social, Personal Health Education Committee (NCCA).*

Children's rights and status within any school tend to be significantly determined by the ethos and whole school approach to the rights of everyone within that school community. Of course this may vary from classroom to classroom, but the reality is that if the school is structured in such a way that all employees feel valued and treated with respect and where parents also feel part of the school in a real sense, then the children are also likely not only to feel valued as partners in the school but also to be respectful of the rights of others because they are treated with respect themselves. The converse is also true. After all, we can hardly expect the children to be shown respect or to have their rights positively reinforced in a school where teachers and parents are not shown that respect. Therefore, whether or not a school is democratically run is also a significant factor in this regard.

I would say that, as principal of a multi-denominational school where we have developed a curriculum to address the issues of rights, respect and responsibilities, I have found that the positive atmosphere generated by such an ethos permeating the whole school community has made it a joy to be principal. Of particular value have been our links with the neighbouring St

Michael's House Special School, where the children from both communities learned to share skills and strengths. There is no doubt in my mind that many schools are the richer for having a structure in place that values the rights of all within and without that community. There is no doubt that the fact that our Patron Body is democratically elected (as is our Board of Management) means that all within our school community feel they are welcome to be involved, and this intrinsically reflects on the rights of the child within the school.

With the advent of the revised curriculum in 1999, it is hoped that methodologies will change to become more inclusive and more democratic. This is based on 'best practice' in existing schools and will be particularly focused on in the in-service for Social, Personal and Health Education (SPHE). The very existence of this curriculum and the fact that dedicated time is being given to this area of the curriculum should ensure that these methodologies may give children a real sense of democracy around their schooling. However, they will suffer the same constraints as the teachers with regard to the allowed number of hours for various subjects.

Added to this is the fact that there is a new programme on the Rights of the Child, which has been developed in a joint venture between Amnesty International (Republic of Ireland and Northern Ireland), the INTO (RoI and NI), the Ulster Teachers' Union (NI) and Education International. This programme has been developed around the UN Convention on the Rights of the Child (1989), and the central character is an alien called CROC. The evaluations of teachers, parents and children are currently being correlated as the programme has just completed its first year of piloting. The initial evaluation response has been overwhelmingly positive and that of the children has been significant. Children have had a voice in this evaluation and their views will affect the next stage of development of the programme. It is hoped that this will be mainstreamed both North and South in all primary schools. It is interesting that again it is methodologies that are central to the programme and again the involvement of the children in their own learning is essential. The programme also seeks to ensure that there is a balance between rights and responsibilities. The children and teachers engaged in the programme seem to have really taken to the implementation of the Convention of the Rights of the Child in a very positive way. This programme would be a subset of SPHE and will help children to understand their rights not only within schools but also within society.

I firmly believe that the enthusiasm of schools involved in this project will be replicated as the programme is extended to more schools throughout the island, and this will definitely enhance children's rights and status within schools.

## Living in the real world

*Kathleen O'Leary is a member of senior management of a post-primary school near Dublin. She has used a wheelchair to get around all her life.*

The notion of a 'disabled world' was a long time dawning. Rejecting that concept has been a life-long reality. Life in rural Ireland in the lean 1950s was not particularly easy for anyone; for someone with a disability it should have been even more daunting. Yet the reality in my early years of involvement and engagement with everyday, domestic activities was one that mirrored the reality of my siblings. The expectations of our parents that we would all share household chores appropriate to age and ability created a climate of independence and inclusion. Their enlightened sense of equity and acceptance of difference was to be the cornerstone of my existence. The question of being different did not arise for me for quite some time.

I was taught to read and write by the age of four by my mother, and my life was happily filled with easy, unconscious learning. No disability organisations peopled my world, no social worker offered guidance and direction in life skills. I had reached my late teens before encountering groups of people with disabilities, so there were no role models of disability to shape my ideas and aspirations.

Looking to expand the boundaries of life, I decided to sit the Leaving Certificate in our local post-primary school. To my amazement, my application was turned down on the basis that I might fail the examination and this would spoil their academic record. The notion of difference had cast its shadow. Luckily for me, the other school in our area approached the matter differently and made me very welcome and encouraged me to excel. Having successfully completed my examination, I approached a disability organisation for the first time, seeking guidance for my next step. Eventually, the social worker recommended that I should take a job in a factory making brushes. There was no expectation that I should have ambition to forge a full and interesting working life, like everyone else.

My brief encounter with the 'disabled world' convinced me that I must make my own way. Three exciting years of learning and personal growth brought me a Bachelor of Arts degree awarded by St Patrick's College, Maynooth. Along with many other students I made an appointment with the Careers Office to discuss my career options. I was advised to be proud of my achievement, frame my certificate but not to expect a place in the world of work. It was evident that there were two tracks, two sets of expectations for people with and without disabilities. This dual reality still exists in the twenty-first century.

My preferred career option of post-primary teaching proved difficult to access. My applications for teaching practice placement always contained the information that I used a wheelchair. The replies from schools usually wished me well but wished me elsewhere! One interview was granted as much from curiosity as genuine interest: no placement was forthcoming. Ultimately, however, I obtained teaching hours in Maynooth post-primary school, the school I have worked in for the past twenty-one years.

These years have been both fulfilling and challenging. Releasing and enhancing the potential of young people as academic achievers and human beings has been a delight. Nevertheless, the novelty of being perceived as a teacher with a disability soon faded. It was obvious to me that to succeed I must seek a greater degree of excellence than others. There is little doubt that if I had required physical assistance in moving from place to place or had other needs identifying me as different or dependent on other members of staff, then my integration into the school would have been unlikely if not impossible. The students' ready acceptance of me as a teacher was a surprise — the 'right side' of the desk and the title of teacher conferred a status I had not foreseen. It is clear that young people have an openness to diversity that is often lost in adulthood as the mores, expectations and prejudices of society take over.

Thankfully, I have long since passed the 'aren't you great?' response from colleagues and parents. I sought and won promotion to senior management. The initial acceptance by my peers has been replaced by hard-won respect. There is little doubt that there was no expectation that I should progress to this stage. Even still, the unsaid and unwritten agenda assigns people with disabilities to lower status and less rewarding positions.

Why should this be so? Undoubtedly, there are many people with disabilities who share the same hopes and dreams of their peers — people with disabilities who have vast intellectual abilities and talents — but barring a small number of notable exceptions they remain largely invisible. The proliferation of disability organisations advancing a charity model of disability must take some of the responsibility for this situation. A fragmented approach does not imply the best use of resources. Their sole purpose is said to be the facilitation of life enhancement of their members and clients, but instead these organisations foster a culture of dependency and acquiescence. Blanket prescription instead of active listening is their common practice. This paternalistic approach further handicaps the individual who has a disability. The education system and schools must share a portion of the responsibility for failing to make these people more visible. Adapting structures and attitudes are of equal importance — both are necessary in order to encourage ambition in all students. An institution of learning that keeps the child safe but suffocated can never release the potential of the child.

It appears to me to be an immeasurable arrogance for a society to consign individuals to categories based on perceived differences from the 'normal'. This creates a tiered system indicating that some people are more valuable than others. Who are the 'disabled'? Who decides? What are the criteria and who measures them? The act of labelling is an act of power by one group to the detriment of another. This is an inadequate and seriously deficient concept. It is incumbent on us all to reach beyond fixed limits and labels into embracing the diversity of all people with pride and not apologies.

*Kevan Thompson* *has taught in both special and mainstream schools and has held senior posts in a variety of special educational settings, supporting children with SLD, PMLD, physical and medical needs. He has experience in developing English and mathematics for children with SEN (Special Educational Needs) and has particular interests in science, history, RE and drama. He gained a diploma in Education, a masters degree in Curriculum Studies and Integration and more recently was accredited with the National Professional Qualification for Headship (NPQH). He has contributed towards training for teaching and non-teaching staff at local and regional levels concerning a range of SEN issues. Kevan was appointed as Teacher Adviser for SEN with Lancashire Local Education Authority in January 2002. Before that he was a deputy head teacher in a local special school for children with medical and complex learning needs.*

It seems very much a pity that Donal Toolan's doctors and other medical professionals did not consider what might have been best for Donal himself (see Chapter 6). It would seem that it was not until Donal was twelve years old that they had the courage to talk to him, and to inform him that the efforts of so many years of trying to get him to 'fit' into a world he had been excluded from had failed — he would never walk. However, what is even more difficult to understand is that for almost twelve years the medical gurus had attempted to get him to walk as a prerequisite of acceptance. It is hard not to believe that Donal himself could have told them the same thing at a much earlier age, if only they had listened to him and, more importantly, simply asked him. He could then have been allowed to get on with the most important aspect of his life — growing up with other children.

It seems that Donal was subject to the medical model of understanding disability, which was seen as a subject that only doctors could comprehend. Disability was a subject much too complex for society in general to understand, let alone Donal's family or Donal himself.

It was clear as I read Donal's account that he was made to feel inadequate from a very early age and that he was considered a problem, the cure being to 'rehabilitate' him so that he could fit into society. The process involved trying to make him like other people, which ironically involved removing him from his family, his friends and finally his clothes and all personal possessions. It was as if they were trying to create another person; all other physical attempts had failed so now the only route left was to remove his personal identity.

Removal of an individual's identity is a tool that has been used in times of war and is still being used effectively by different regimes as a cleansing agent to rid undesirables from the preferred group. But Donal was not at war, he was a child who wanted friends, wanted to be with his family, wanted to experience a childhood. All the medical practitioners succeeded in doing was to rob Donal of his childhood. In doing so they showed a total lack of empathy and made him feel inadequate to the point of believing that he was a problem, which was further underlined by giving him a label.

Donal expresses that having a label seemed to present itself as a double-edged sword. Firstly, the doctors needed it so that they could in the end feel satisfied that they had done everything possible — once a diagnosis had been applied they were able to make decisions about what he was able or, more appropriately, unable to do. Secondly, while a label effectively pointed a finger and said 'you are different', Donal soon realised that it was a necessity for acceptance among his disabled peers.

As Donal grew up he expresses his awareness that inequality in the education system exists simply because disabled children and young people are not seen as being equally productive as their able-bodied peers. This fact seems to be underpinned even more starkly in the current climate of target setting, testing and performance tables, where children with disabilities are often seen as a threat to the overall picture. Indeed, Donal cites the notion that disabled children may draw valuable time from 'other' students, which may make their experiences less accessible and valuable. From my own experiences concerning inclusion and integration opportunities, there seems to be a notion that there has to be a 'trade off' from the able-bodied sector, who adopt a 'what's in it for us?' stance.

From Donal's writing it would seem that the attempts during his early years to rehabilitate him were a result of problems with society and not with Donal. Doctors and the medical gurus were effectively playing God by deciding who should be included in society and who should not. The provision of a label would not meet Donal's needs, but it would meet the needs of the majority, who could then point the finger and say, 'Ah yes, I understand what's wrong with you.' What was actually needed was a label for the majority, so that they could point a finger at themselves and realise what was wrong with them.

It is interesting that at the end Donal recounts his experience of New York as a positive one — here everyone is an outsider and so he has become what he describes as 'the majority who are staring back'. If this is the case, does it not tell us simply that rather than excluding those who are different by sending them to isolation, if the opposite had been done earlier, the staring back would have happened much sooner. Donal would at least have had an opportunity to be seen as part of and not apart from the whole picture.

## The great silence

*Brian Sheehan is the former Director of Gay HIV Strategies, a non-governmental organisation core-funded by the Department of Health to build the capacity of the gay community in health promotion, community development and HIV prevention. In that capacity he has worked with the education sector towards including and developing supports for gay and lesbian students. He is also the co-chair of the National Lesbian and Gay Federation.*

> Lesbian, gay and bisexual youth sit in every classroom, in every school in our communities. Often invisible, they are required by law to attend institutions which often ignore or stigmatise them. Some of their teachers are unprepared to recognise their existence publicly or to respond appropriately to their needs. Other teachers, including many who are themselves lesbian, gay or bisexual, are engaged in ongoing efforts, often in the face of tremendous resistance, to ensure that the school experiences of such students are positive ones.[1]

It is estimated that 10 per cent of any population group are lesbian or gay —

whether that population group is a school classroom, a group of disabled people, or a group of Traveller young people. In the study by Anne Lodge and Kathleen Lynch, reported in Chapter 2 of this book, it is shocking, but not altogether surprising, the extent to which this 10 per cent are silenced in Irish schools. There were no gay or lesbian voices. They were silenced both within the student body and within the teaching body. Equality around sexual orientation received scant mention, from both students and educators. Where that silence was broken, it was only in discriminatory, pejorative and possibly dangerous terms. It is no surprise that school is the most vulnerable time for young gay people.

This silence around the 10 per cent has significant consequences for young lesbian, gay and bisexual people. Some of these consequences have been documented in Irish and international studies:

- 50% became aware of their sexuality before the age of fifteen.
- 66% stated that gradual awareness had caused them problems.
- 57% experienced problems at school because of their being lesbian or gay (isolation, depression, poor self-esteem and harassment and bullying).
- 8% left school earlier than anticipated as a result.
- A quarter of respondents had been punched, beaten, hit or kicked because they were assumed to be gay — half in their own locality.[2]
- Gay men are seven times more likely to attempt suicide than their heterosexual counterparts; lesbians 2.5 times more likely.[3]

In a UK study of 4,000 gay people, of those under eighteen:
- 61% had been harassed, 44% in a school environment.
- 40% experienced violence at school.
- 24% had been attacked by fellow students.
- had been 79% called names by fellow students.[4]

Not only are young gay people at risk, but also those who are perceived to be gay, or those who may have lesbian or gay parents and family situations. Very high numbers of reports of bullying complaints involve harassment because of assumed or perceived sexual orientation. Refusal to recognise or respond to these circumstances perpetuates the silence that surrounds difference on the grounds of sexual orientation.

The Lodge/Lynch study highlights that Irish schools have so far failed to provide an inclusive learning environment. That this damages the individual student who is perceived as 'different' is obvious. However, it also damages the other students, at best illustrating the denial of difference and diversity, and at worst fostering prejudice that inadequately prepares all students for life after school.

Education and the education system have a crucial role to play in transmitting our values as a society, values that need to include a commitment to equality and a respect for diversity and difference. Legislative progress in Ireland means that all children are entitled to equality of access to and participation in education, as well as freedom from harassment and discrimination within school. There is a long way to go to fully implement this legislative imperative, though successful programmes are emerging which contribute towards an integrated equality approach within schools. It is not enough to wait for these programmes; simple measures can have quick and positive impacts. Lodge/Lynch suggest that where space is provided to name and discuss diversity and difference, when young people had come knowingly in contact with others who were 'different', a more positive and enriching learning environment can be created, with significant positive impacts on prejudice.

There are challenges in schools in responding to the needs of young lesbian, gay and bisexual people. These are challenges that all partners in education have to overcome. However, the guiding principle should be that schools have a legal, ethical and professional duty to care for the needs of all students, regardless of their 'differences', perceived or otherwise.

As the Lynch/Lodge study suggests, an explicit acknowledgement of the diversity within every school is a good place to start breaking down this 'great silence'.

***Moira Leydon*** *is Assistant General Secretary with responsibility for education and research in the Association of Secondary School Teachers of Ireland (ASTI). Her responsibilities include contributing to the development of ASTI policy in a wide range of education areas, including teacher professional development, curriculum, educational disadvantage, special educational needs and educational legislation.*

The publication of *Encouraging Voices* could not be more timely. The consultation process on the Education for Persons with Disabilities Bill, 2002 is almost complete and there is an expectation that the ensuing legislation will mark the commencement of a new era in terms of guaranteeing the rights of young people with disabilities to education. For those of us involved in the consultative process, the message presented in *Encouraging Voices* is compelling and humbling. Many of the young people and their families directly affected by the legislation do not have the opportunity to shape its content or direction. Those of us who have such opportunities must be aware of the advantage we possess and use it wisely in the interests of the child and the young person.

The issues raised by Máirín Kenny, Eileen McNeela and Michael Shevlin in Chapter 9 of this book indicate the challenges facing young people with disabilities in our second level schools. At a systemic level, the paper succinctly identifies the core issues undermining the educational opportunities of young people with disabilities. These include lack of infrastructure to support integration initiatives; lack of professional development for teachers; and lack of awareness of the needs of young people with disabilities and their experiences in school. One can only optimistically hope that the forthcoming legislation will, once and for all, begin to address some of the infrastructural problems in our system, such as the provision of assessment and diagnostic services; the development of individual education plans; the provision of resources to schools; providing opportunities for inter-agency and professional cooperation; and securing the involvement of parents in the decision-making process on their children's education.

We should not, however, become complacent about the capacity of legislation to effect change. Genuine and far-reaching changes will only come about in our schools when teachers 'buy into' the rationale for change and when they are assisted to engage in a wider range of professional practice at both classroom and whole school level. Looking at the last decade, a major criticism of policy in relation to interventions to address educational disadvantage, for example, has been its neglect of the need to secure the commitment of the teaching profession to engage in a sustained process of innovation at school level. One has to be concerned that similar problems will occur in the area of special educational needs. Unless and until the State is willing to provide adequate teaching resources in schools — special and mainstream — to meet the needs of young people with disabilities, then major changes cannot be expected from the teaching profession. This is an unavoidable fact. However, this does not mean that the teaching profession must shirk from addressing some fundamental issues in relation to the education of young people with disabilities. As the seminal work *Hidden Voices: Young People with Disabilities Speak about their Second Level Schooling* (Kenny *et al.*, 2000) so eloquently demonstrates, some of the most fundamental problems faced by such students relate to teachers' perceptions of their capacity to access and achieve within the curriculum. In the opinion of these students, this is indicative of the seriously flawed 'common sense', individual, tragic view of disability which is the norm in schools and, indeed, in the wider society. There is an urgent need for an ongoing disability awareness training programme for teachers and for students in schools as the social matrix in personal and social development takes place.

All of the young people in *Hidden Voices* were unanimous in their identification of the impoverished nature of their social experiences in schools, largely arising from the lack of awareness of their needs, in particular their need for dignity, for autonomy, for being seen as a person in the first instance rather than as 'disabled'. These are fundamental developmental needs. They cannot be dismissed as secondary to more formalised educational needs but, rather, are intrinsic to personhood. The real challenge of integration will be to enable cultural and normative changes to take place that will enable these needs to be met in the classroom and in the wider school community. It is a challenge that can no longer be ignored.

*__P.J. Drudy__ is the parent of a young man (fifteen years old) who has Down's syndrome. In his professional life, P.J. is a fellow and associate professor of economics at Trinity College Dublin. He is chairman of the National Institute for the Study of Learning Difficulties recently established at Trinity College. In addition, he is also director of Trinity's Centre for Educational Access and Community Development. Recently P.J. has published a number of papers on the housing problem in Ireland and is currently carrying out an evaluation of residential provision for people with learning disabilities.*

The research being carried out by Richard Rose, and reported by him in Chapter 8 of this book, is particularly important and timely from an Irish viewpoint. Submissions have been sought and a detailed series of consultations are currently taking place regarding two legislative proposals relevant to those with disabilities in Ireland. Both were withdrawn on the dissolution of the Dáil in May 2002, but they will be presented again after further consultation has taken place. The Education for People with Disabilities Bill, 2002, proposed to set out a statutory framework for the education of those with disabilities, while the Disabilities Bill, 2002, was intended to deal with a broader range of issues affecting those with disabilities. When presented to the Dáil, both Bills aroused considerable controversy. The most important criticism was that both failed to incorporate a rights-based approach and therefore would do little to resolve a range of fundamental difficulties. In its *Programme for Government* published in June 2002, the new government committed itself to include 'provisions for rights of assessment, appeals, provision and enforcement' in new legislation, but the precise outcome remains to be seen.

While Professor Rose would not claim that all is well in the UK educational system, he points out that many (though not all) special schools are making serious attempts to move towards a rights-based approach by involving students in decisions affecting their lives. The school examined in his study showed a strong commitment to pupil involvement, and the object of the research was to assess the impact of such involvement and whether or not the approach adopted could be refined and improved to the benefit of the pupils.

It transpired that those pupils who became most 'involved' had acquired a number of key, yet complex, skills in relation to 'negotiation', 'recognition of potential' and 'prediction'. Arising from this it was possible to assess the extent to which other pupils had acquired such skills and to enable the teachers and pupils to work together towards further development. The acquisition and recognition of skills would of course have a positive self-reinforcing effect on increasing pupil involvement. One particularly important outcome of this work was the realisation by the teachers themselves of the critical need to have 'high expectations' and to encourage full participation and inclusion of all pupils from an early stage in educational provision.

Arising from his work Professor Rose rightly advises against an environment that encourages dependence and inability; rather he espouses the principle that pupils should take far more responsibility for their own learning throughout the school and that parents, teachers, carers and pupils should work in partnership to ensure the acquisition of the necessary key skills from an early stage. He further convincingly argues that the above approach must progress well beyond the school itself — 'into all aspects of a pupil's life'. He thus points to the need for participation, enjoyment and inclusion in a whole range of activities. In effect, this research work points towards the inescapable conclusion that, unless a rights-based approach is adopted in relation to a range of central concerns such as lifelong learning, residential and health services, social and recreational activities, and employment, many people with disabilities will remain marginalised and even excluded, both within and outside the educational system.

## Common concerns
### Michael Shevlin

*The Encouraging Voices Conference attracted participants from a wide range of backgrounds: people from marginalised communities and their advocates (where necessary); representatives from governmental and non-governmental organisations; and a number of teachers, service providers and researchers. Feedback from conference participants focused on the issues concerning voice, representation and identity in relation to young people from marginalised groups within the education system. Participants were asked to identify barriers to good practice and to formulate the implications for educational policy. This account is based on feedback from workshops facilitated by conference rapporteurs Mary Byrne, Sean Griffin, Mike Timms and Marion Wilkinson.*

It was observed that as a general rule children did not have a 'real voice' in their education. This reality has serious implications for children from marginalised groups. There was an awareness that listening to these children and valuing their voice involved a whole school response involving the school culture, teaching methodologies, assessment procedures and school/community relationship. Every school needs to ask searching questions about whether every child is equally valued or whether certain professional voices dominate the discourse. It was suggested that minority concerns could be represented through student councils. Reservations were expressed about the capacity of student councils to equalise the unbalanced power relationships within schools and adequately represent the minority voices. Sometimes, teachers may feel threatened by students voicing their concerns and fear a loss of control in the classroom. For others, student feedback forms an essential element in developing responsive, effective teaching practices and a healthy school environment.

Barriers to good practice were identified at the level of national policy and local implementation. Within society, it was felt that there was a lack of consensus with regard to social inclusion. As a result, interactions and structures involving people from marginalised groups were dominated by a culture of welfarism rather than a culture of rights. Policy and practice in this area has been restricted by the fact that rights are not automatically conferred but only 'as far as resources permit'.

The continual battle for rights has had a demoralising impact on people and their advocates from marginalised groups. Making resources and services more widely available would reduce the stigmatising effect on those people who avail of them. It was recognised that the complex process of initiating meaningful change had been limited by the lack of support structures to prepare all interested parties to enable the full participation of these young people within society. Knowledgeable professionals were required in all settings to support this process of change.

The current competitive environment in education was acknowledged as a powerful factor militating against the full participation of young people from marginalised groups within our schools. Disclosure of needs is more difficult within this type of competitive environment. The failure to develop cohesive individualised approaches to education creates difficulties for every child, but particularly for those children from marginalised groups. Schools face the dilemma of how to offer support to these children without further emphasising the differences between them and their peer group. A useful starting point would be to encourage an acceptance that any child can encounter difficulties in an aspect of learning and that these difficulties need not be permanent. Then, receiving support would become a 'normal' and integral aspect of the process of education. In addition, the traditional low level of expectation for marginalised children can be challenged and structures put in place to ensure equitable access to the positive attitudes and resources required for a successful education.

Many strategies were suggested to inform and develop policy in relation to this issue at national and local levels. Equality of opportunity requires a focus on equality of access, participation and outcome. This involves a principled commitment to rights-based provision. A transparent mechanism is needed for the delivery of services locally; this process should be governed by nationally agreed criteria. At school level, the inclusion of diversity can be developed within school culture and practice. The school takes responsibility for inclusion rather than the individual student and/or their families. For example, schools can develop a listening culture through structured consultation with students, and as a first step schools could be audited for the existing level of consultation and the identification of opportunities to develop this process of empowerment. Teachers, as part of their practice, can create opportunities for children to develop decision-making/choice-taking skills in all aspects of the curriculum. The sharing, collaborative culture that thrives in some schools needs to expand to include all schools. The 'cotton wool', over-protective approach commonly used with marginalised children needs to be replaced by a culture of fostering independence and self-reliance within a supportive environment.

Participants observed that there was a real opportunity to develop inclusion policies and supportive practices within our education system. They pointed to a number of salient factors: the momentum for change generated by high-profile court cases; upcoming legislation on education; the emphasis on meeting 'individual needs' within policy proposals; and the social partnership approach in Irish politics. Given this progress, the question remains: Will the concerns of marginalised children/young people be listened to and acted upon to create a more equitable education system?

## References

Kenny, M.; McNeela, E.; Shevlin, E. and Daly, T. (2000) *Hidden Voices: Young people with disabilities speak about their second level schooling.* Bradshaw Books, Cork.

## Notes

1   Monahan M. (1997). 'Making the grade: responding to lesbian, gay and bisexual youth in schools', quoted in *Education: Lesbian and Gay Students. Developing Equal Opportunities.* Gay HIV Strategies/Nexus.

2   All from Combat Poverty Agency/GLEN, *Poverty—lesbians and gay men: the social and economic effects of discrimination,* Ireland, 1996.

3   Garofalo, R.; Wolf, C.; Wissow, L. S.; Woods, E. R. and Goodman, E. (1999). 'Sexual orientation and risk of suicide attempts among a representative sample of youth' in *Archives of Pediatrics and Adolescent Medicine* 1999 153: 487–493.

4   Mason, A. and Palmer, A. (1996) *Queer Bashing: A study of 4000 lesbian, gay and bisexual people.* Stonewall, UK.

# 16

## RECOGNISING VOICES

### MICHAEL SHEVLIN AND RICHARD ROSE

In this concluding paper Michael Shevlin and Richard Rose provide an overview of the critical issues explored in this book. The authors identify common themes emerging from the diverse voices of young people from marginalised groups. These young people clearly want to be valued and accepted within the 'real world' and enabled and encouraged to make their unique contribution to society. They are acutely aware that their experience of marginalisation will continue unless the individualised approach to meeting their needs is replaced by a collective will to develop an education system that can support their ambition. Their voices are included in this final paper through direct quotations interspersed through the text.

The voices of young people from marginalised groups make explicit a number of common, recurring themes. These themes include the desire of these young people for a normality that involves the facilitation of access to education, achievement within the educational system and beyond, and ambition for their success from teachers and policy makers. These young people want to contribute to a world where difference is accepted and valued, and they want to participate in the real world as opposed to the shadow world governed by paternalism and dependency. Also, they would like to take part in a mainstream setting where their normality is taken for granted rather than constantly contested and challenged. Creating this type of mainstream setting will involve the affirmation of the right of these young people to have a powerful voice in the decisions affecting their lives, so that these young people will not be expected to change fundamentally in order to be accepted.

Commentators have observed (Lewis and Lindsay, 2000; Lynch and Lodge, 2002) that the notion of voice has been very problematic in educational discourse. For example, the voice of children has been noticeably absent from the educational decision-making processes. It is assumed that to have a voice that will be acknowledged, children must attain a degree of maturity; although when this will happen in childhood is never specified. Research and teaching experience strongly suggest that children from relatively young ages are capable of reflective activity and communicating their opinions cogently. So the absence of the child's voice cannot be solely attributed to their perceived lack of maturity. Evidently the explanation can be found elsewhere, and the perspectives on exclusion from people within marginalised groupings offer an alternative and compelling view. Within this perspective, it is evident that a discourse of power prevents young people from marginalised groupings from influencing vital decisions about schooling, curricular access and career choices.

Certain voices within society have tended to be ignored, isolated and patronised as the discourse of professionals and policy makers have dominated. It is hardly surprising to discover that these voices have belonged to people from the most marginalised groupings within society, including disabled people, ethnic minorities and the poor, among others. Equally these voices rarely appear in the educational debates, although it is arguable that the outcomes of these discussions and subsequent policy initiatives will affect their lives proportionally more than the rest of society. People from marginalised groupings have remained on the periphery of decision-making processes in education, and despite their belated involvement in case conferences about their own future, consultation has often been token and patronising. The power relationships that dominate educational discourse are rarely examined or challenged. Despite the rhetoric concerning parental choice and stakeholder involvement, people from marginalised groupings encounter substantial difficulties in having their voices heard. Even where these voices are heard it is still relatively easy for policy makers and professionals to sideline these views in pursuit of greater efficiency or the efficient allocation of scarce resources. People must be labelled before these resources can be accessed. The effects of this categorisation, though well intentioned, can be to further marginalise and alienate people already excluded from the mainstream of society.

Within the Encouraging Voices research project, common themes have emerged that link the experiences of children who have a disability with their counterparts from ethnic minorities and those children who have been bullied. The dominant theme has been the powerlessness of children in relation to the adult world. As our writers have observed, there is a huge disparity between official policy documents that recommend the inclusion of the child's perspective and the reality of minimal consultation. Children are keenly aware of the inequality in child–adult power relationships within schools. They point to their experiences of a lack of privacy and autonomy in everyday school life. Creating a democratic 'listening culture' within schools is an obvious first step. However, it is doubtful if the creation of student councils can seriously address the issues raised by young people from marginalised groupings in relation to the imbalanced power relationships they experience within schools. Listening in this context can involve simplistic assumptions that ignore the reality of how decisions are made and implemented in schools. There needs to be greater analysis of the complexities of encouraging and affirming voices traditionally suppressed, and enabling these voices to have a significant impact on school policy and practice. Many children with learning difficulties are treated with a mixture of benevolence and concern. There is the inherent risk that these young people become overly dependent on adult approval. As a result, their voice will rarely be expressed or acknowledged, since adults believe they know best and these young people appear happy to acquiesce. Creating opportunities for greater autonomy must permeate the curricula design, delivery and school practice. A more radical approach is urgently required. Young people with disabilities recognised the need to have a teacher advocate to ensure their curricular and social inclusion within schools. Our young disabled researchers realised that while their voice was heard and they were given access to influential decision makers when policy initiatives were announced, it was evident that their voice had been effectively ignored and marginalised. In addition, they felt undervalued by the education system, as they had no effective role in shaping their own learning experiences and education outcomes. While the rights discourse has attained prominence within marginalised communities, this view is not necessarily shared by policy makers or professionals in schools. In reality, rights and status are closely related to the ability to have one's voice recognised and heard.

## Access, ambition and achievement

'If you don't go to secondary — you ain't going to have no exams — when you get a job. You'll be stuck in some field all your life. There's no future in that! You need at least two GCSEs to get into college.'

'The parents have a dream for their daughter. They want her to live 'where she could receive visits from her family and friends without intrusion''.'

Across the diverse studies in this book, there was an overriding concern about issues relating to access, achievement and ambition. It is apparent that access is a complex and multi-layered process. For children with physical/sensory difficulties and Traveller children, getting into school was not a major problem.

Ensuring participation and achievement was another matter. One of the key issues identified by the young people concerned the ambition or lack thereof from teachers towards them. Research has demonstrated that teachers' expectations for young people from marginalised groups are a critical component in school success or failure. There were indications across studies that minimal levels of achievement and participation were acceptable for certain individuals and marginalised groups. Guarantee of access was no guarantee of full participation. The young people were certainly aware that they were experiencing lower levels of teacher expectations in comparison to their mainstream peers. Generally, these children were expected to adapt to mainstream norms and expectations, although their dominant experience was one of oversight and sometimes denial of their existence. This was particularly true where there was little curricular modification or adaptation. Often these young people internalised these deficit views and developed a stoic acceptance of the dominant status quo. This type of neglect often led to difficulties with retention for Traveller children, for example, and a peripheral and erratic presence in school for those with disabilities. The young disabled researchers, for example, were certain that with the appropriate level of structured support, examination success would have been a real possibility much earlier within their education. The fact that they eventually succeeded in gaining accreditation and recognition for their achievements was largely down to their own determination.

The barriers to full participation experienced by the young people have serious implications at both organisational and pedagogic levels for schools. It should be relatively straightforward to tackle physical access issues. It is totally unacceptable that such issues can inhibit the social and academic participation of these young people. Attitudinal and awareness issues may be less amenable to change. Schools often reflect and sometimes reinforce societal perceptions of young people who are viewed as different. The categorisation of these young people into distinct groups with presumed similar educational and emotional needs has resulted in fragmented and often piecemeal inclusion of these young people into mainstream settings. Inclusion has tended to be on an individual basis; thus generalising 'good practice' to all mainstream settings is very difficult. It is assumed that the individual needs of young people viewed as different are qualitatively different to the needs of their mainstream peers.

It is fair to say that these young people have often had their ability underestimated, and have experienced low teacher expectations as a result. They observed that the most responsive teachers generally listened closely to their concerns and helped them to identify their learning strengths and shortcomings. This direct involvement in the education process resulted in greater learning confidence and assurance. Generally, the young people themselves were very self-aware and their expectations for themselves were realistic and possible with sensitive support. A key element in ensuring equal opportunities must be to work towards a system in which all pupils, regardless of their background or need, are viewed as being able to achieve. Low expectation is clearly a major factor in denying access to an effective education. Enabling young people to become more self-reflective and to take greater responsibility for their learning has been demonstrated to be effective in working with young people who have severe learning difficulties. These pupils often present a particular challenge to teachers who need to explore alternative means of providing communication and access to learning. The teachers who have demonstrated that this is possible for this section of the population provide a positive model for other teachers who work with pupils of diverse need and ability. Exclusion from involvement in aspects of the curriculum, such as physical education and extra-curricular activities, can marginalise these young people even further from their mainstream peers. The opportunity to participate at whatever level is valued and this type of exclusion was keenly felt. These young people were aware that being treated differently to their peers reinforced the sense of difference and, despite the best intentions, could reinforce negative stereotypes that emphasise dependence. Schools may be seduced into creating a protected artificial world for their young people who are viewed as different. This superficially attractive option may appear to provide a risk-free environment; however, the corollary is that these young people can remain unchallenged and passive observers of the 'real world'. This approach does a disservice to both the young people involved and the schools.

It represents an almost fatalistic acceptance that these young people will not achieve their potential or participate in the 'real world' of employment, autonomy and interdependence alongside their mainstream peers.

## Social inclusion

> 'Before [student] came to the school if I looked at a person in a wheelchair I really didn't know a lot about them. But when [student] came I realised he's just another person.'

Being accepted by their mainstream peers and establishing viable relationships with their mainstream peers were perceived to be priorities for the young people from marginalised groups. Often, social acceptance was perceived to be more important than academic success. However, for many, social inclusion proved elusive. The difficulties in establishing and retaining social relationships with their mainstream peers were often exacerbated by the lack of basic structural supports for young people with disabilities. The lack of attention to vital access issues meant that social relationships were construed as dependent rather than reciprocal. The young people transferring to mainstream from special provision perceived that they had to be adroit in adjusting socially to mainstream demands and priorities. Failure to be adept in this area could result in being the target of verbal and/or physical bullying. Young people who are deaf or hearing impaired felt most comfortable when engaged in structured classroom activities. Outside this environment, these young people felt their disability excluded them from meaningful social relationships with their mainstream peers. Yet, the mainstream peers appeared totally unaware of this difficulty or of the divergent perceptions of the young people who are deaf or hearing impaired. Traveller young people and refugee children also experienced exclusion based on hostility and an incomplete understanding of the norms and cultures of ethnic minorities. It appears that the status of the young people who are viewed as different within school and society in relation to their mainstream peers predominated in all their social interactions. Concepts of difference appeared to be based on a deficit model where the identity of the young people was totally dominated by the labelled difference.

Most teachers were kind and supportive. However, the young people maintained that despite teacher benevolence, some of their basic needs remained unmet within the school environment. The young people recognised the inherent danger of being overlooked, bullied or not achieving their potential. Taking into account the sensitive perceptions and feelings of these young people and the possibility of isolation, it is essential that schools must avoid any actions that might, even inadvertently, reinforce negative perceptions of these young people among their peers and the teaching staff. In addition, helping these young people to raise their own self-esteem and ensuring that they are held in high esteem needs to be a school priority. Specific changes to the current school programmes are required to fully include the young people from marginalised groupings. Teacher awareness of the issues affecting these young people is critical as they, in particular, need to be publicly valued for their work and affirmed as full class participants. For a variety of well-documented reasons, these young people may feel insecure in mainstream provision. This may require that we take a different view of the future role of special schools, ensuring that they work collaboratively with the mainstream in developing a more balanced continuum of provision. Providing opportunities for the development of positive peer relationships can help to overcome these feelings. Classroom activities can be organised to maximise the potential for healthy peer interaction, as in mixed-ability groupings and collaborative learning processes within the classroom. Inviting these young people, where appropriate, to assume class or whole school responsibilities can enable their effective engagement in the life of the school.

## Acceptance of difference

'It would become normal, just everyday life and people would be able to understand it, 'ah sure we don't even know what that is, we just know it's a normal thing [he's] like everyone else'. When it comes like that we would get good jobs ... '

While young people in mainstream schools appeared acutely aware of the inequality governing their relationships with adults, there was little awareness of equality issues concerning those belonging to marginalised groups. This was attributed to the lack of heterogeneity in Irish schools and limited opportunities for mainstream children to interact with their peers from marginalised groups. Generally, these young people displayed lack of respect for, and recognition of, the cultures and perspectives of minorities, including those from racial or ethnic minorities, those with disabilities, those belonging to minority religious groups and those who are gay, lesbian or bisexual. Difference was not really tolerated, particularly where difference was associated with lower status identity. Teachers shared this lack of awareness of minority issues. Curriculum content, teaching approaches and school ethos can all contribute to the exclusion of students from marginalised groups from full participation in schools. Travellers, in particular, were the target of hostility, and with the recent arrival of migrant workers, refugees and asylum seekers there are indications that these groups are also regarded with fear and a rejection of racial difference. People with disabilities tended to be viewed from a charity perspective emphasising dependence and pity. How can schools challenge the negative stereotypes adolescents have of those from marginalised groups? The ways in which support is offered to marginalised groups can have a significant impact on mainstream attitudes towards individuals in these groups. Where support is conceptualised according to a deficit model of difference and need, it is probable that the recipients of support will be accorded an inferior and dependent status.

## Concluding comments

Within these diverse studies, we have heard the concerns expressed by young people who have been marginalised for one reason or another within our education systems. These voices demand a proactive response from policy makers and professionals. Many examples of 'good practice' have been documented. For example, young people with disabilities have been centrally involved in research design and the promotion of policy formulation. Others with learning difficulties have participated in augmenting their own learning through structured teacher support. A few individuals, with perceptive support from schools and families, achieved success and made the transition to an adulthood shared with their mainstream peers. However, the dominant tone of the contributions consisted of frustrated opportunities, lowered expectations and a general sense of disappointment. Despite and sometimes due to teacher benevolence, these young people experienced their difference as a restriction and a barrier to full academic and social participation in mainstream education. Often, difference became the defining feature of their identity. Some young people from devalued cultures, such as Travellers, implicitly rejected their identity in order to 'pass for normal'. Society's emphasis on homogeneity and preference for single approaches to complex issues has resulted in a narrow and limited response to diversity. Often young people viewed as different can find themselves hovering on the margins of the world of their mainstream peers, isolated and undervalued. Sometimes these young people are firmly rooted in special provision and follow this track into adult life. Others have attempted to take the mainstream route and, because of lack of success, have reverted to the 'safe' world of special provision.

How do we begin to create education systems that value diversity? Listening to the young people from marginalised groups and really hearing their perspectives and concerns provides the ideal starting point. Teachers and others charged with the responsibility to work with young people need to be supported through training and by policies that recognise the full value of pupil participation. Where diversity is truly valued, the conventional education system is challenged to become inclusive. Young people from marginalised groups are becoming more embedded in mainstream provision, and some schools have demonstrated the capacity to develop a more inclusive philosophy. This involves creating a flexible, responsive school organisation and supporting teachers in developing teaching approaches that will ensure that these young people and their mainstream peers are given equal opportunities to access the curriculum and make a valued contribution to school life. By establishing such principles within schools, we will better equip young people to play a fuller part in post-school life and to support the future development of more participative societies.

## References

Lewis, A., and Lindsay, G. (2000) 'Emerging issues'. In A. Lewis and G. Lindsay (eds), *Researching children's perspectives*. Buckingham: Open University Press.

Lynch, K., and Lodge, A. (2002) *Equality and power in schools: redistribution, recognition and representation*. London: Routledge Falmer.

# INDEX

NATIONAL DISABILITY AUTHORITY
ÚDARÁS NÁISIÚNTA MÍCHUMAIS

The National Disability Authority will, on behalf of the State, promote and help to secure the rights of people with disabilities. The Authority will achieve this

by influencing public policy and legislation;

by working to ensure that services to people with disabilities are of the highest standards and quality.

Specifically the National Disability Authority :

develops, co-ordinates and advises on policy;

promotes equality, participation and inclusion;

advises on and monitors the implementation of standards for programmes and services;

prepares codes of practice;

undertakes and commissions research;

collects and disseminates information.

For further information contact:
**National Disability Authority**
**25 Clyde Road**
**Dublin 4**

**Tel. (01) 608 0400**
**Fax.(01) 660 9935**
**www.nda.ie**

# NDA Publications

1   *Disability related research in Ireland 1996–2001*
    Free of Charge

2   *'A matter of rights'. NDA Strategic Plan 2001–2003*
    Free of Charge

3   *Building for everyone — 2002*
    €45.00, €25 PWD

4   *'Ask me'. Guidelines for effective consultation — 2002*
    Free of Charge

5   *Irish National Disability Authority: IT accessibility guidelines — 2002*
    Free of Charge

6   *Guidelines for including people with disabilities in research 2002*
    Free of Charge

7   *Public attitudes to disability in the Republic of Ireland 2002*
    Free of Charge

8   *Equal citizens proposals for core elements of disability legislation 2003*
    Free of Charge

9   *Responding to violence against women with disabilities 2003*
    Free of Charge